P9-DWB-533

# WHERE MEMORY LEADS

# *Where Memory Leads*

## MY LIFE

Saul Friedländer

Other Press
New York

Production editor: Yvonne E. Cárdenas
Text designer: Julie Fry
This book was set in Fournier by
Alpha Design & Composition of Pittsfield, NH

10 9 8 7 6 5 4 3 2 1

Library of Congress Cataloging-in-Publication Data

Names: Friedländer, Saul, 1932- author.
Title: Where memory leads : my life / by Saul Friedländer.
Description: New York : Other Press, [2016] | Volume Two of
    Saul Friedländer's autobiography. Volume One was originally
    published in New York in 1979.
Identifiers: LCCN 2016008344 | ISBN 9781590518090 (hardback)
Subjects: LCSH: Friedländer, Saul, 1932- | Jewish historians—
    Biography. | Jewish learning and scholarship. | Holocaust,
    Jewish (1939-1945)—Research. | Holocaust, Jewish (1939-1945)—
    Influence. | BISAC: BIOGRAPHY & AUTOBIOGRAPHY
    / Personal Memoirs. | HISTORY / Middle East / Israel. |
    BIOGRAPHY & AUTOBIOGRAPHY / Political.
Classification: LCC DS135.F9 F75 2016 | DDC 940.53/18092 [B]
    —dc23 LC record available at https://lccn.loc.gov/2016008344

*For Orna*

# PROLOGUE

How do you say "aubergines" in Hebrew? I've eaten hundreds, maybe thousands of aubergine dishes in my lifetime, particularly in Israel, and suddenly the word for it was gone. Strangely enough, the American English term surfaced immediately: eggplant. But never mind the English, it was the search for the Hebrew word that kept me awake.

It was our last night in Paris. A few days earlier, in October 2012, we had celebrated my eightieth birthday. Tomorrow we'd be on our way back to L.A. At dinner we had a *salade d'aubergines* in a small restaurant close to the hotel and now, well past midnight, my wild chase continues. I notice that my wife has somehow half woken up. "What's the salad we ate last night called in Hebrew?" In her half sleep, Orna manages to whisper, "*Hatzilim.*" Of course, *hatzilim*! What a relief! Now I can finally fall asleep. Damn it! What was the English word that had come up so easily? Oh yes: eggplant. That's probably how the Dutch felt when they drained off seawater and secured a further patch of land: a victory against nature!

———

Starting a book of memoirs with an episode of memory loss may seem like a joke. It is not; it is a real situation that nonetheless can be dealt with, as I will explain at the end of this prologue.

Thirty-eight years ago, I published *When Memory Comes*, a memoir about my childhood and adolescence, focusing on my early life in Prague, the war years in France, adolescence in Paris, and my departure for Israel in June 1948. Some short glimpses of later years were included, up to 1977.

In these pages, I turn to events that I hardly mentioned, or, in most cases, did not mention at all, between my return as a student to Paris in 1953 and the year preceding the publication of the early memoir, 1977. Then the narration goes on to this day (2015). As this text frequently deals with my reactions to and, sometimes, my involvement in public events, I opted, for the sake of clarity, to keep to an essentially chronological narrative. It so happens that the main clusters of events that I shall evoke indeed followed each other; thus, the text tells of a sequence that took place in real time.

First come the years of apprenticeship, in which I move from place to place, from country to country, in search of an identity and a calling. The second part deals with Israel, at the very outset, then from about 1967 — when I started teaching in Jerusalem — to the early 1980s and, less intensively so, in the subsequent years. Germany follows, from segments of my early life to this day, but mainly as I experienced it during the eighties. The fourth part turns to life in the United States.

No life progresses along such neat divisions, and issues dominant during one stage may carry over to all that comes thereafter. In this memoir in particular, the main issues — possibly less so regarding the American experience — are interwoven throughout. In short, these divisions represent temporary accentuations of one central issue during a given period, accentuations that are often narrated within the context of the minute incidents of everyday life.

This book shows the influence of the Shoah (the Holocaust) on my personal life and on my reactions to Israel, Germany, and ultimately America. And, as the narration progresses, it also increasingly centers on the writing and teaching of history, particularly the history of the Holocaust, the essential work of my life. Thus, the writing of that history and, in my case, the unavoidable relation of memory to history is a recurring theme in each of the succeeding parts, even the first one.

Beyond this central theme, by dint of circumstances, I became deeply involved at times in places and issues that continue to attract intense general interest; they are presented here from a subjective perspective, but as openly and candidly as possible and from as detached a viewpoint as I can manage. I also intend to share with the reader my doubts, debates, and regrets about this or that attitude or decision and, finally, the false starts and the right intuitions inherent in the history-writing process.


I started writing these reminiscences after my eighty-first birthday, under the constant threat of some loss of memory. At my age, though, long-term memory is present, usually with added clarity, while the short-term past fades away at times. I have kept written traces of some recent events and integrated them into the text; it helps, but, all in all, they are only a tiny part of it, mere ripples on the course of the later years.

# PART I

## *Changing Places**

---

* In homage to David Lodge

# CHAPTER ONE

# Nirah

"Dear Sir, when this letter reaches you, I will have left Paris for Palestine . . ." Thus began the letter I sent to my guardian, Isidore Rosemblat, in the early days of June 1948.

> *You will probably be astonished, but don't worry: I am with a group of Betarim [members of the right-wing Betar, the youth movement linked to Menachem Begin's semiclandestine Irgun], entirely safe. Mainly, don't alert the police or any other organization of the kind; it would only create additional problems and be of no help as, when you get this news, I will already be on the ship.*
>
> *Don't worry about what my uncles may say as, before you even write to them, I shall be with them and I am sure that they won't be terribly displeased.*
>
> *Let us now turn to concrete matters: I took with me, in my backpack, all my linen as well as my gray suit, my beige suit, and the leather jacket. Before leaving, I carried the yellow suitcase, the briefcase, and the textbooks to a friend who will return them to you as soon as possible.*
>
> *I must also ask you to send word to the lycée to inform*

*them that I am leaving the establishment and that I am not
presenting myself for the baccalaureate [the first part of the
final high school exam, taken at the end of the eleventh
grade]. Thus everything will be settled.*

*I will send you a long letter as soon as I arrive; I would
have liked to say goodbye and thank you in person for all you
have done for me but I was worried about the possibility of
some obstacle to my departure. In any case, don't consider it
as ingratitude on my part. While waiting to see you again in
Palestine, I kiss you affectionately,*

*Paul\**

*PS (very important): Please do pay my third quarter boarding
expenses as, otherwise, they will not return 1 pair of sheets,
2 shirts, 2 underpants, and 2 pairs of socks I left at the lycée.*

On June 5, two days after I had written that letter, the principal of the Paris Lycée Henri IV (where I was a boarder) wrote to my guardian:

*Sir,*

*I regret to inform you that young Friedländer, a boarder
student in First A [eleventh grade, classic] surreptitiously
left the lycée yesterday at 4:30 p.m., using the exit of the day
students. According to our investigation he intends to join the
Jewish forces in Palestine.*

*Please excuse my reminding you on the same occasion that
the April–June quarter has not been paid. Please accept . . .*

*P. Camenen, Principal*

News travels fast.

---

* Paul was my original name; I became Saul on arriving in Israel.

Thus, in June 1948, a few weeks after the creation of the State of Israel, I disembarked in the new country. One of my maternal uncles, Paul Glaser, whom I managed to phone, took me in. Paul lived in Nirah, a small village in the Plain of Sharon, close to Natanyah. The village had been established by newcomers from Prague and other Czech towns who, like my uncle, immigrated to Palestine in 1939, around the time of the German occupation of the Czech part of Czecho-Slovakia (the hyphen was added after the Munich agreements, in 1938).

That same year, my parents and I, then six years old, left Prague for France. We were fleeing one sinking ship for another — though no one could have known that at the time. The approaching Germans cut short our precarious existence in Paris from April 1939 to June 1940. I don't know how my father managed the impossible: to buy my mother and me two seats on a train departing southward in early June and, a few days later, one for himself. This must have cost a fortune.

We made it to what became the "nonoccupied" zone of France and settled in a small resort town, emptied by the war: Néris-les-Bains. The local population went on living in Néris but soon refugees, mostly Jews, replaced the usual visitors to the spa. Some Jews were French, though the majority was foreign. Eventually the difference between these two groups would mean the difference between life and death.

When the roundup of foreign Jews started in our zone in the summer of 1942, my parents, with the help of Catholic friends, hid me in a seminary in nearby Montluçon while they attempted to cross the Swiss border. They were arrested by the Swiss, delivered to the French, then to the Germans, transported to

Auschwitz in November 1942, and murdered. The French Jews were pariahs, but most of them managed to hide; the foreign Jews were "dead men walking."

As I described some four decades ago, at the seminary I was baptized and became a staunch Catholic. In early 1946, the temporary guardian appointed by my uncles (my mother's three brothers) compelled the nuns to let me go. I first became a boarder in the provincial *collège* of St.-Amand-Montrond, a small town in the center of France. After a year in St.-Amand, I transferred, as a boarder once again, to Lycée Henri IV in Paris. In the meantime, I lost my Catholic faith, became a Communist for a few months, and then a Zionist.

From my Paris lycée, I passionately followed the events unfolding in Palestine and soon decided that instead of standing for the first part of the baccalaureate, I would somehow get to Eretz Israel (the land of Israel). On May 15, the State of Israel was officially established and was immediately invaded by armies of the neighboring Arab states; its chances of survival were scant. I wanted to fight. After one Zionist youth movement rejected me because of my age, I changed the birth date on my ID card from 1932 to 1930 and was accepted by the Betar, the youth movement of the right-wing Irgun. I had not the faintest idea who they were or what aims they pursued, but when asked, "What do we want?" I delivered the slogan a friend of mine told me to repeat: "Both shores of the Jordan." It sufficed. But what the hell did "both shores of the Jordan" mean?

In early June, after getting a message from the organizers, I "surreptitiously" left the lycée, walked to the Gare de Lyon, and joined my group. We made it to Marseilles, then to nearby Port-de-Bouc. After two days of waiting, we boarded a converted Liberty ship of D-day vintage, the *Altalena*, flying the colors of

Panama, which had been bought by American supporters of the Irgun. I sailed with nine hundred companions and hundreds of tons of weapons donated by the French government. It was the first time I'd ever seen the sea.

David Ben-Gurion, now prime minister of Israel, viewed the Irgun as a terrorist group. He feared that the additional Irgun fighters and weapons would incite a coup. He demanded that the movement's leadership prevent the *Altalena* from sailing, while it was still anchored in Port-de-Bouc. Menachem Begin, the Irgun's leader, wanted to avoid a confrontation and relented, but hotheads in Paris overruled his orders; the ship departed, and there we were, on June 20, 1948, anchored off the coast of Israel. None of us knew what was in store.

On the shore of Kfar Vitkin — where the *Altalena* unloaded mounds of weapons and ammunition and disembarked most of its passengers (including me) — Israeli army units were waiting. A few hours later, after an ultimatum to surrender the ship expired, they started shooting. The ship sailed to Tel Aviv and we were moved to a camp of the Irgun. By the end of that dramatic day, the Irgun had disbanded. For me, it meant the end of the affair. My uncle Paul, whom, as mentioned, I had managed to call, picked me up. Instead of my initial plan of joining the army, I went to live with him in Nirah. As for the ship, artillery shells sank it near the coast of Tel Aviv. Sixteen of the passengers who had remained on board were killed, some as they attempted to swim ashore. For about two years, I think, when you strolled along the Tel Aviv seashore, you saw the massive hulk of the *Altalena* emerging from the shallow water. Then it was towed away and sold as scrap iron.

In my previous memoir, I may have described the life in Nirah and its inhabitants somewhat too idyllically. That was my perception at the time. I also didn't say much about my uncle Paul. In Rochlitz, in the Sudeten area, where the Glasers lived, Paul had managed the family textile factory before 1938. After his arrival in Nirah, he took over the management of a very small local factory, producing mainly camouflage nets for the British and, after 1948, for the Israeli army.

A bachelor who had become rather morose over the years, Paul, the oldest of the Glaser siblings, was in his early fifties when I arrived in Nirah. He probably considered me a burden after a while and packed me off to an agricultural school, to learn a profession useful for my new life. "Enough with intellectuals in the family," he used to say (I suspected he was referring to my father; though resenting his remarks, I kept silent).

Ben Shemen — that was the name of the school — was an excellent technical and agricultural learning institution, but I showed no talent whatsoever for any of the crafts they taught: I'd clearly been blessed with two left hands. Moreover, I desperately wished to get back to a regular high school. My uncle wasn't moved by my pleas. After a while I decided to risk a rejection and, on my own, I paid a visit to Shaul Levin, the director of the high school in Natanyah. Easily convinced, Levin talked to my uncle, and, in the spring of 1949, I joined the eleventh grade at Shaul Tchernichovsky High. To this day I remain grateful to Levin.

My relationship with Uncle Paul didn't improve. Sometime in 1950 he underwent prostate surgery at the Hadassah hospital in Jerusalem; it led to complications and he became incontinent. It turned him, understandably, into an increasingly unfriendly person. Some two years later, uremia developed, which apparently caused paranoid delusions: he became convinced that I'd been spending his money, and that I harbored hostile intentions toward him. Luckily, by then I was in the army and did not live in Nirah anymore.


## 2


While Israel was winning its War of Independence, momentous events shook my native Prague: the Communists, backed by the Soviet Union, came to power. Soon a wave of refugees left the country and thousands of Czech Jews arrived in Israel, some of them to our village. There was even family in their midst, whom my uncle took in.

It was then, in the spring of 1949, that I received an unexpected visit. I've since forgotten what my visitor looked like and the name he gave me. I remember only that he arrived on a powerful motorcycle. He asked me to follow him and, once assured that we couldn't be overheard, told me that he worked for the government. It obviously meant that he had something to do with security. "You came on the *Altalena*," he said without much of a preamble. "That's not good. If you want to make up for it, you have to help us. Among the new *olim* [immigrants] from Czechoslovakia, there are Communist agents. I want you to listen to conversations and report anything that could sound suspicious to me." He gave me his address — not far away by bus — and departed.

I understood that to erase my original sin, to become a real Israeli, one not infected by the *Altalena* virus, I had to observe and report. I did . . .

You may wonder how the would-be informant could understand conversations in Czech. My Czech returned within two or three weeks of hearing the language spoken again all day long, as the case had previously been with German. However, my mission soon ended, after I conveyed totally irrelevant details and demonstrated my complete lack of talent in this line of work. But I had watched, and although I was sixteen at the time and utterly disoriented, I cannot get over it to this day.

My readiness to "watch" can be explained by my intense desire to belong to the community I had enthusiastically joined. Yet this need probably had deeper roots: upon the disappearance of my parents (I should add that I was an only child), I embraced my new identity — Catholicism, and the seminary that hid me — with all the intensity of a ten-year-old, taken in by a collectivity that was strong, protective, and nurturing. I ran away once, at the very outset, but was brought back and relented; ultimately, I fully submitted. The nuns believed that my path to priesthood was assured.

But after leaving the seminary in early 1946, and after my stint with Communism, I found another community, an even more compelling one, to which I became irresistibly drawn. I embraced the idea of Israel and the dream of total acceptance. Under those circumstances, arriving on the *Altalena* could look like a sin that needed to be redeemed; after all, I had seen with my own eyes that we had not been welcomed and that the Irgun had been disbanded.

Yet, notwithstanding my initial enthusiasm to strike roots in my "ancestral homeland," I increasingly felt an urge to return to France — for a while at least. I didn't understand at the time (and grasped only years later) that as much as I craved to belong, I feared it. During the war, I knew that the Catholic milieu into which I had assimilated was not naturally my own and that if I did not adapt *corps et âme* (body and soul) I could be rejected, possibly even delivered to some mortally dangerous "elsewhere." My submission was genuine, but I couldn't remain totally unaware of the fact that it was a guarantee of survival.

Over the following decades, a kind of seesaw between these two opposing drives — fervent commitment on the one hand, constant search for an escape route on the other — would come to define most of my life. This is probably why I was holding teaching positions in two countries — simultaneously — for the major part of my university career. I never found a compelling argument that could explain this strange pattern.

Thus, during these first years in Israel I did everything in my power to become an Israeli through and through. I was my high school's valedictorian, worked as a messenger boy at the Foreign Ministry, became a civilian employee in the army for six months, then served in the same highly secret intelligence unit (Intelligence 2, the earliest form of what was to become Unit 8200, the Israeli NSA) for another two and a half years.

Yet the urge to return to France grew nonetheless. (During my service I had drawn the map of the Paris underground, the Métro, from memory, and got it partly right.) Such nostalgia for France occasionally materialized in strange ways. Thus, when a documentary showed the Piscine Deligny (the Deligny public swimming pool, possibly the most famous in Paris), I felt such a sudden pang of homesickness that I vividly remember it to this day. As I had never been inside this *piscine* — nor any other, for that matter (except in Prague, at age five), as I'd never learned to swim — this reaction was especially absurd.

The explanation I provided for returning to France sounded plausible enough: the teaching of political science was, at the time, better in Paris than at the Hebrew University in Jerusalem.

## 3

My cultural identity has remained essentially French throughout my life. On the occasion of my German publisher Wolfgang Beck's sixty-fifth birthday in 2006, most of his authors contributed a short essay on books that changed their lives, for a volume entitled *Ein Buch, das mein Leben verändert hat*. In the opening paragraph of my essay, I mentioned — without giving it too much thought — that I would avoid the "great books" that I read and reread, such as Proust's *Recherche* or Flaubert's *Éducation*, and turn instead to a slender novel that, for my generation and for a prior one, defined the field of adolescent dreams: Alain-Fournier's *Le Grand Meaulnes*. I hadn't even noticed that in the first paragraph of my text I had referred to three books that, each in its own way, were quintessentially French.

In my essay, it was the primary school of Sainte-Agathe — from where the narrator and Meaulnes, the main protagonist, set out on their dreamlike adventure — that became my very specific "site of memory." It appeared to me as the model of the *école communale* which I attended for two years in Néris-les-Bains, from the summer of 1940 to 1942 (half a century after Meaulnes). To stress that point, I entitled my text "L'École communale." As in Sainte-Agathe, and probably as in schools all over France at that time, my *école* comprised one elongated building, subdivided into three parts: *la petite classe* (the lowest grade), *le cours moyen* (the middle grade), and *le cours supérieur* (the upper grade); the building opened onto a vast courtyard with a covered section (*le préau*); you had to cross the courtyard to reach the gate and the street.

I didn't make it to the *cours supérieur* but in the *petite classe* and in the *cours moyen* I became irrevocably French. There was nothing more hegemonic (at the time, in any case) than French education; it led you, step by step, whether you wanted it or not (and I certainly wanted it), into a unique mode of perception and expression. (Today, I write in English for practical reasons as I live in the United States, but I still think in French — and would do better writing in French.)

Such attachment to a culture actually goes well beyond basic schooling. In my case at least, I fell in love with the sheer beauty of the French language. From early on, maybe from the second year at the *école primaire* but certainly during the years spent at the seminary, we had to take a weekly *dictée*, a dictation, to check our progress in orthography. For me the *dictée* was a special moment: I loved the texts chosen from some volume of selected excerpts illustrating perfect style. I didn't mind whether it was Jules Renard's *Poil-de-Carotte* or Bossuet's *Oraisons funèbres*; I simply loved the style: "*Madame se meurt, Madame est morte.*" It reminds me that Kafka had this same love for beautiful French style, particularly in Flaubert's *Éducation sentimentale*; he quoted sentences from it to his friend Felice Bauer, sentences he deemed perfect both in their diction and their structure.


The avatars of memory that I experience are by far more mysterious to me than I put it in the Prologue. Over the last few months I have noticed that the disappearance of words and mainly names of people I know well is worsening. How come, however, that these words and names reappear, sometimes days later, after a relentless quest or just so, on their own? Does it mean that when words disappear they are not entirely effaced? Is there a "hard disk" of human memory? Are there various levels of effacement and various modes of retrieval? How is it, also, that when a forgotten word reappears, I know immediately that it is the right one?

Long-term memory is even more puzzling. As time goes by, I notice that poems I must have learned by heart in high school and entirely forgotten since, are reappearing in their pristine forms (parts of them at least). Thus the first strophe of Paul Valéry's "Le Cimetière marin" ("The Graveyard by the Sea") is suddenly present, in full. Where was it stored for seventy years or so? And why did it reappear instead of Lamartine's "Le Lac," for example, of which only a verse here and there returned?

No less strange is the working of "traumatic memory." While studying interviews with Shoah survivors, Lawrence Langer noticed that if the interviewer managed to break through the "standard" story of the interviewee, a sudden outburst of chaotic reminiscences surfaced, some kind of "deep memory" overcame the previously built defenses. I guess that in many cases, deep, traumatic memories reappear on their own in old age, like forgotten poems. They carry along forgotten fears.


Aside from French, significant fragments of a Prague-Jewish/ German heritage that had vanished for a few years during the war slowly resurfaced, refusing to be ignored anymore. This earliest identity linked up somehow with the Israeli one; it never left me since, although there were fluctuations. The only cultural environment that does not seem to have left an imprint is the American one with its added Los Angeles hue. There is nothing intentional in this resistance; it probably derives from the simple fact that I was too old for adding one more identity when I arrived in Los Angeles for my first extended stay in 1982 (at age fifty) and then, more permanently so, in 1988.

The Prague-Jewish part became the "guiding impulse" of *When Memory Comes*, which dealt primarily with my childhood and adolescent years; the title of the book derived from the reshuffling of a quote belonging to Gustav Meyrink's *Der Golem*, a somewhat gothic novel that my father loved and of which he possessed a magnificent copy, illustrated by the lithographs of Hugo Steiner-Prag. He took it along into exile. The book is all about the magic of Jewish Prague, about the labyrinths of the ghetto and the no less mysterious ones of memory and knowledge. Later, when I read it, it triggered in me the nostalgia for a world about which I knew very little; it revealed traces hidden until then. It reminded me of my father. Decades later, I wrote a small essay on Kafka; here was Jewish Prague again, to a point.

There was more than nostalgia to my Prague heritage. The main component, one that influenced my life and possibly even saved it, turned out to be my parents' total assimilation. They were "non-Jewish Jews," to use Isaac Deutscher's term, to the point of not having me circumcised. During a long and serious illness in the seminary (diphtheria), the physician who took care of me may, politically, have been on any side. Luckily, there was no visible indication that I was a Jewish boy, hidden under a false name. Later, after I came to Israel, this "omission" bothered me. The Nirah physician to whom I talked before joining the army told me that many immigrants from Central Europe shared "my fate." He gave me the name of a surgeon, just in case. I did not pursue it. When I underwent the initial medical examination at the draft and later, during several weeks in a military hospital, nobody seemed to pay attention.

It is by way of language that my cultural belonging to Israel is evident. Two years after my arrival, I successfully took the high school final exams in Hebrew. To pass, I had to study the Tanach (the Hebrew Bible) and an entire Talmud chapter (with commentary, partly in Aramaic, on objects lost and found). I enjoyed it as much as somebody allergic to pollen enjoys strolling in a flower garden in the spring, but I complied and passed the exams.

Both my first and second wives were born in Israel, and throughout these two marriages, from 1959 to this day (2015), we've spoken Hebrew at home and also with the children (and some of the grandchildren). For several decades, first at the Hebrew University in Jerusalem and then at Tel Aviv University, I lectured only in Hebrew and, quite naturally, went through daily life in Israel in Hebrew. Yet — and there is a small "yet" — I never quite enjoyed reading books in Hebrew, nor have I ever written a book in Hebrew. And, strangely enough, whether I lecture in Hebrew or in English, to this day I still write my notes in French.

One last element has to be added to my cultural profile: traces of Catholicism. As I indicated, after some initial resistance, I became a devout — even ecstatic — Catholic. Some of Catholicism's marginal impact resides in its aesthetic dimension: Romanesque, Gothic, and Baroque churches and cathedrals fascinate me to this day, and religious music (particularly organ music) touches me very deeply, as do religious choirs. It could have been so even without my Catholic adolescence, but I believe that those years added intensity to my listening emotion as an echo of the bliss which that music evoked in me at the time. More important by far, however, was the fact that, as a consequence of the religious force-feeding to which I was submitted, I became from adolescence on, and remain so to this day, totally indifferent to any religious belief. I am not a militant atheist; I simply don't care.

By far more consequential, though, was the deep and pervasive sense of guilt that the fundamentalist brand of Catholicism practiced at my seminary ingrained in me and, I am sure, in many others like me. We were constantly reminded of our sinful tendencies, warned against indulging in any *mauvaises pensées*, and sent weekly to confession. The *mauvaises pensées* were thoughts about sex; this was never stated and the notions we had about sex were utterly vague for most of us (including me); the word "sex" was unknown.

Incidentally, I do not remember any sign of sexual abuse or homosexual relations. I remember that the older boys were quite taken by one of the nuns, younger than the others and quite pretty (I liked her too). One of them said that he had once seen her in a bathing suit, which I doubt. Notwithstanding the innocence of it all, pervasive, indefinable guilt remained.

While for most people cultural identity merges with the feeling of "home," it never was so for me. I like being in France but I certainly do not have any sense of arriving "home" when the plane lands at Roissy — or, for that matter, anywhere else in the world.

This being said, if anyone were to ask me what I consider my core identity, beyond any cultural imprint, something I would never be willing to deny or give up, I would answer without the least hesitation: I am a Jew, albeit one without any religious or tradition-related attachments, yet indelibly marked by the Shoah. Ultimately, I am nothing else.

———

Life's ironies are not always amusing. This one, however, is to a point: that I, with my European "roots," my French education, my love of much that derives from it, will most probably end my life in Tarzana, California, where Orna and I live now. This is quite paradoxical, to say the least.

Moreover, at the time of writing, it is the place where I do little else than follow Israeli politics. On the eve of the March 2015 elections, I, like so many others, hoped for a long-overdue change. It was touch and go, as for years the nationalist religious right, supported by over 50 percent of the population, has dominated the political scene. Add to it the growing rift between the Israeli prime minister and the American president and you are facing a downward slope partly of Israel's doing, in fact a series of provocations coming from its side. It reminds me of a drawing by the Israeli cartoonist Dosh, printed some decades ago on the occasion of some other Israeli confrontation with the United States: a tall Uncle Sam leans toward the small Israeli boy (Dosh's typical representation of Israel) wearing the equally typical *kova tembel* (a hat that makes you look silly) and offers him a handful of dollars. While the little boy extends one hand toward the money, with the other he directs his peeing on Uncle Sam's shoes.

Today, Israel is no little boy anymore; he has turned into a defiant adolescent who still doesn't hesitate to pee on the shoes of his protector against much of the world.

*4*

My various identities found their expression in a series of name changes. I was Pavel, called Pavlíček, in Prague, Paul on arrival in France, Paul-Henri-Marie Ferland in the seminary, Shaul after my arrival in Israel (where I also Hebraized my family name for a short while), then Saül in France again, and finally Saul, a compromise between Paul and Shaul.

Some names, usually the most familiar ones, remained hidden from me for decades. My mother's first name was Elli. I assumed (and never asked my uncles about it) that this was a diminutive of Elisabeth or, in Hebrew, Elisheva. Thus, when filling out forms where the mother's name was required, I confidently put Elisabeth or Elisheva Glaser. It was only some years ago, when working on my Kafka essay, that I discovered that one of Franz's sisters, Elli Kafka, was in fact named Gabrielle, which was shortened to "Elle" and more commonly to "Elli."

My father was Hans in German and Jan in Czech; that much I knew. But other than his sister, Martha, who lived in Prague and whom I dearly loved, I knew nothing of my father's family. I never inquired whether he was born in Lemberg (Lwów or Lviv) or in Prague. In recent years, somebody discovered my father's place of birth, near Prague, and the names of his parents: Arnold and Babette. Arnold and Babette? I had no clue, and I still wonder in what context my paternal grandmother's nickname, Babette (for Barbara?) could have emerged.

For a long time, I was puzzled by one of my own middle names. Officially, I had been given the following middle names (here in their French version): [Paul] Henri Félicien (Felician in German). "Félicien" was particularly unusual ("Henri," at least, was relatively common). By pure chance, I discovered the likely origin of "Felician" in two unrelated stages. First, when I met with my childhood nanny Vlasta in Prague, in 1967, she told me that before I was born, my mother had had a miscarriage and that she had been advised not to become pregnant again. That, in itself, led nowhere, except that I've since wondered whether my conception was intentional or not.

Years later, in Berlin in 1985, I read Arthur Schnitzler's 1908 novel *The Road into the Open* (*Der Weg ins Freie*), and suddenly it clicked. In Schnitzler's novel, an Austrian aristocrat, Georg von Wergenthin, has an affair with a middle-class woman he loves, Anna Rosner. She becomes pregnant. Georg, who is encouraged and supported by his brother Felician, wants to give his brother's first name to the newborn. Anna has a miscarriage, and Georg promises her that should there be another child and were it to be a boy, they would call him Felician. Thus, little by little, I discovered the literary origins of my strange middle name and the events that led to its choice.

## 5

The books I read during my first years in Israel should have expressed the various facets of my fragmented cultural self. They did not. Although I somewhere found Eugène Fromentin's novel *Dominique*, that was more or less all the literature in French I got hold of in my new surroundings (I don't remember when I first read *Le Grand Meaulnes*; it probably was in my Parisian lycée). At some point and for a very short while, I started reading in Hebrew, not mainly Israeli literature, but translations: Dostoevsky, Thomas Mann, in short the "great books." I should add nonetheless that I managed to read S. Y. Agnon's *Tmol shilshom* (*Only Yesterday*) in Hebrew, no small achievement.

I truly loved the "great books," but this wasn't the literature that I devoured during those years. My English was good enough and public libraries supplied me with novels and plays by writers mostly forgotten nowadays — Charles Morgan, Louis Bromfield, A. J. Cronin — but also by some who haven't yet fallen into complete oblivion like Somerset Maugham and J. B. Priestley. And, there was Aldous Huxley's *Point Counter Point*, Galsworthy's *Forsyte Saga*, and Richard Llewellyn's *How Green Was My Valley*. Sometimes, I reached even higher: Thomas Hardy's *The Return of the Native* and *Jude the Obscure*, as well as Rainer Maria Rilke's *The Notebooks of Malte Laurids Brigge* and *Letters to a Young Poet*.

Don't misunderstand me; I didn't abandon my French "heritage": I read in English what I couldn't get in French. I plunged into existentialism (I had started at Henri IV with *L'existentialisme est un humanisme* and *L'étranger*, maybe even with some more) and read any translation of the new masters I got my hands on. In short, Nirah, maybe even Natanyah, received its first existentialist settler; all that may have disappeared when I left. I don't recall ever reading historical books about Nazi Germany or the war; it simply didn't occur to me.

*When Memory Comes* may have appeared to some readers as a memoir describing utter loss, followed by a retrieval of self and the construction of a normal life. I have to correct or at least to nuance this impression. People who, like me, lived their childhood under catastrophic circumstances, may have built a "normal" exterior. Yet, no matter how ornamented the façade may appear, some flaw invariably remains at the very core of their personality. A strange dynamic often ensues: you can't get rid of the flaw, but to offset it, you tirelessly improve the exterior — which does not help much and, for many years, will keep you desperately toiling, never secure, always anxious. This recurrent feeling gets ultimately numbed but it did accompany me as some kind of *basso continuo* through the ups and downs of a good part of my checkered existence. And, as unique as each individual story may be, it can, when told, produce some sense of recognition.

In my case, the inner flaw manifested itself mainly in emotional paralysis. At some stage in the seminary, I stopped longing for my parents and started worrying about how I would express happiness upon their return. I cried profusely when told they would not come back, but wasn't that expected of me? Soon thereafter, mainly after I left the seminary, I recognized that nothing could touch me profoundly. Later I often used a metaphor to describe my incapacity to establish a normal emotional relationship: I was like an insect whose antennas had been torn off. It was not easy to recognize this from the outside — I smiled a lot, knew the right things to say, and readily adapted to fast-changing circumstances. People who knew me well were not fooled, however. "You are incapable of emotion," I was not infrequently told. "Your soul is arid."

The emotional paralysis applied to my relationships with people only. I could become enthusiastic about a cause (Zionism, for example) or very emotional when watching a film, reading a book, or listening to music. In short, there was hope for change — over time.

# CHAPTER TWO

# Paris

In June 1948, I'd left the Paris Gare de Lyon for Marseilles (Port-de-Bouc) and sailed to Israel on the *Altalena*. Five years later, I sailed from Israel to Marseilles on the *Theodor Herzl*, took the train to the Gare de Lyon, and was back in Paris. (My uncle Paul refused to pay for my ticket. I had no choice but to sell those of my father's books and lithographs that I found in Nirah. I left my uncle without regret.)

After emerging from Métro station Saint-Paul on Yom Kippur (the Day of Atonement), 1953, I schlepped my only suitcase to my former guardian's address, rue de Birague, next to the Place des Vosges. I had been accepted as a second-year student at Sciences Po, as I had completed three years of evening classes at the Tel Aviv School of Law and Economics during my service in the army.

The difficult part was finding a job that would allow me to attend Sciences Po at least once a week, for the mandatory seminar. Working for my former guardian as a textile rep (I tried it for three weeks) wouldn't do. I had a letter of recommendation to the Israeli embassy, and made an appointment with the second in command, Counselor Ziama (Zalman) Divon, to whom the letter was addressed. He looked at the letter and at some other documents. Then, eerily echoing my Nirah visitor of 1949, he remarked, "You came on the *Altalena* . . ." I got the job nonetheless, thanks to my "native" French.

Recently a German colleague who had read a few pages of the memoir asked me what was so terrible about arriving in Israel on the *Altalena*. It may be hard to convey the atmosphere of political fanaticism and suspicion that swept the fledgling state of Israel during its War of Independence; its survival was far from certain. While the socialist leadership, with Ben-Gurion at its head, was keeping the ship (no, the raft) of state from sinking during the first phase of the war against the Arab coalition, any internal political opponents were considered direct threats. In particular, Begin's right-wing Irgun, which had allowed the *Altalena* to sail with almost one thousand "fighters" and tons of weapons, was regarded as a terrorist group possibly intent on organizing a military coup. Neither Begin nor anybody around him planned anything of the kind, but Ben-Gurion thought otherwise and for a long time, as we saw, arrival on the *Altalena* carried an unmistakable stigma.

*2*

Nothing of the majestic presence of Paris had changed, but the atmosphere, the feel of the city, was entirely different from when I had left. In 1948 I had escaped from a place in which, for many of its inhabitants (myself included), food and other essentials were still scarce. During the winter of 1947–48 the dormitories of Lycée Henri IV were freezing cold and the meals provided were woefully insufficient. Most boarders received food packages from home and were warmly clad. There wasn't much sharing, however, as the needs of all were hardly fulfilled by what came from the outside.

Moreover, daily life was disrupted by major political demonstrations and strikes, orchestrated by the Communist-dominated trade unions organization, the CGT (Conféderation Générale du Travail); the mass rallies, also led by the Communist Party, protested against the Marshall Plan and the like. For a short while I took part in some of these demonstrations. At least once the strikes included the staff of schools and lycées and sent us boarders scurrying to students' restaurants, where the fare was even worse. In short, the Paris of 1947–48 was hardly a city of unmitigated pleasure for me. Leaving for Israel was both the fulfillment of a dream and a deliverance from daily Parisian reality.

When I returned to Paris in the fall of 1953, everything seemed different. Yes, political life remained unsettled, mainly as a result of hopeless French attempts to keep control of Indochina (later Vietnam) and of the growing threat of a full-scale war to subdue the incipient national rebellion in Algeria. Governments followed each other with increasing speed under the nominal authority of President Vincent Auriol, followed by President René Coty. The Fourth Republic was dying.

I watched the events like everybody else, particularly when Pierre Mendès-France became prime minister (*président du Conseil*). He extricated the country from the war in Indochina and started doing the same in North Africa. The anti-Semitic attacks against Mendès grew, particularly among the populist movement of Pierre Poujade. Some opposition also came from more traditional political old-timers, one of them being another Jewish politician, René Mayer, much more "French," in his own eyes, than Mendès; it led to novelist François Mauriac's stinging article in *L'Express*. Mauriac compared *"Le grand Israelite français, René Mayer"* and *"le petit juif, Mendès-France"* (the great French Israelite René Mayer and the little Jew Mendès-France), invoking the contemptuous attitude of the old French Jewish families of Alsatian background to the more plebeian Sephardic "little Jews"). I supported Mendès, not that it helped . . .

However, all of this political turmoil had no major impact on the course of daily life. Even in the eyes of an impecunious student, paid a meager salary by the Israeli embassy for work in the press department at first, then in the military attaché's office, Paris in the mid-fifties was a feast; I felt like a ravenous guest standing at the threshold of the banquet hall.

For a year or so, I shared an apartment on rue Ampère (close to the embassy, located on avenue de Wagram), with my friend and colleague Meir Rosenne, who worked in the visa office of the consular section. I had received Meir's address from his brother, who had been a fellow passenger on the *Theodor Herzl*. I called and when Meir told me that he also had a job at the embassy, I suggested that we rent an apartment together, close to our workplace. So we did. On many a morning when we arrived at avenue de Wagram, on foot of course, and the ambassador's limo was idling in front of the building with driver in livery at the ready, Meir prophesied that one day he would ride in that kind of car with that kind of driver in uniform. And he was right. Another of our colleagues, who participated in many of our escapades, Eliahu Ben Elissar, also became an ambassador in Paris.

I had practically no contact with the ambassador, Yakov Tsur, and not much with his second in command, either. Most of my work kept me in the basement of the building, the domain of the press department, where I started working sometime in the late fall of 1953. It was headed by a most congenial attaché of Italian background, Dan Avni (or, in the original, Vittorio Segre). I couldn't have wished for a nicer boss, and I soon was a frequent guest at the Avnis' (Dan, Rosetta, and the first of their boys, Emanuel).

My work involved summarizing the daily press articles about Israel and meeting with journalists — Israeli correspondents needing assistance, journalists of the local Jewish press, and, of course, French journalists of all hues. Elie Wiesel, who at that time worked for the Israeli evening paper *Yediot Ahronot*, often came by. And sometime in 1954 or early 1955, I met a journalist from *Haaretz*, Shabtai Teveth, who became a very close friend.

And there was Sciences Po. It was a *Grande École* (French higher education was divided between its universities and its *Grandes Écoles*, which were much more selective institutions). The name "Sciences Po" was a remnant of the former elitist "École Libre des Sciences Politiques," which, after the war, became "Institut d'Études Politiques," a democratized school preparing for various branches of the civil service and more. If you were French, once you completed the three years of Sciences Po, you could compete again for admission to the École Nationale d'Administration, which led to the higher civil service. Foreigners like me, and like quite a few Israelis at that time, were limited to the first three years. Most of us chose the Relations Internationales department, which could lead to our own foreign service.

Once a week, we attended a mandatory seminar, but beyond that, attendance was never checked. Most of the time, work prevented me from getting to the lectures. Moreover, you could buy the mimeographed texts of these lectures in a bookstore opposite the entrance to the school, on the hallowed rue Saint-Guillaume. At the end of the year or of your stay at Sciences Po, you could sell back your mimeographed texts; thus the same copies were passed on to the next cohort, often with additional comments scribbled in the margins. As the lectures remained largely unchanged year after year, your predecessors even noted the exact spot of a lecturer's standard joke.

I vividly remember some of the professors I occasionally listened to in halls packed with several hundred students. There was Pierre Renouvin, a revered professor of international relations history, who dealt particularly with the 1870–1914 period. When he entered the hall in his dark blue suit with one empty sleeve — he had lost an arm during the Great War — everyone stood up. There was an apparently excellent professor of economic history who "lost" me once he started explaining Ricardo's theory of surplus value. Some teachers were downright amusing: François LeRoy, for example, who, from year to year, opened his lecture on French postwar foreign policy with the same outline: "French foreign policy after the Second World War was fuzzy in its aims, feeble in its means, and null in its results. Part one: 'Fuzzy in Its Aims' . . ."

2

Apart from the embassy and Sciences Po, Paris offered its streets, theaters, cafés, and restaurants, its music and its dance halls.

This last item demands a short preface. A further consequence of my strict wartime Catholic education was shyness around girls. This eased somewhat in Israel. In the army I had a few girlfriends; they allowed much, but not everything (and I probably did not insist strongly enough). The moment, however, I boarded the *Theodor Herzl* for Marseilles, I decided to change all that — and fast.

At the time, Paris harbored any number of expensive nightclubs and dozens of affordable dance halls with live orchestras; you didn't go there with a girl but in order to find a girl or vice versa. (These dance halls were packed with young men and women with similar intentions.)

During my army service I had taken dance lessons in a studio on Ben Yehuda Street, in Tel Aviv, so that, technically, I could manage. The trick was not in the dancing, however, but rather in overcoming your inhibitions. You had to spot a girl you fancied in the crowd and then, while a dance was ending, rush to her and ask: *"M'accorderez-vous la prochaine danse?"* (Would you grant me the next dance?) If the answer was yes and the girl pleasant, you didn't wait too long to ask her for the following dance. During all that time you had to talk your head off; in French you call it *baratiner. Baratin* (the noun, translated as "blah-blah" in the dictionary) demanded a special talent and I wasn't bad at it. Then, if the response to your new request was positive (and you were already slow-dancing, glued to one other), you could start planning further ahead. Some dance halls were popular (Mimi Pinson on the Champs-Élysées, for example), others more subdued and select, like the Whisky à Gogo on rue Jean Mermoz (where in fact records had replaced the live band). The *caveaux* where you went to listen to jazz more than to dance represented a special category: thus, at the Vieux Colombier, for example, you could spend the evening with Claude Luter's orchestra and Sidney Bechet playing the saxophone.

I became something of an authority on these institutions. I used to declare that if I ever chose to write a dissertation it would be on Parisian dance halls. Today, it would be a great topic in cultural history but I am afraid that this kind of dance hall has disappeared. Some of my "conquests" were just casual encounters, others turned into relationships that may have lasted for several weeks; one became a two-year-long affair that ended with my departure from Paris. Incidentally, Meir and I shared a large apartment where each of us had his own room and reasonable privacy. In short, I was "sowing my wild oats," albeit very late in the day by present standards.

There was a special treat that didn't cost much: students could buy tickets for a very low price to a famous nightclub off the Champs-Élysées: the Villa d'Este. You had to be well-dressed, tie and all, come relatively early, and sit leisurely with a bottle of pseudo-champagne, so that the place seemed already partly full when, somewhat later, tourists started looking in. There, at the Villa d'Este, you could hear the best of the best: Georges Brassens, Gilbert Bécaud, and the comedian Fernand Raynaud, among many others.

Finally, there was the world of theater and film. In that domain, the fifties were an extraordinary time. In theater, Jean Vilar's TNP (Théâtre National Populaire) was revolutionary in many ways since its founding in the late forties, the opposite of the august but stuffy Comédie Française. One of the TNP's stars, Gérard Philipe, had also become an admirable film actor: I shall never forget *Le diable au corps*, which I probably saw in 1947 or 1948. In the 1950s, I went to all of Gérard Philipe's movies from *Belles de nuit* on. This was not yet the French "new wave," but these more traditional films and their more traditional directors (Carné, Clément, Renoir, Clair, Autan-Lara, among some other great names), most of whom were already famous well before the war, created a world of unique sensitivity and beauty.

I shouldn't forget to mention one of the magic moments of daily life: the meals. For me, at the time, food was not only about nourishment; a meal turned into a ritual, the occasion of a daily celebration. I had been hungry during the war, then during the postwar years in France, and a year after I arrived in Israel, *Tsena*, the austerity period and the rationing, began. The main staple, tuna fish, delivered in endless shipments from Denmark, became the unavoidable daily fare for months on end.

In Paris, I usually had lunch in the same restaurant, close to the embassy. It turned into a fixed repeat ceremony: *oeuf dur mayonnaise, steak frites (saignant), chèvre, meringue Chantilly,** espresso, and red wine, mostly Côtes du Rhône. How could I work after that? I did, without any problem — like most Frenchmen. This was nothing compared to the dinners (oysters, *steak au poivre,*† etc.). I hadn't heard of weight issues, nor, incidentally, of the dangers of smoking. I enjoyed indiscriminately one or the other brand of cigarettes: Gitanes or Gauloises bleues, without filters. Smoking a pack a day was common.

One question, though, kept flashing on an otherwise peaceful horizon: How and where would I prepare for the end of second-year oral exams and, mainly, for the third-year finals? The second-year orals were no major problem, thanks to the mimeographed lectures. As you were informed on which specific course you would be examined each day during the two-week

---

* Hard boiled egg with mayonnaise sauce; steak (rare) with fries; goat cheese; meringue with whipped cream.

† Steak with pepper sauce.

exam period, it sufficed to memorize the lecture notes on the eve of each interrogation, regurgitate the answers the next morning, then forget everything you'd just studied and repeat the process for the following day's exam. At that time my memory still functioned as it was expected to, and fatigue was overcome with pills the name of which I have since forgotten. When all was over, I fell ill from exhaustion, but within a few days I was back on my feet.

The end of the third year did not allow a repeat performance, as the exams were both written and oral and, except for knowing that they would cover the history of international relations, international law, and international economics, any topic that had been taught over the three years could come up. As chance would have it, about three months before the finals, the physician of the embassy, whom I visited for some minor complaint, had me x-rayed and found dark patches on the lungs that he interpreted as early signs of tuberculosis. He ordered three months of paid leave and full rest. A second opinion, which I sought on my own, did not confirm such an ominous diagnosis. I kept this second opinion to myself (after all, the embassy was responsible for a diagnosis by its own physician . . .) and took my three months' pay.

I settled in Saint-Rémy-lès-Chevreuse, a small town some forty minutes by local train from the Gare du Luxembourg. La Créssonière, a charming little inn, offered me full board for the money I could pay. Nearby, the ruins of the famous Jansenist convent of Port-Royal, where Blaise Pascal and Jean Racine had lived for some time, attracted tourists. My own inn was also well-known but differently: I soon discovered that it was a choice retreat for couples from Paris who wished to remain anonymous. I worked hard for three months and became ready for the finals.

The regular written and oral exams were no major problem, but then at the end came the most dreaded exam, the notorious *exposé oral* (oral presentation), a specialty of Sciences Po. You drew a topic from any of the subjects you had studied during your three years at the school, received half an hour to prepare, and then had to present it in front of a jury of three professors in exactly ten minutes (you were stopped if you went overtime). This was the "endgame" in a sense. It so happens that I drew a topic I had read about shortly beforehand: "The Institutional Structure of the British Commonwealth." Today, I wouldn't have the faintest idea.

By ordinary standards, I reacted strangely on receiving my Sciences Po results in the early summer of 1955: I had made it to top student (*major*) in Relations Internationales that year. However, instead of attending the "champagne reception" for the four *majors* of the year (one for each department), hosted by the director of the school, Jacques Chapsal, I went to a *thé dansant* (five o'clock tea with orchestra and dancing) somewhere on the Champs-Élysées. It took me some years to understand that strange behavior: I was probably so terrified of any success that I used quasi-magical rituals, not to cancel it, as I needed it like the air I breathed, but to welcome it and at the same time establish a safe distance. Over the years I acquired the almost automatic habit of belittling any achievements. In short — and please excuse the oxymoron — I became an artist in false modesty.

More importantly, my life could have changed there and then. Given my results, Michel de Boissieu, one of the adjunct professors and a very high official at the Banque de Paris et des Pays-Bas (today "Paribas," I think), offered me a position at the bank, one of the most important ones in France. It meant, among other things, becoming French almost automatically. I was duly grateful but rejected the offer. It did not occur to me to turn my back on Israel. However limited my desire to live in Israel at the time could have been, I felt inexorably attached to that country. In fact, however critical my present attitude may be, this sense of attachment is not yet extinguished.

## 3

Once back at the embassy, in the summer of 1955, I moved from the press department to the military attaché's office, and again I was lucky. The military attaché, Colonel Emanuel Nishri, a French-trained officer, was a bon vivant with an eye for the ladies; he ruled his office like an enlightened monarch. Always spick and span — and very different from most Israeli officers, who, in that regard, exhibited a studied nonchalance — Nishri, when considering some trying issue, would puff at an inexhaustible pipe while exclaiming from time to time, "A scandal! A scandal!" (*Biẓayon* in Hebrew). Nobody got upset.

On the other side of our three offices, you entered the domain of the air attaché, Lieutenant-Colonel Paul Kedar: during the war, he had fought as a Royal Air Force pilot, stationed mainly in South Asia (Ceylon, I think). Paul, as I would soon call him, had not acquired British superciliousness. As at the Avnis, I was to become a frequent guest at the Kedars' (Paul and his wife Ruthie).

Very soon after I joined my new post, a hectic period started. The special relations between Israel and France were tightening rapidly, and a constant stream of high-ranking Israeli officers and Defense Ministry officials visited Paris in what soon turned into preparations for a common operation against Colonel Gamal Abdel Nasser's Egypt. In 1955, as Egypt controlled the straits of Sharm el-Sheikh, Nasser closed the Gulf of Akaba to ships sailing to Elath, the Israeli Red Sea harbor. In July 1956, Nasser nationalized the Suez Canal, a waterway supposedly open to all shipping under international law, although Israel had been barred from using it since the creation of the state. The Soviet Union was sending military advisers and massive quantities of heavy military equipment to the Egyptians. We saw a short film secretly shot in the harbor of Alexandria: huge Soviet tanks were being disembarked and loaded on trailers by Egyptian crews. It didn't bode well. Moreover, incidents between the two countries, mainly incursions by fedayeen from the Gaza Strip and Israeli retaliations, grew in number and scope.

As for the French, they believed that Nasser was helping the Algerian rebellion. In short, common interests between Israel and France were leading to preparations for common action. Moreover, the French prime minister Guy Mollet and his entire socialist government were friendly to Israel and set on helping the Jewish state against the growing danger from Nasser's Egypt and its Soviet ally. The memory of Munich, the abandonment by France of a small state threatened by a powerful neighbor, remained strong.

As a symbol of the military rapprochement between the two countries, in early 1956 the commander in chief of the French army, General Maurice Challe, decorated the Israeli chief of staff, General Moshe Dayan, with the medal of *Grand Officier* of the Legion of Honor. We all attended the ceremony; it took place on a cold and rainy day in February in the courtyard of the École Militaire, the same courtyard where some sixty years earlier the Jewish captain Alfred Dreyfus was publicly stripped of his rank after having been (falsely) found guilty of treason because he was a Jew. And it was this blatant manifestation of anti-Jewish hatred that prodded the Paris correspondent of the Viennese *Neue Freie Presse*, Theodor Herzl, to come up with the idea of fighting anti-Semitism by establishing a Jewish state.

What a sneer on the face of history! One cannot escape the fact that the Jewish state, which should have saved the Jews from a monstrous paroxysm of anti-Semitism, came too late. And one cannot help recognizing that, nowadays, the Jewish state contributes, not only by its misguided policies but by its very existence, to the surge of a new/old anti-Semitism. I often think of that tragic evolution, which, in part, is the background of my own life. Even in 1956, our "natural allies" in the French army (the government, as I said, was different) were friends of Israel, but no friends of the Jews.

Soon the British would join the secret alliance to reestablish control over the Suez Canal, but warily, and with persistent hostility toward Israel. Painful memories of the mandate period lingered in London, and while Prime Minister Anthony Eden mainly worried about a negative reaction from the United States, Foreign Minister Selwyn Lloyd, who participated in tripartite talks near Paris (in Sèvres) in October 1956, was typically wary of Jews, and mainly of Israel (in the tradition of his predecessor, Ernest Bevin, and of the Foreign Office more generally).

The French were delivering Mystère (or was it already "Mirage"?) jet fighters, Ouragan fighter-bombers, as well as AMX tanks to Israel. The jets flew from a military airport near Paris (Villacoublay) to Bari in southern Italy and from there to Israel. We followed the landings in Bari over the phone. I suppose communicating in Hebrew was enough of a code for these occasions, even if some Soviet agents were listening. In any case, it didn't remain secret for long, as within a few months the Suez campaign would start and all these French planes would then fly Israeli colors.

4

During all those years in Paris, not once did I bother to look for the places in which my parents and I lived after our arrival in April 1939. At that time, I had forgotten the name of the hotel where we spent our first weeks in France, along with the name of the street on which my parents had later rented a small apartment. But I clearly remembered the areas (Pigalle in the first case, Porte de Versailles in the second), and I certainly remembered the Jewish children's home to which I was sent while my parents were learning some useful profession (my mother became a beautician and my father learned cheese making). I recall getting tied to a tree and beaten up by yarmulke-wearing boys for being a *goy*. The home was in Montmorency, scarcely beyond the northern suburbs of Paris. In short, I didn't wish to reach beyond what I already knew. And what I knew did not weigh on me, or so I thought.

Nevertheless, during the years 1953 to 1956, I regularly met with people who knew my parents in Néris and now lived in Paris, particularly the Macé de Lépinay family, who, in 1942, had established the contact with the seminary, and the Chamboux couple, who had become close friends of my parents. The Macé de Lépinay family stayed regularly in Néris, where they had a pleasant secondary residence during the summer season. The husband, a physician, attended to patients who came for treatment to the spa; the water was supposedly beneficial for nervous disorders. Madame de Lépinay, a formidable lady, ruled over the local lending library, over her family, and over whoever came under her spell, like my father, her German teacher. She told me much later that she was born Jewish but converted to Catholicism early in life. That may have been a good reason for staying in Néris during the war. As for the Chamboux, they were both Communists; that, again, may have been a sufficient reason to choose our small town.

Somewhere, deep down, I may nonetheless have kept some traces of emotion. Thus, I went at least five times to see René Clement's film *Les jeux interdits* (*Forbidden Games*), the story of a little French girl, Paulette, whose parents are killed during the *débacle* (the flight of millions of people ahead of the German advance). She finds shelter with a peasant family, where she falls in love with the son, Michel, approximately her age, about six. The idyll cannot last: a Red Cross delegate takes her away. As the crowd in a large refugee hall mills around, Paulette hears a voice calling "Michel!" The film ends as she shouts desperately, "Michel! Michel!" I cried each time.

## 5

I forgot to mention that when I left Paris for Saint-Rémy, Meir and I had to give up the apartment on rue Ampère, which was leased to us by the most eccentric landlord I ever encountered: a dowser. I wonder how many people still know what a dowser is; it so happens that I knew the word in French, *un sourcier*, and reached for the dictionary. A dowser discovers underground water, lost objects, and more by using a twig that supposedly vibrates the closer he gets to the object of his search.

From the spacious apartment on rue Ampère, I moved to a *chambre de bonne* (a maid's room) on the sixth floor, under the eaves of an apartment building on boulevard Berthier. At the time — and possibly even today — housemaids lived in those tiny single rooms, with a sink in the room but common toilets at the end of the corridor. It was in such a room that my girlfriend Maryvonne, whom I met at Mimi Pinson, and I spent much time, and also where we later had to induce a hemorrhage in order for her to be admitted into a hospital and have an abortion. We both agreed on it: Maryvonne already had a son who lived with her parents; she didn't want another child.

Abortions were strictly forbidden in France at the time, except if prior bleeding or any kind of related complication occurred. These were messy affairs: you had to call somebody, usually a midwife (whose phone number you kept, just in case), who would induce the bleeding for a substantial sum. I felt quite guilty, notwithstanding our agreement, a feeling intensified by my certainty that this relationship wasn't going to last.

Two months before the beginning of the Sinai campaign (which started at the end of October 1956), I resigned from my temporary job at the embassy and left Paris for Sweden.

In the next two years, I would change countries three times again. Was I replicating the migrations of my childhood? Was I acting out geographically, so to say, the repeatedly shifting changes in my sense of identity? I don't know. I only remember that, at the time, I was proud of my "lightness of being." I liked living on the surface of things. Possessions, I had none; deep attachments to people, I hadn't either. My commitment to Zionism was real, but I preferred it nonbinding as far as life in Israel went, so that I could quickly escape, if need be. Thus, at twenty-four, I was a luftmensch in the true sense of the word.

# CHAPTER THREE

# Sweden

To reach Saltå Arbetsskola, you take the train from Stockholm to Järna, via Södertälje; from there you can choose between a short drive or, on a nice summer day, a pleasant one-hour walk downhill. The school appears after the road turns sharply to the right (it is on flat ground by then): a cluster of small houses built in the typical red wood of Swedish country homes, surrounded by trees and, beyond them, by cultivated fields. If you look down the road, you will notice, about half a mile away, the dark line of a forest. After reaching the edge of the forest and climbing a gentle slope, the road winds down toward the waters of a sound and a ferry wharf.

The Saltå Work School (as its name could be translated) was (and maybe still is) an anthroposophical institution for mentally disabled boys from approximately age twelve to an undefined upper limit, as most of the patients would never be able to adapt to the outside world. Sometime in the 1940s, my uncle Hans Glaser became Saltå's director. He had chosen Sweden, together with my maternal grandmother, in the fall of 1939.

By pure chance — but he would have objected to "chance" — Uncle Hans had become an anthroposophist in the early 1930s. His brother Willy (my mother had three brothers: Paul, Willy, and Hans), a chemical engineer, was returning home via Switzerland. As he had to wait several hours in Basel for the train connection to Prague, he decided to visit the world center of anthroposophy in nearby Dornach, mainly, I think, to see the peculiar architecture of the Goetheanum (the headquarters of the movement) designed by its founder, Rudolf Steiner. During the visit, he took some literature and left it lying around in the Glaser family home in Rochlitz; Hans discovered it, read it, and saw the light.

Steiner had founded anthroposophy on the eve of the First World War. The movement derived from Theosophy but seceded from it. Anthroposophy aims at spiritual enlightenment, achievable, according to Steiner, by a series of rational steps that can be scientifically validated. The movement became influential in introducing its methods and insights into education (it established its own schools, the "Waldorf schools"), special education, medicine, agriculture, and art.

I don't know what Hans had read in the thirties and how far he had internalized Steiner's teachings. Whatever the case may be, the Swedish anthroposophists — who probably helped him get a visa for himself and for my grandmother — must have been sufficiently impressed by his commitment and also, probably, by his practical experience in agriculture and business, to put him in charge of the school in Järna.

Apparently my uncle did very well in his new position, and Saltå Arbetsskola also became recognized as something of a model institution by the Swedish health authorities. Some of its young residents came from state mental homes, others were sent privately. I'd visited the school for the first time in 1954, and liked it. After leaving my temporary job at the Paris embassy, I thought that Saltå would be a good place for pondering about a more permanent future. I informed my uncle and set off from the Gare du Nord: Brussels, Amsterdam, Hamburg, Copenhagen, Malmö, Stockholm, Södertälje, Järna.

I would have to earn my keep. At first, I didn't consider taking a job at the school and rather hoped to find something in Stockholm and come to Järna occasionally. I talked to people at the *Dagens Nyheter* (the Daily News) and at some commercial enterprises, all in vain. The two months' salary that I had received upon leaving the embassy would not last for long. I enjoyed being down and out, sitting till late at night in a café at the Central Railway Station, watching the trains, eating my only meal of the day, a hot dog with a lot of mustard and a cup of coffee, basking in real, penetrating melancholia.

In October 1953, I had arrived in Paris with one suitcase that contained all my belongings, and here I was in Stockholm, three years later, with the same suitcase and all my belongings. In 1954, my uncle Paul had died of uremia following the botched operation I mentioned previously. Willy, who also lived in Nirah, took over Paul's house, gave me some paltry sum — and that was it.

2

I returned from Stockholm to Saltå and joined the staff of caretakers (a few Swedes and some Germans). I started learning basic Swedish, and in the late fall of 1956 became a full-fledged orderly. That stay would become a significant, albeit short, episode in my life.

My uncle Hans must have been in his late forties at the time of my arrival: he was a small, squat man with a ducklike walk, at each step balancing his entire frame from one leg to the other. His wife, Lissa, was as tall and emaciated as he was small and squat. A German Jewess, she had fled from Fürth to Norway and from there, in 1942, to Sweden. Like Hans, she was an anthroposophist. I haven't encountered many families of Protestant pastors of the old European hue; I imagine that in their appearance, Hans and Lissa would have fitted in nicely. They were good people, entirely devoted to the youngsters in their care — and to anthroposophy.

Most of the caretakers were young men and women; some were attracted to anthroposophy but the majority had merely heard of the place and come as volunteers for a year or two, in search of their future, like me. The odd man out was Herr K.: he had served in the Waffen-SS on the Eastern Front and, after a few glasses of aquavit, he would tell of the Russian villages his unit had set ablaze and the like. My uncle said that K. had come out of remorse. I didn't think so.

I don't remember how many youngsters lived in Saltå during my stay, probably around thirty, all of them Swedes, all of them very ill. Some became quite unruly at times and had to be physically restrained, but mostly for a short while and never in the harsh ways used in state institutions. During my stay, only one patient turned truly dangerous and chose me of all people as his target. Whenever he saw me, his face contorted, clearly indicating a mysterious but irrepressible rage. Had it gone on, he certainly would have attacked me physically. I had to leave for a week or so to a neighboring farm; when I returned, Pär (that was the youngster's name) had been transferred to another institution.

The very basic Swedish I soon acquired sufficed for exchanging a few words with my charges when we went on walks (usually I would take three or four of them along). No level of linguistic mastery could help, however, when a member of my little group decided to run into a snow-covered field and lie in the snow, arms and legs flailing in all directions, resisting any attempt at pulling him up. I described one such incident in *When Memory Comes* (it involved young Hans Z. and not Arne as I mistakenly wrote; Arne could not speak). Although Hans's speech was limited to just a few sentences, he followed some internal monologue with indistinct mumblings and wild gesticulations. On a day I will never forget, we walked by a local school just as the children were coming out. They saw Hans and the fun began: standing in a wide circle they imitated his gesticulations while taunting him in words incomprehensible to me. My shouting made no difference, and an infuriated Hans threw himself down into a nearby snowfield in a total loss of control. When I reached him and tried to calm him, he suddenly turned his snot-covered face toward me and desperately shouted, "Herr Friedländer! Herr Friedländer!"

Generally though, the daily routine ran smoothly: gardening, weaving, eurythmic dancing, reading aloud, and taking our meals in Saltå's large dining hall. The weaving and the eurythmic dancing stemmed from the same principle: instill in the patients a sense of order (the weaving followed simple patterns and so did the dancing, created by one of Rudolf Steiner's early adepts). The reading in common had a somewhat different aim: every day, one of the Swedish caretakers read some old legend to the assembled youngsters for about an hour. Although, in ordinary terms, most of them were not capable of understanding the story, the assumption was nonetheless that such legends carried archetypal contents (the Jungian concept was not used, but the notion was the same) that, in subconscious ways, had a healing effect. Naturally, this insight could not be verified, but during the readings the youngsters were absolutely quiet and seemed to follow along.

Belief in the reincarnation of souls underlay these various therapies. Mental illness was but a phase in a long series of mutations; accordingly, all individuals were to be treated with respect and care — as beings who would heal at some stage. No state institution would encourage such attention. Medication was used, but only in homeopathic dosage.

Don't be mistaken: we felt strong compassion for our wards, but on occasion we had to laugh at their idiosyncrasies. Göran, for example, the oldest patient and a very big fellow, always impeccably dressed with tie and hat, would never fail to shake your hand and then, while mumbling some incomprehensible incantation, bring his fingers to your throat — not to strangle you, but rather to button your collar for tidiness's sake. Now imagine Göran (with a caretaker) getting on the train to Stockholm for a visit to the dentist. He would shake hands with all the passengers in the compartment; in turn they would invariably get up to greet this polite newcomer. A few minutes later, though, Göran would suddenly lunge at some traveler's throat before the caretaker had the time to utter a word . . .

Or take Karl-Georg. Day in, day out, he held forth in angry monologues against the Catholic Church, God, the saints, and any related topics; he spoke with blazing eyes and agitated movements, totally impervious to his environment. The angry youngster's bowel movement took place once weekly; he shunned the toilets and opted for a chamber pot that he filled to the brim. Then came the crucial moment: if no caretaker was around — and you never knew when Karl-Georg would hit the pot — he would open the window of his second-floor room and fling his chamber pot into the courtyard. During my stay no passerby was ever struck by it, but this remained a distinct possibility.

Arne, the young resident I mostly took care of, was about thirteen. All day and all night long he sang the same three syllables: "*Svalla Ble*"; it meant nothing. Usually he sang quietly but at times he would raise his voice and yell the "*Svalla Ble*" at the top of his lungs. It sufficed to say "*Tyst!*" (Silence!) and the volume would return to normal. Arne had been a bright child, but at some stage a degenerative — and irreversible — illness set in. If you gave him a printed page, he could read the text automatically, in a robotic way, but he could not speak on his own. He died two or three years after my departure.

### 3

What was it that so strongly impressed me during my stay in Saltå? Not anthroposophy, to which I was never attracted, nor caretaking of the mentally ill, which I performed as well as I could but never considered a calling. I could have stayed, but I left at the end of one year, in the summer of 1957. And yet, as long as my uncle was alive — and that brings us to the mid-1980s — I returned several times to visit him and Lissa and to see Saltå again.

The strong impression left by Saltå was probably due to several elements. Belonging to a community cut off from the "noises" of the world certainly had its importance (in this, my cloistered childhood had left another imprint: I often longed for some kind of retreat, for living in a secluded community); Saltå was not secluded in the least but lay somewhat outside of the real world, given its inhabitants and mainly the melancholy of the

Swedish countryside that surrounded it. In the winter one hardly saw the light of day, and during endless summer nights, when you sat on the shore of the sound, nothing broke the deep silence, except, occasionally, a flight of wild geese.

After leaving Paris — probably during my stay in Saltå — I shed my gregariousness and became much more prone to keeping to myself. The quest — sporadic at that time — for some "spiritual" content played a role. I don't like using the word "spiritual," as it may give the impression of my turning toward religion. It certainly does not mean starting to believe in God or adopting any kind of religious doctrine. No, it could rather be defined as a meditative tendency, without the trappings of the form of "meditation" that became so common in the West from the late sixties on. I never meditated as a kind of exercise, as some search for "personal improvement" or "growth." At times, I simply longed for interior stillness, for just letting the surrounding world take over, wherever I might be at that moment, and emptying my mind of all thought.

Finally, did the very existence of the Saltå youngsters influence me in a way that I may not have clearly perceived at the time? Most of them carried within themselves something that could not be reached, something that overwhelmed them, thoughts they could not articulate, feelings they could not express. Of course, there was an unbridgeable gap between their mental illness and the kind of emotional blockage in a life like mine. But, symbolically speaking, in both cases a path was closed, some inner domain remained inaccessible. Without realizing it, I may have found in Saltå's patients the reflection — albeit a distorted one — of a mute self, that may have attracted me to the school, kept me there, and brought me back several times over three decades.

The impact of that first prolonged stay also found an expression some thirty years later, which I rediscovered only recently when browsing through old letters. In the early eighties, I planned to write a novel; the title I gave to a publisher was The Journey to Sweden (Le Voyage en Suède). I even signed a contract.

My stay in Saltå came to an end. In July or early August 1957, thanks to some money I had just received (as I will explain in the next chapter), I took the train to Göteborg. As the train started, a German caretaker and a good friend, Habermann (first name forgotten), stood on the platform, took out his guitar, and intoned a hit apparently famous in Germany in the fifties: *"Alles liegt so weit, so weit; schön war die Zeit"* (All lies so far, so far; beautiful were the days . . .). And, with this touch of kitsch, I was on my way. The next morning, I boarded the *Gripsholm* for New York.

The Swedish story has an epilogue, however. On the *Gripsholm*, a very modern liner, my cabin was located on the lowest deck; I possibly even shared it. I have forgotten the details of the voyage, with the exception of one memorable incident. I met a very nice young American couple from Seattle, Pat and Pete, who were returning from their European honeymoon. We spent much time together during the trip, so that quite naturally we also sat together at a small table of four during the captain's dinner, on the eve of our arrival in New York. The fourth diner at our table was a youngish ship officer, as is customary.

Our Swedish companion arrived late, which is unusual on such occasions, and when he finally showed up, it was quite clear from his stumbling gait, his perspiring reddish face, his open collar, and his hardly comprehensible greeting, that he was quite drunk. We started eating and he started speaking. He spoke erratically but without stopping. Pat and Pete tried desperately to make some conversation with him while I gave up from the beginning and kept silent. It was a mistake.

Suddenly our officer — who had of course been briefed about the identity of the three other guests — turned to me and exploded: "You arrogant Jew! You consider yourself better than us, you look down on us, you despise us!" I cannot remember the exact words, yet it is impossible to forget the gist of his tirade. Pat, Pete, and I were paralyzed as he proceeded to hurl one anti-Semitic insult after another. He was enraged, yet could not be overheard at the other tables because of the general hubbub in the dining room. I could do nothing except get up and leave, which I did.

I don't know anymore whether I expected my Seattle friends to leave with me or to intervene in any way. They did nothing. I met them the next morning; they apologized and told me that our table companion had been an officer on the *Stockholm*, which had rammed into the Italian liner *Andrea Doria* a year beforehand. The *Andrea Doria* sank, and some fifty people died in the shipwreck. They had heard it all from another officer, to whom they spoke of the incident. Since then, our companion was drinking heavily and had become something of a problem. I understood the explanation. What I couldn't understand as easily was the anti-Semitic torrent that had erupted. Was I walking on thin ice during my stay in Sweden?

At the time, it didn't even occur to me. After all, hadn't the Swedes taken in the Jews who fled Norway and Denmark? Hadn't the Swedish diplomat Raoul Wallenberg saved thousands of Jews in Budapest during the last months of the war? Yes, the Stern gang had killed the Swedish mediator in the Israeli-Arab conflict in 1948, but it was an assassination that could be attributed to Israel and not to Jews as such. In short, our host's outburst came from some personal source of hatred. And yet, in its fury, it drew upon common lore, upon something present in his cultural background, something still widely present all over Europe. It still was taboo but the taboo could disappear after a few drinks.

# CHAPTER FOUR

# New Horizons

When Karl Rossmann, the protagonist of Kafka's first novel, *The One Who Disappeared* (often entitled *Amerika*), sails into New York harbor, he sees the Statue of Liberty holding a sword. I don't remember anything as ominous when the *Gripsholm* approached its pier. Yet, instead of the rich uncle who welcomes Karl into a brief life of luxury, I was thrown into the unbearably damp summer heat of New York City and into what was probably its dingiest hotel, somewhere around Forty-second Street. Did I mind? Not really. My suitcase was safely with me, the night went by, and in the early morning I was on my way to the Greyhound station, heading for Boston.

*l*

Let me backtrack very briefly.

In 1949, my uncle Paul took in the four members of the Neumann family who had arrived from Prague: the mother, Herma, was a cousin of my mother and thus of my uncles. Herma and her husband, Emil, an engineer, stayed with us for a longer period while their twin daughters, Irena and Alena, soon went to live and work in Tel Aviv. Both daughters were about seven or eight years older than I. They had been deported with their parents from Prague to Theresienstadt and then, in late 1944, to Auschwitz, from where they were sent to some German factory. The entire Neumann family survived the war and returned to Prague. The Communist "coup" of 1948 convinced them to leave; although they were not Zionists, the best available option at the time was Israel.

Both sisters were sophisticated young women and strikingly beautiful. Within a short time, Alena got married to a South African Jew, Norman Lurie, who, ardent Zionist that he was, had built a very posh hotel, the Dolphin, in western Galilee. In the early 1950s Irena got involved in a long and tumultuous affair with Nahum Goldmann, then president of the World Jewish Congress and of the World Zionist Organization. She later married Lane Kirkland, an American labor union leader who became president of the AFL-CIO.

Irena told Goldmann about my success at Sciences Po and he offered me a job as "political secretary" (whatever that meant), which induced me to leave my temporary position at the Paris embassy. The embassy colleagues organized a farewell party for me and told me how lucky I was to have landed such a great job. On the morrow of the party, I received a telegram from Goldmann informing me that he was sorry but, on second thought, he didn't need a political secretary. Out of the embassy, without work, uncertain about what I wanted to do in the longer run, I decided on Sweden. I also wanted to put an end to the affair with Maryvonne. This perhaps better explains the voyage.

After a while, Goldmann realized that he had left me in the

lurch. He knew from Irena that I wished to start graduate studies and sent me a check for $2,100 (that went a long way at the time), allowing me to purchase the ticket to New York and even leaving me some money for a few months. Thanks to my Sciences Po results, I had been accepted as a graduate student in the Harvard Department of Government, so that from Boston I proceeded to Cambridge and to some motel on Mass. Ave.


Why the Department of Government? And why, moreover, did I specifically choose Middle Eastern studies? Probably, as in choosing Relations Internationales at Sciences Po, I kept to the vague idea that, ultimately, this would lead me to the Israeli Foreign Service; in other words, I would become a staunch representative of Israel but spend much of the time outside of Israel.

Back to Cambridge. During the few weeks preceding the start of the academic year, my material circumstances improved: I moved from the motel to a large apartment together with three other Israelis, all of them advanced graduate students at MIT. I had a girlfriend named Franny and some of the Goldmann money left over; at that point, there was nothing to complain about.

I greatly enjoyed the peace and quiet of Harvard before the beginning of the school year. Most of the time, I sat in the reading room of Widener Library and read eclectically. Some texts I remember clearly to this day. As I had chosen Middle Eastern history and politics, I systematically went through issues of the *Middle East Journal* and discovered an article that quite unsettled me: a detailed comparison between Israel and the Crusader Kingdom. Necessarily, the author argued, Israel's fate would ultimately be the same as that of its medieval precursor. In other words, as the kingdoms established by the European invaders during the crusades lasted barely two hundred years before succumbing to Muslim armies, so would Israel's fate not be different. As with the medieval forerunner, the presence of the Jewish settlers before 1948 and of the State of Israel that followed were considered intrusions of foreign elements into the body of the Umma (the Muslim commonwealth); they had to be expelled before health was restored. Although the outcomes of the war of 1948 and of the recent Sinai campaign did not point in that direction, the argument seemed historically plausible to me at that time.

Apart from my intellectual pursuits, I discovered hot pastrami, Reuben sandwiches, and many varieties of pizza that in those years were not very common in Paris or Sweden.

The academic year started and everything changed. I soon realized that I had no compelling interest in learning Arabic, in the history of Islamic civilization, in village life in Anatolia and all that went with it. The teachers were good, but as Richard II would say, "not greatly good," with the exception of Sir Hamilton Gibb, who had just arrived from Oxford. At least one Israeli student, Menachem Milson, was his devotee. Later, Milson would become a professor at the Hebrew University in Jerusalem and, in due time, the first Israeli civilian governor of the West Bank.

One of the freshmen that year was Guido Goldman, Nahum Goldmann's younger son. When Goldmann senior came for a visit, we met and talked. Goldmann renewed his offer to hire me as his "political secretary" in New York. As my funds had dried up and as Middle Eastern studies bored me, I left Harvard in January 1958, without too much regret.

## 2

I remained Goldmann's secretary for about two years, from early 1958 to early 1960. At the time, my boss was, as I've mentioned, president of the World Jewish Congress, which he had helped to establish in the mid-thirties. The Congress was a worldwide federation of Jewish organizations created to fight for Jewish political rights, inform the world of anti-Jewish policies and crimes in an increasingly anti-Semitic period, and extend help to Jewish refugees wherever possible. After the war and mainly after the creation of Israel, the Congress was particularly active regarding the situation of Jews living in camps for displaced persons, in the Communist world, and in Arab countries, in addition to its global political mission.

Goldmann had also been elected president of the World Zionist Organization, whose aim, since its creation by Theodor Herzl, was to fight for the establishment of an autonomous Jewish political entity and, later, for the establishment of a Jewish state in Palestine. After the creation of Israel, the World Zionist Organization became mainly active in helping immigration and early integration of immigrants in their new country. Combining those two positions as well as the chairmanship of the Jewish Agency, the executive body of the World Zionist Organization, made of Goldmann the most important Jewish leader in the Diaspora.

Working with Goldmann as a personal assistant meant spending half my year in New York and the other half in Jerusalem. In New York, I lived in various hotels, mostly at the Alamac, on Broadway and Sixty-seventh. The Alamac was already well past its prime when I became a resident. The hotel's glory days extended through the twenties; I was told that Babe Ruth had once lived there (but, I wondered, without daring to ask, who the hell was Babe Ruth?). I still remember that it is in my room at the Alamac that I read Boris Pasternak's *Doctor Zhivago*, which I loved and which made quite a splash at the time because of its criticism of the Soviet regime.

In New York, I responded to a growing number of dinner invitations from Jewish families that had unmarried daughters and thought that Goldmann's secretary, an Israeli with a French accent to boot, was a young man with a future. Nothing came of it, except that I found the film *Marjorie Morningstar* — a satire of the 1950s about "Jewish American Princesses" — quite familiar. I also discovered Yorktown, the German district, around East Eighty-sixth Street, with its restaurants and dance halls. I vaguely remember that the girls there were coarser in behavior than my partners in Paris, but then a few Manhattans made everything look fine.

My daily secretarial duties were light: answering some of the letters addressed to Goldmann and meeting people who requested his support. I vividly remember some of the persons who regularly gravitated around him: his secretary Vera; the president of Hadassah, Rose Halprin — who, each time she was annoyed by something, bought a new hat; Sam Haber, who had performed miracles in helping the DPs in postwar European camps; the fawning Leon Dulcin, who couldn't have been more subservient to Goldmann at this early stage of his career and later turned against him in a most despicable way: as we shall see, he opposed Goldmann's burial among the great figures of Zionism. I also met there the *Haaretz* correspondent Amos Elon, a future friend, and the ubiquitous Joe Golan, Goldmann's very able emissary in any kind of somewhat covert international mission.

Goldmann paid me $500 a month, which in New York in the late fifties was just enough to get by for somebody like me. In Israel, though, it was a fortune.

In the spring we moved from New York to Jerusalem. Jerusalem in those years was a real backwater. Only the Jewish half of the city belonged to Israel, while Jordan ruled over the Arab part, including the Old Town. For Israelis, there was no access to the Jordanian sector that comprised the most important religious site of Judaism, the Western Wall of the Temple Mount, dominated by two magnificent mosques built on the site of the Jewish temple. Since 1949, Jerusalem had been the capital of Israel; it didn't much alter its sleepy nature.

Goldmann stayed at the King David Hotel, the best in the country. I lived in rented rooms and took my meals at Pension (Hilde) Wolf (?) on Kikar Salameh, where, day in, day out, I met the other three or four regular guests: the scholar of Islamic art Leo Mayer, the historian Yakov Talmon, and two other university professors. The university itself, after losing access to its buildings on Mount Scopus, moved to a temporary location in town, the exiguous facilities of the Terra Santa monastery.

In Jerusalem, I was much busier than in New York, with meetings and the vast correspondence that reached Goldmann from all sides. I also had the occasion to make new acquaintances such as the always welcoming and friendly Itzhak Navon, Ben-Gurion's "political secretary," and, decades later, president of Israel.

### 3

Goldmann was a brilliant negotiator and he certainly wasn't shy in expressing his opinions. As a negotiator, he contributed greatly to the success in September 1952 of the Reparations Agreement among Germany, Israel, and the Claims Conference of Jewish Organizations, by establishing warm personal relations with Chancellor Konrad Adenauer, as he later did with chancellors Erhard, Brandt, and Schmidt. He negotiated with the king of Morocco, with the Soviets, and, of course, with the State Department. Before most Israeli politicians, he also understood the need for peace with the Arab world and the plight of the Arabs in Israel.

In 1958, the Arab "citizens" of Israel were still under a military administration and brazenly discriminated against as potential enemies. This became tragically clear in October 1956, at the beginning of the Sinai campaign, when a curfew was imposed on all Arab villages in the country. Information about the curfew had not reached the inhabitants of Kafr Kassem, who returned from the fields after the curfew was already in force. Instead of being warned, they were shot at. About fifty of the villagers were killed, including ten women and seven children. The officers in charge were put on trial and sentenced to lengthy jail time, but soon pardoned and set free. In fairness, it should be added that a duty to disobey illegal orders became part of Israeli legislation as a result of this event.

Goldmann helped the few groups in the country that supported these second-class citizens, particularly the left-wing Mapam party. He regularly contributed funds to keep the Mapam English-language periodical *New Outlook*, edited by Simcha Flapan, afloat. I didn't know much about Israeli Arabs and Palestinians more generally (the term "Palestinians" was not yet in use). At that time, like hundreds of thousands of Israeli Jews, I believed in the official version of the events: After the United Nations' decision to partition Palestine between a Jewish and an

Arab state, in November 1947, the Arabs of Palestine unleashed violence in opposition to the partition plan. As the fighting turned against them, they fled of their own initiative, encouraged to do so by their leaders, who promised a quick return with the victorious Arab armies.

Very few Israelis admitted in those years — and for several decades — that in quite a number of cases, it was the Israeli army that forced the Arabs to leave, probably on orders from the top: tens of thousands of Palestinians were the victims of a brutal military expulsion. During the following years, many Arab villages in the country were forcibly evacuated, often destroyed, and when reoccupied by Jewish inhabitants, they received Hebrew names.

My first real awareness of the fate of Israeli Arabs occurred on the occasion of a trip that took Goldmann (and me) to several Arab villages in the area along the armistice line with Jordan, called "the small triangle." One image remains in my mind as a perfect expression of abject submission and humiliation. We drove to the mayor's office in one of the villages. The mayor and his aides received us with coffee and sweets. Two portraits were hanging above his desk: on one side, that of the founder of Zionism, Theodor Herzl; on the other side, that of the founder of the state, David Ben-Gurion.

Despite such brief moments of "awareness," we were all — I mean Ashkenazi ("white") Israeli society — unconscious or semiconscious racists, not only regarding the Arabs, but mostly in our attitude toward the hundreds of thousands of new immigrants arriving from North Africa and, in lesser numbers, from Iraq and Yemen. The *mizrahiim* (Orientals) often spent years in transit camps (*Maabarot*) in miserable conditions. They were deemed best suited for menial labor, cleaning the homes of the upper classes, voting "the right way" and adding manpower to Israeli infantry units. At the time, it never occurred to me to see things differently, and I don't think that Goldmann spent much time worrying about such a disastrous social situation, although these immigrants had been brought to Israel under the auspices of the Jewish Agency, over which he presided. In part, their integration was in his purview as well.

Our "racism" toward Oriental Jews ultimately led to dire consequences for Israeli politics. These consequences first appeared in 1977, when Begin — the political leader who for years had appealed to the "Orientals" and thus restored their dignity as citizens and who by then represented almost half the population — won the elections. The Ashkenazi left didn't learn its lesson, and in the elections of March 2015, Netanyahu came in ahead by appealing, once more, to the by now traditional supporters of the right: the voters of Oriental background.

I personally liked Goldmann, yet I wasn't very happy with a job that didn't require initiative, even though it paid well (during the Israeli part of it). In Jerusalem, I was busy, but that wasn't enough. I was waiting, though without any clear idea for what. During my free time I regularly took the bus to Tel Aviv, and although I couldn't be counted as a member of the local bohemia, the fact that I could pay for treats (even for dinners) gave me access to its headquarters, the Kassit coffeehouse on Dizengoff Street. I have to admit, however, that I was never invited to shake hands with the greats of that establishment: Nathan Alterman (a national poet of sorts); the flag bearer of the Israeli bohemia, the writer Dan Ben Amotz (whose specialty was to shock the bourgeois); and the writers and journalists Haim Hefer, Amos Kenan, and a few others. After all, standards had to be kept.

During one of these stays in Tel Aviv, in the spring of 1959, I met Hagith Meiry. She was a young pianist who had actually studied in Paris at the École Normale de Musique with Magda Tagliaferro during my last year at the embassy. I had heard of her porcelainlike beauty from several Israelis and also from her boyfriend, the painter Avigdor Arikha, with whom I was on excellent terms. I took him out for lunch dozens of times, and in return he promised that once he was anointed king of Israel, he would appoint me prime minister. In Paris, though, he never introduced me to Hagith.

Hagith put an end to their relationship and returned to Tel Aviv in early 1959. Avigdor soon followed in the hope of bringing her back. It is then that the three of us met for dinner, as Avigdor expected my support in urging her to return to him and with him. I wasn't convinced, and Avigdor left for Paris without Hagith. She was indeed beautiful in a fragile kind of way, and quite perceptive. I told her the story of my aristocratic descent, as I had told it to many girls before her and always with great success: Schiller, in his play about Wallenstein (the greatest Austrian military leader of the Thirty Years' War), called him *der Friedländer*, as Wallenstein came from Friedland in the Sudeten area, from where my mother's family stemmed. Hagith was not impressed. "Isn't Friedländer your father's name?" she asked. She was an only child. Her parents, Meir and Rivka, were Russian Jews who had arrived in the country several decades beforehand. Her father was a high official in the new Israeli administration: director general of the State Controller's Office.

We got married in London in August 1959, in great secrecy, to avoid the news reaching Avigdor, as he threatened suicide in the near-daily letters he was sending to Hagith. The passage of time would make things easier. Avigdor, incidentally, was convinced his entire life that I was responsible for Hagith's separation from him; he avoided me like the plague and we never met again. Of course, I had to say goodbye to the premiership that he had promised me . . .

Hagith and I left for New York in the fall, as I had to return to work for Goldmann. Incidentally, Goldmann and his wife Alice invited us for dinner at their New York apartment to celebrate our marriage. On that occasion we met a remarkable representative of the early Central European Zionism, Hans Kohn. Kohn was part of a group of like-minded intellectuals (Martin Buber, Gershom Scholem, Hugo Bergmann, Ernst Simon, Arthur Ruppin, and a few others) whose main political aim was to achieve peaceful relations between the Jewish community and the Arab population of Palestine within a binational state. The creation of the Brit Shalom or "Peace Alliance" movement followed, but remained without any political influence. Whether the ideals of Brit Shalom had a chance, whether they would have ever encountered an adequate response on the Arab side, we can only guess. The history of Arab-Jewish relations became, as we know all too well, one of deepening conflict.

Marriage excluded my previous kind of back and forth between New York and Jerusalem; we would stay in Israel and I would look for some job in the country, a plan that turned decidedly more urgent once Hagith became pregnant. As melodramatic as this may sound, for me our son Eli's birth in July 1960 was a revenge — a revenge against fate.

Feet on the desk, soles facing me, Shimon started talking about a biography of Sun Yat-sen, the founder of the Chinese republic, his latest discovery. The year was 1960 and Shimon Peres was vice minister of defense. The boss, the "old man" (*ha-ẓaken*), as they all called him, was Prime Minister and Minister of Defense David Ben-Gurion.

Shabtai Teveth, my journalist friend from Paris days, introduced me to Peres. When "Sabi," very close to the Israeli defense establishment, heard that I was looking for a new job, he simply called Shimon (the widespread use of first names among people at all levels of a workplace or simply in social contacts was very much part of Israeli culture during those years, and remains so to this day, a remnant of a long-gone pioneer mentality and of American movies).

Once again, I got the job, and this time, my title was even grander than before: "Head of the Scientific Office of the Vice Minister of Defense." The title didn't mean much in my case and it didn't take me long to understand this. My predecessor, however, Shalheveth Freier, for ten years scientific attaché at the Israeli embassy in Paris (whom I had not met there), was a remarkable and influential individual — and an eccentric as well. He supposedly lost his job — though I am convinced this belongs to legend — for throwing an ashtray at Shimon's head. Whatever disagreements there were between Shalheveth and Shimon, they certainly were linked to the one crucial project both were involved in at that time: the building of a nuclear reactor and assorted installations in Dimona near Beersheba, in the northern Negev Desert. Why I, of all people, was chosen to replace Shalheveth, I never found out.

Although I liked to spend time there during my work with Goldmann, let's admit it: Tel Aviv in those days was an ugly city with its back to the sea. Many of its houses had not been repainted for years and the closer you came to the shore the more decrepit the façades appeared, as if afflicted by some form of leprosy. On average, though, the hotels and restaurants offered better fare than in Jerusalem, theater life was expanding beyond the iconic Habimah, and there was a first-rate philharmonic orchestra. We lived at my wife's parents' place, a large enough apartment on Rothschild Boulevard in a relatively genteel part of town, but even there, as all over, we were in the Levant.

The Ministry of Defense, located in the center of Tel Aviv in an area called *HaKiryah* (the City), which we shared with the army headquarters, did not look more impressive than its surroundings: merely a set of rectangular, two-story buildings (the army headquarters could boast of five stories) as nondescript as thousands of housing projects emerging all over Israel to offer cheap lodgings to the waves of new immigrants. The heart of our ministry was a little house with an ivy-covered façade; Peres's office occupied the ground floor while the "old man" ruled on the second (and top) floor. I never saw Ben-Gurion but quite often got a glimpse of his most faithful and secretive aide, Haim Israeli, shuttling up and down the stairs. As for Shimon's office, it was run with remarkable efficiency and good spirits by Israeli's downstairs counterpart, the affable Avraham Ben-Yosef.

An intense feeling of mission and empowerment animated Shimon's inner circle; it did not, however, exclude tensions and rivalries. I've since forgotten the details of internal squabbles, which were generally about the allocation of budgets and the enforcement of power boundaries, except for the fact that the notoriously most difficult individual among those very difficult individuals was the man in charge of the actual building of Dimona, Colonel Manes Pratt.

Pratt had the reputation (justified or not) of being an engineering genius, a stellar administrator, and (justified) a very unpleasant person. Getting on his bad side didn't make life easy. Peres was the only one able to handle Pratt, which he did as he handled other department heads, by mastering the essential technical aspects of the highly complex tasks each of them was dealing with and also perfectly grasping the general picture with its manifold financial and political ramifications. All in all, he had an unusual ability to maintain the modicum of peace necessary for the rapid progress of work (except in Shalheveth's case, manifestly). In that sense, Peres, younger than most of his main acolytes, proved to be an outstanding leader with one formidable asset: Ben-Gurion's full support.

There I was then, inside the holy of holies of the Israeli defense establishment, included in a project surrounded by rumors but so secret that, in 1960, even Foreign Minister Golda Meir did not know the crucial details I was privy to (she would soon have to face some of it, to her distress).

Within my limited ability, I contributed. In Shimon's name I kept in touch with various departments of the ministry, drafted the letters to some outside agencies, particularly the International Atomic Agency in Vienna, and, when it came to humdrum issues, took care of things on my own; I summarized French correspondence and at times even made some suggestions. To this day, I do not regret having belonged, albeit briefly, to a project that, ultimately, may be the only guarantee of Israel's survival. I never forgot the article about the fate of the Crusader Kingdom that I had read at Harvard in the summer of 1957.

The world I became part of under the name of Shaul Eldar (the hebraization of names was compulsory for government employees) had been given its decisive dimension in a series of audacious secret agreements between Israel and France, initiated by Shimon Peres in 1956. According to these agreements, France would assist Israel in the building of a nuclear reactor and related installations and, in due time, would provide Israel with the necessary uranium fuel. On the French side, notwithstanding the secrecy of the project, quite a number of officials took part in various stages of the negotiations. However, throughout, the main driving force remained the defense minister, then prime minister, Maurice Bourgès-Maunoury. The political alliance and personal friendship between Peres and "Bourgès" overcame all initial obstacles. Soon Dimona was teeming with French engineers and technicians of all kinds.

"In Israel," Michael Bar-Zohar writes in his Peres biography, "Peres started building a huge organization of manpower, scientific personnel, construction companies, budgets, and, primarily, weaving a watertight cover of concealment that would hide the daily activity of thousands of people. The success of the project depended on preserving absolute secrecy; any leak might set off heavy international pressure that could kill the project."* Leaks occurred, nonetheless.

## 5

During my work with Peres, three major crises shook the defense establishment. All three were centered upon Dimona.

---

* Michael Bar-Zohar, *Shimon Peres: The Biography*, New York, 2007, p. 218. The biography was first published in Israel in 2005.

The first crisis was close to home. I had become quite friendly with Israel Bar, an old-timer at the ministry who, as far as I remember, filled the role of free-floating adviser but one who participated — as I did — in all meetings of the senior staff and with whom one could discuss any of the most confidential issues. Easygoing and amusing, Bar told me how close he was to Ben-Gurion (true) and to Shimon Peres (also true) but how thoroughly he despised the chief of staff, Moshe Dayan. Dayan, it so happens, distrusted Bar.

One of the stories Bar told to illustrate how he felt about Dayan was that of the turtle and the scorpion (a story that has a long pedigree). A scorpion and a turtle arrive at a riverbank and want to cross. Since the scorpion can't swim, it begs the turtle to take it across the river on its back. "You'll sting me while I'm swimming," objects the turtle. "Why should I do that? We would both drown," the scorpion replies. The turtle sees the logic of the argument, takes the scorpion on its back, and starts swimming. Midstream, the scorpion stings the turtle. "Why did you do that?" cries the dying turtle. "We are both sinking!" "It's my nature," answers the scorpion, a.k.a. Moshe Dayan.

Bar told me — and everybody else — that he was born in Vienna, studied at the university there, fought in 1934 in the Schutzbund (a socialist militia) against the authoritarian government of Engelbert Dollfuss, moved to Spain when the Civil War started there, became a Communist, and joined the International Brigades. In 1938, he opted for Zionism and immigrated to Palestine. Soon his military experience brought him close to Itzhak Sadeh, the leader of the Palmach (the elite unit of the Jewish underground army, the Haganah), and eventually to Ben-Gurion, Peres, et al. Bar knew practically everything about

Israeli military doctrine, strategic planning, defense installations, and procurement. He knew about Dimona.

Bar had been a Soviet mole before the creation of the state and an active spy thereafter. The Israeli Security Service arrested him sometime in 1961, as he returned from one of his frequent trips to Germany. The head of the Mossad, Isser Harel, shared Dayan's suspicion of Bar but for a long time Ben-Gurion dismissed any such allegations.

Peres told us of Bar's arrest and, among other things, of a diary he had been keeping during his recent trip to East Berlin. Each day was marked by several names of women. As Bar was a notorious ladies' man, he argued at first that these were merely some of his conquests. It soon became obvious, however, that they were code names for various contacts in the East. Bar died in prison in 1966 and, to this day, his true identity remains in doubt.

What the Soviets probably got to know about Dimona from Israel Bar, the Americans learned from U-2 overflights and other sources. Golda Meir had to face difficult questions from the U.S. ambassador about installations linked to the reactor she had just heard of. As a result, President Kennedy pressured Ben-Gurion to open Dimona for inspection. I still remember the first visit of American inspectors to the site in the spring of 1961, to ascertain its peaceful aims; the tension was palpable. The visit proceeded without incident, but each following inspection probably became a source of some jitters (by then, I was long gone).

The potentially most serious crisis of all developed at about the same time as the U-2 affair. After deciding to accept the National Liberation Front's demand for the independence of Algeria, French president Charles de Gaulle, who had returned to power in May 1958, sought to reestablish his country's traditional influence in the Arab world. This meant, among other things, considerably loosening many of France's secret ties with Israel, and particularly, putting an end to its assistance in the construction of Israeli nuclear installations. Ben-Gurion, accompanied by Peres, traveled to Paris to persuade de Gaulle to reconsider. A compromise was reached: although official French help stopped, some private French firms were allowed to continue working at the site.

I saw Peres almost daily throughout this period of overlapping and highly stressful events. Much criticism has been directed at him throughout his career — some of it quite justified, as we shall see — but to one thing I can attest: Peres remained unflappable during the crises just mentioned, although pressure on him at the time was immense. He steadily continued to work on his major projects — and kept talking about the latest book he had read.

I remember only vaguely today what made me decide to leave my position at the ministry in the summer of 1961 and opt for a different course altogether. I recall mulling for months about the possibility of resuming graduate studies. I even had a rather clear idea of what I was specifically not interested in: Middle Eastern topics. I was attracted to the history of Europe between the wars and during the Second World War, without yet clearly linking it to my personal story. I wanted to make my own decisions and face my own choice of challenges in an area in which I felt confident that I could achieve something on my own. In other words, I sensed that it was the world of books and of scholarly work that came closest to what could be seen as a calling.

CHAPTER FIVE

# Geneva

The Graduate Institute of International Studies stood on the shore of Lake Geneva. From the Villa Barton, its main building, painted an unusual rose color that made it look more like a candy box than a site of learning, a few steps led to the "promenade," along the bank of the lake. To your right you could see the scenic Geneva fountain rising tens of feet into the air, behind it the Mont Blanc bridge that linked both parts of the city, the old town above it, and — as Proust wonderfully wrote about the church of Combray — the Saint Pierre Cathedral "*résumant la ville*" (summing up the town). To your left the lake extended along shores you knew (but could not make out), toward Lausanne, Vevey, and Montreux. And, on many days of the year, looking straight ahead, you could see, over the opposite French shore and the lower mountain ranges, snow-covered Mont Blanc dominating the landscape.

And, if you drove along the French side for an hour or so, you would reach Saint-Gingolph, the small border town where my parents were arrested in September 1942. It took me seventeen years after arriving in Geneva to make the trip to Saint-Gingolph.

Sometime in September 1961, I left Hagith and one-year-old Eli in Tel Aviv, drove to Haifa in my brand-new Peugeot, and boarded a ferry to Genoa on my way to Geneva or, more precisely, to the institute.

During my early months of work with Peres I had been "lent back" to Goldmann for a few weeks to organize the first international conference on Soviet Jewry scheduled to take place in Paris in the fall of 1960 under the auspices of the World Jewish Congress. It meant traveling all over Western Europe to convince prominent personalities to attend. I still remember how, during a short stay in Amsterdam to invite a Dutch bishop, Msgr Ramselaar (who attended), I read with amazement in the morning paper that Adolf Eichmann had been abducted from Argentina and was safely held in Israel to stand trial. I felt proud.

In the course of this mission I had also paid a visit to Jacques Freymond, the director of the Geneva Graduate Institute of International Studies (who, I believe, also attended). A year later, after leaving my work with Peres, I applied to the Hebrew University in Jerusalem and spoke with both historian Jacob Talmon, the widely known author of *The Origins of Totalitarian Democracy* and a recognized stellar lecturer, and with political scientist Benjamin Akzin, the undisputed ruler of his department (both of whom I knew from my Goldmann days). I asked for a teaching assistantship in either domain, as I didn't have the means to take care of a wife and son without some income. Both, generous with advice, turned me down. I remembered Freymond. He promised a modest fellowship in exchange for some tutoring. I gratefully accepted.

----

I just mentioned Eichmann's capture. Still working with Peres, I couldn't get to the trial in Jerusalem, but, notwithstanding all my "defenses," I followed the radio reports as much as possible. Many years later, while I taught at Tel Aviv University, in the late 1970s or early 1980s, I read the protocols of the interrogation preceding the trial, an interrogation conducted with great skill by police officer Avner Less, who was of German background and interrogated Eichmann in German. What struck me — and hadn't been mentioned as far as I know — was a strange aspect of Eichmann's way of referring to superior authority. Here he was, in an Israeli prison in 1960, fifteen years after the collapse of the Reich, but when he mentioned Himmler, each time he added the full title: Reichsführer SS und Chef der deutschen Polizei Heinrich Himmler; of course, the same happened with Hitler (Führer und Reichskanzler). In short, as apparently candid as Eichmann was in his answers, inwardly he still stood at attention. Whether this ongoing subservience to his past masters influenced his answers cannot be proven, but it is not impossible.

Hagith and Eli joined me a few weeks after my arrival. Very soon the institute's fellowship did not suffice to support a family of three. I appealed to a wide variety of funding sources and finally got a positive reply from the Rockefeller Foundation. However, as the foundation was also financing the institute as such, they asked me to find another academic sponsor to supervise the transfer and use of the money. The Hebrew University seemed to me the obvious choice and, once again, I naively turned to Talmon and Akzin. Their answer was immediate: since I had not enrolled at the Hebrew University, they could not help me with the Rockefeller fellowship. After I explained my predicament, I received the fellowship nonetheless and soon thereafter a teaching assistantship.

Six years later, forgetting that he had refused to give me even a lowly assistantship, Talmon asked me to replace him as visiting professor of history at the Hebrew University while he spent a year in Princeton. Sometimes, life has its sweet little ironies.

After reading through the summer of 1961, I concluded — and rightly so — that the topic I had thought of for my dissertation had hardly been dealt with and manifestly not on the basis of archival work. The title I chose was self-explanatory: "The American Factor in German Foreign and Military Policy between September 1939 and December 1941" (that is, between the beginning of the war in Europe and Hitler's declaration of war against the United States). I wrote to Freymond about my suggestion and he accepted right away.

I had squandered too many years, I thought, and had to make up for lost time. Consequently, I adopted an unusual working routine: I wrote a first draft with whatever material I had on hand, along the general lines that I could establish on the basis of my reading; then came a second draft and a third and so on (ultimately there could be ten such drafts or more), each integrating more material, each eventually adapting to new archival material, until I sensed that the text was ready. It allowed me to keep a constant overview of the entire manuscript and organize its chapters accordingly. It meant working simultaneously on content and on form.

To this day I work in the same way, even on this memoir. As I write, new perspectives open that I had not perceived before and much that seemed forgotten suddenly reappears, imposing new reshufflings, new drafts, and so on. At the time of my dissertation, I also adopted a very strict discipline: six pages every day, except during archival research. If I didn't complete my daily chore, I had to add the missing pages on the following days. (I have become more lenient since . . .) The really strange aspect of this obsessive approach to work was, and remains, writing a draft in longhand and, as I was (and am) unable to type myself, having somebody type the manuscript, then reworking the newly typed draft in longhand, having it typed again, and continuing this process to the very end. It was a very expensive method at a time when I hardly could afford it. Such was the price of obsession: I couldn't do without a cleanly typed draft for each round.

There was another price exacted by my obsession. Barreling, as I did, toward the completion of the dissertation didn't leave time for any unrelated subjects. The immediate consequence was a huge and cumulative gap in my education. After finishing high school in 1950, I had gone on reading eclectically but studied neither history nor political science in any organized way. I managed — and managed well — at Sciences Po because I briefly concentrated on my exams and nothing else. When I finally returned to my studies, in 1961, eleven years after high school, I had swallowed bits and pieces from here and there: evening courses in law and economy, the Sciences Po fare in a very "concentrated" mode, then nothing from 1955 to 1961 (the last year at the embassy, Sweden, Goldmann, and Peres). Now that I was back in a doctoral program, I avoided courses or readings that could deflect me from my dissertation. The dissertation would be solid, but any other area I dealt with was just a cobbling together of bits and pieces, or, as the German poet Christian Morgenstern put it, "a picket fence of interstitial excellence."


During our first two or three months in Geneva, we lived in a studio belonging to Hôtel Mon Repos, just opposite the institute.

We then moved to our first rented apartment on rue Gauthier, a small street not far from the lake, and remained there until well after the completion of my dissertation. We liked that small but cozy abode, in walking distance from Eli's *jardin d'enfants*. Eli must have been about three when Hagith was summoned by the *directrice*. There had been a crisis. The children had been given some drawings of animals that they had to color and put in an envelope. Eli had nicely colored the figures but instead of putting them in the envelope, he had dropped them on the floor. "Madame," said the lady director to Hagith, "if your son continues to behave in that way, he has no future in Switzerland." "No future in Switzerland" remains a frequent family expression to this day.

As I went on working in my monomaniacal way, the doctoral exams in law and in economics could have been a problem. Yet I somehow survived both the quizzing on "repressed inflation" and the one on "compulsory arbitration." The history of international relations went well; I spoke of my dissertation topic and Freymond waved me through.

I liked Jacques Freymond. A native of the Canton de Vaud, he had been a professor of history at the University of Lausanne before being chosen as director of the institute in the late fifties. "What, a foreigner?" must have been the reaction of quite a number of Genevans upon his appointment. In fact, he had something of the crafty Vaudois peasant in him, together with a very amicable personality. Here (in California) you would say that Freymond was "a people person." When he wanted to talk to you, even about the most banal issue, he would hold you by the arm, call you *mon cher*, and create an instantaneous feeling of trust and complicity.

The institute could be considered as liberal-conservative in terms of the political leanings of its director and its senior teachers. I guess that this overall tendency, supported by the identical philosophy of an affiliated institution, the Institute of European Studies, under the aegis of Denis de Rougemont, made it a natural venue for at least one gathering of the Congress for Cultural Freedom's governing board. I didn't know at the time how thoroughly anti-Communist the Congress was; not that I minded or felt otherwise. Freymond invited me to attend the discussions.

Thus I met Robert Oppenheimer; Melvin Lasky (the editor of the organization's periodical, *Encounter*); G.L.S. Shackle, one of Churchill's economic advisers during the war and later professor of economics in Liverpool; Oskar Morgenstern, who, with John von Neumann, invented game theory; and a few other luminaries whose names I have forgotten (I think Karl Popper also attended). The organizer of the meeting, and its supervisor, if one could call him this, was Michael Josselson. Part of the funds came from the Ford Foundation. Many years later it became known that the Congress and *Encounter* were "guided" by the CIA — and that Josselson may have been its main operative in Europe for these and related matters.

I never tried to find out whether a parallel intellectual enterprise, Futuribles, run from Paris by the political philosopher Bertrand de Jouvenel and also funded by the Ford Foundation, belonged to the same CIA anti-Communist intellectual campaign. It probably did. Be that as it may, in 1964 (after I had finished my dissertation), a much larger conference organized by Futuribles took place in Paris. I spoke on "Forecasting in International Relations." Despite my excruciating fear, I delivered the lecture reasonably well and Jouvenel had it duly published. It was my first semischolarly article.

My first scholarly text in a traditional sense dealt with American policy regarding Vichy-dominated North Africa during the months preceding the Anglo-American landing of November 1942. It was published by the *Revue Suisse d'Histoire*, whose editor at the time was Jean-François Bergier. Thirty-seven years later, Bergier presided over the Independent Historians' Commission, of which I was a member, set up to investigate the history of the relations between Switzerland and Nazi Germany, particularly during the war.

My first political article, a paean to Israel, an excerpt of which was published in 1962 in *Le Figaro Littéraire*, angrily answered an essay by the famous French sociologist, historian, and regular contributor to *Le Figaro*, Raymond Aron. Aron had questioned the ability of a tiny state like Israel to produce anything of significance in the fields of science or culture. As a true believer, I protested.

Let me return briefly to Jouvenel, and to Aron in fact. In the sixties, I knew little about Jouvenel's past, except that he had been Colette's lover and that in 1936 he had been granted a notorious interview by Hitler (the Führer probably ignored that Jouvenel was half-Jewish). Twenty years later, thanks to my friend Zeev Sternhell's book *Neither Right Nor Left* (*Ni droite ni gauche*: *L'idéologie fasciste en France*), I discovered some of Jouvenel's shocking political choices during the late thirties and under Vichy. What subsequently astonished me no less was Aron's testimony in favor of Jouvenel in the lawsuit that the author of *Après la défaite* (After the defeat), first published in Berlin in 1941, had brought against Zeev and his publisher, Seuil. I had come to like Aron personally, but his right-leaning politics may have misled him in this matter, out of loyalty to a like-minded intellectual of the postwar period.

## 2

The dissertation demanded archival work in Bonn, Koblenz, Freiburg, and London. I added quite a few interviews, even one with former admiral Karl Dönitz, whom Hitler appointed as head of state before committing suicide.

I wanted to ask Dönitz whether, before December 1941, the German navy was preparing for the possibility that the United States would join the war on the side of Great Britain. I wished to know particularly whether the Germans were staging war games (*Kriegsspiele*), during which military units practice responses to hypothetical battlefield (or naval) situations involving a probable enemy. Submarines (which Dönitz commanded until 1943) would have been the weapons of choice in such exercises. I drove all the way from Geneva to Aumühle in Schleswig-Holstein, where Dönitz lived after spending the several years in jail to which the Nuremberg tribunal had sentenced him.

I was often asked what I felt while en route to meet the man Hitler appointed as his successor on the eve of his suicide. I felt nothing.

Regarding naval preparations for a war with the United States Dönitz not only denied that war games that assumed such a possibility had ever taken place, he even declared that, before the outbreak of the war in Europe, no games forecasting a war with Great Britain had ever been organized. This last claim seemed highly dubious, mainly in view of the tense international situation between mid-1938 and the last months of peace in 1939. In short, according to Dönitz, Germany had avoided any step that smacked of "preparing a war of aggression," one of the indictment counts in Nuremberg.

I then decided to confront the admiral with the Jewish issue, unaware of the anti-Semitic repertory he flaunted throughout his career. It also shows how naive I was: would Hitler have appointed as his successor somebody whom he wouldn't have considered ideologically reliable through and through, that is, first and foremost, a thoroughgoing anti-Semite? Thus, without thinking of the obvious declarations I would get, I asked him at what point he became aware of the extermination of the Jews. "Never," he answered. Only after Hitler's death, once he became head of state, was he told about it, he claimed. This was even less believable than his statement about the war games. I ignored that he had made the same declaration at Nuremberg and told him that I was not convinced. The discussion went back and forth until, as a last resort, I ventured a question to which, I thought, he would be unprepared: "*Herr Grossadmiral*," — I used his full German title — "do you give me your word of honor as German grand-admiral that you knew nothing about the extermination of the Jews?" The answer was immediate: "I give you my word of honor as German grand-admiral that I knew nothing about it."

Dönitz had misinformed me about the war games involving Great Britain before September 1939, as I soon found out. Both the head of the historical section of the British Admiralty, Commander Saunders, and a former German naval officer, *Korvettenkapitän* (Lieutenant Commander) Bidlingmeier, wrote to me that such war games had taken place. Bidlingmeier clinched the issue: he had personally participated in one of them. If Dönitz lied on a minor matter, then he most likely lied about one of utter importance: his knowledge of the extermination policy. As I previously mentioned, I should have expected it.

The meeting with Dönitz reminds me of an Israeli-German documentary about Himmler, *The Decent One*, that we recently saw. It is essentially based on Himmler's letters to his family. I had read his early diary, his service diary, most of his orders, exhortations, and speeches, and some of his letters. These previously unpublished private letters do not add much to what we knew of the man: obsessive, power hungry, a true believer in Nazi ideology, enthralled by Adolf Hitler. I found the rejection of his father's entreaties to save some old friend from Dachau and the ultimate break with his father as the most interesting part. He did not attend his father's funeral. There was a fanaticism in the Nazi leadership that Dönitz shared and just tried to camouflage after the war.

At the end of 1963, my dissertation was ready. The "defense" would take place before a jury comprising at least two members external to the institute. In my case, Freymond would preside, while two well-known historians, the Paris professor Maurice Baumont and the Zurich professor Jean Rudolf von Salis, would be the external members.

During that same year Baumont used to come once a week from Paris as guest professor at the institute to lecture on the diplomatic history of the Second World War. I hadn't attended his course and had never spoken to him. Naturally, I worried about his attitude. As I arrived at the institute, one hour or so before the *soutenance* (the French equivalent of the dissertation defense), I saw Baumont sitting in one of the offices, with the door ajar, reading my dissertation. I walked in and introduced myself. "How old are you?" he asked me. "Thirty-one," I said. "At your age," he commented, "Jesus had almost finished his career." I am usually quite bad at quick repartees, but at that moment, I was struck by some momentary inspiration: "Yes," I said, "but without a doctorate." Baumont laughed, and I knew that he would be friendly.

The defense went well. My main argument was simple, although uncommon at the time. Instead of accepting the view that Hitler's ideological contempt for the United States blinded him to the military significance of its eventual intervention, I showed — on the basis of much new archival material — that, notwithstanding his outbursts against the American medley of races headed by Roosevelt and his Jews, the German leader, well aware of the country's enormous potential, made considerable efforts to prevent the U.S. entry into the war, all the more so from November 1941, when his Russian adventure was slowing down. Thus, aware of the fact that his Japanese quasi-allies were intent on conquests in the South Pacific that would mean war with the United States, Hitler tried strenuously to convince them to attack the Soviet Union in Siberia instead. Moreover, notwithstanding Roosevelt's repeated provocations in the Atlantic (to overcome strong isolationist opposition in Congress and join the war on Great Britain's side), the German leader manifestly avoided an escalation of the naval incidents. Once Japan attacked, however, Hitler's anti-American rage exploded and he took the initiative and declared war.

In the course of the discussion, I heard for the first time a comment that apparently belonged to French examiners' arsenal of nasty remarks. It came from Baumont, but he turned it around from negative to positive: "One cannot say about your dissertation," he quipped, "what has been said more than once: 'Sir, in your work there is much that is right and there are also some original ideas, but what is right is not original and what is original is not right.'"* Old Baumont was a character. Later

---

* I recently mentioned this anecdote to my colleague and friend Carlo Ginzburg, who told me that this was first said about Rossini's music during the composer's life in Paris from the 1830s on.

on, we used to chat, and he told me that General Maxime Weygand, whom he knew, still remained convinced that Dreyfus was guilty. Weygand was commander in chief during the last part of the campaign of 1940 that led to the French surrender (he died in 1965).

When the post-dissertation dust settled, Freymond informed me that, notwithstanding all my good work, there was no teaching position available at the institute. But, as chance would have it, a young assistant professor, who had just started teaching, fell ill and had to take a long-term break. Freymond asked me to replace him from January 1964 on. I did so, and a few months later was asked to stay.

The overall theme of my dissertation, namely the foreign and military policies of Nazi Germany, was attuned to the general trend of historical research and publications at that time, the early 1960s. I remember that while working in Bonn, I often discussed my work with a historian of the war generation, Hans-Adolf Jacobsen, who had already worked on an edition of the OKW (the High Command of the Wehrmacht) diary and related material. This was, all in all, a kind of history still keeping its distance from the criminal dimension of the regime, although Hitler's military orders were duly investigated.

It was no longer the period of overall German historiography's silence about Nazi crimes; the first major German trials (the trial of an Einsatzgruppe in Ulm in 1959, the first Auschwitz trial in 1963), as well as the Eichmann trial in Jerusalem in 1961, demanded massive documentation and drew widespread attention for a while. In that sense, the early sixties were a transition phase and the same Hans-Adolf Jacobsen must have already started research for his forthcoming publication on Hitler's "Commissar Order" (the order to shoot all political commissars of the Soviet army, considered as the carriers of Bolshevik ideology and, for Hitler, all Jews), issued in early June 1941, two weeks before the attack on the Soviet Union. More generally, German historians of the Reich were well aware of any new material that came up in the various trials. And yet, for the general public, the open awareness of the full dimensions of Nazi crimes and the demand for full information of a largely repressed past were still a few years away.

## 3

I loved teaching and I think that for years I was a good teacher, in Geneva, Jerusalem, Tel Aviv, and Los Angeles. One should sense, however, when to stop. Among the refugee scholars at the institute in the 1930s, one of the professors of international law, Hans Wehberg, did not heed the signs and remained with a single student sitting in his course. His widow didn't know what to make of it: "I don't understand; at the beginning my husband attracted dozens of students, and at the end only one stayed. Yet he taught exactly the same material."

In fact, apart from my decreasing enthusiasm for teaching and even for shepherding dissertations over the last few years, what particularly induced me to retire was the sense that my memory was in decline. The sudden disappearance of words or names became an annoyance in and of itself, with the added worry of facing a blank in the midst of the Q&A period, after a lecture. It is not yet a problem in writing, as usually, after a while, the forgotten word comes back. For now . . .

Age is one explanation of my memory issues; the medicines I've taken for the last fifty-six years are another. The symptoms that led me to doctors and their prescriptions started in Israel somewhat before the time I decided to get married. No complex psychological theories are needed to explain a sudden surge of anxiety, which began with claustrophobia.

The symptoms spread. At first, I couldn't sit in the middle of a row in theaters. After some time, sitting near the exit didn't help either, and I started avoiding enclosed spaces in general. Imagine what flying to New York meant during my last year with Goldmann, the more so that I was afraid of flying. Those unbearably lengthy trips offered one saving grace: in the age of propellers or turbojet engines, the planes had to land every few hours: Tel Aviv–Rome; Rome–Shannon; Shannon–Gander; Gander–New York. I tried drinking myself to oblivion: it didn't help much.

When my anxiety and phobias started, the medicine prescribed (Equanil) didn't work, and dizzy spells, very frequent ones, followed my bouts of claustrophobia. Much worse were the repeated nightly attacks of tachycardia: I was terrified and no physician could convince me that I suffered only from anxiety and wasn't dying. Such assurances would work for a few days and then the anxiety returned. The symptoms became much worse shortly before our marriage, when Hagith and I, during a few days of waiting for some documents from Israel, left London for a very welcoming inn in Hartford. I simply could not stay in the restaurant without feeling that I would faint, so that on several occasions I had to leave dinner and flee to our room. The same occurred — even more intensely — at the hotel in Flims, a Swiss resort where we spent three weeks after the wedding. I was desperate and Hagith utterly at a loss.

From Flims we were to travel to Zurich and from there fly to New York, via Paris. We used the opportunity to make an appointment with a professor of psychiatry at the University of Zurich whose name I have since forgotten but who had a great reputation. After hearing me out and performing a few tests, he recommended a stay at a famous clinic established by Ludwig Binswanger. In short, my psychological state didn't bode well. We left for New York nonetheless and I started my last stint of work with Goldmann. I don't know how many doctors I saw, but it was a long list that included several psychoanalysts. When I told the analyst I saw in Israel that I planned to leave my job with Peres in order to resume my graduate studies, he answered with authority, "I am not sure that given your state you will be capable of concentrating enough to pursue any studies."

Strange as it sounds, apart from those closest to me, nobody noticed a thing. Even stranger was the fact that I could do my work and later pursue my studies. In Geneva, anxiety became almost unbearable: agoraphobia (the fear of open spaces) was added to my claustrophobia. At that point, I became tempted to drop everything. I thought that I would never recover and that, ultimately, I would have to be relegated to a psychiatric institution, as the Zurich specialist had recommended. But how would I pay for it? Putting an end to my studies and returning to Israel remained the only option, as in Israel comprehensive health care was available to all.

Still, work on the dissertation never stopped, and, as I mentioned, sometime in October 1963, the manuscript was ready. When I was about to take a copy of the text to Freymond, I got so dizzy that I fell. Hagith had to deliver the manuscript, explaining that I was suffering from an upset stomach and a fever.

In Geneva, I saw an analyst for four years. She was a very congenial lady from North Carolina who had married a Swiss psychoanalyst, the son of the famous linguist and Geneva patrician, Ferdinand de Saussure. Saussure junior died and his widow Janice went on living in one of the most impressive palatial homes of the old town. Unfortunately, for patients the entrance was through a side door. At least it helped one to fantasize about Janice's hidden palatial life.

The analysis (five times a week) seemed orthodox Freudian. I read all I could about it (I "enjoyed" particularly Otto Fenichel's *Psychoanalytic Theory of Neurosis*) — supposedly not a good idea as it created intellectual obstacles to spontaneous reactions. Yet I liked J. de S. and looked forward to my visits (let's call it a bit of "transference"). I do not remember much of the therapy itself beyond some of my recurrent and obvious issues, except for a short dream that, without knowing why, I never forgot. I am walking down a mountain road when I see, coming in my direction, a strange herd guarded by two or three policemen. The thirty or forty members of the herd are "monsters" physically speaking, but clearly they are humans, deformed humans with contorted human faces; they have breasts, although they appear to me to be men. I ask one of the guards where they are leading this strange group. "We are going to kill them," he tells me, and adds, "It's horrible." Then he adds again: "It's horrible because they cry." Could the tears be those I was unable to shed in real life?

At the time I believed in the therapeutic effect of analysis more than I do today, so that I cannot say whether it was the analysis that kept me afloat or whether, ultimately, hefty daily doses of Librium, then of Valium, and years later of Xanax, Zoloft, and Klonopin did the trick, although sporadic bouts of anxiety never entirely disappeared. Perhaps a measure of academic success became the real therapy. Whatever helped, the fact is that gradually the various manifestations of anxiety from which I had suffered day in and day out for some five to six years lost in intensity and then disappeared, as did the fear of flying and other phobias as well. But in the meantime, I had become addicted to tranquilizers.

I have left the most obvious question for the end: How did all of this affect my marriage? When Hagith and I met, I was nothing more than Nahum Goldmann's employee, without much to show for myself, and I soon started to get mysteriously ill. No physician, psychiatrist, or analyst seemed capable of curing me of ailments that were evidently psychological with some psychosomatic consequences. The Jerusalem analyst who attempted to dissuade me from leaving the job with Peres for uncertain studies had seen Hagith in private and told her outright that she had to separate from me.

Another warning followed that I haven't yet mentioned. To prepare the conference on Soviet Jewry, I worked from Paris, where we stayed for several weeks and from where I left on my various visits. And it is there that a duodenal ulcer of which I was unaware bled for the first time. Two years or so later, I left for my trip to Geneva. I had barely reached my destination when the ulcer bled again. This time I was hospitalized, received blood transfusions, but was not operated on, as the physicians thought that given my age, the right diet would suffice. Many years later, Hagith told me that, at a loss regarding all my ailments and the bleak future they heralded, she had considered divorce.

# CHAPTER SIX

# Turmoil

The last weeks of 1964 were one of the happiest periods of our stay in Geneva. Our son David was born at the end of November, I had a regular position at the institute, and, mainly, I started feeling much better.

One of the "magic moments" of those same days was a program that French television (I think there was only one channel at the time) offered for the holidays; it had been conceived and directed by Claude Santelli and included two miniseries that I still remember fifty years later: *David Copperfield* and Jules Verne's *Les Indes noires* (Black Indies). This was television at its best, or so I thought.

And, from the spring of 1964 on, there had been some excitement of a very different kind.

*l*

Over the years, my "Catholic past" hadn't particularly been on my mind, except possibly during analysis, and of course as far as guilt feelings were concerned. Yet its very background presence made me aware of matters that, otherwise, I may not have noticed at all.

Be that as it may, while working on my dissertation in the Bonn archives, I came upon a misplaced document in a file on the United States. It was a cable sent to Berlin in December 1941 from the German embassy at the Vatican. According to the message, a Vatican official had addressed a letter to the *Intendant* (director) of the Berlin State Opera about to visit Rome, asking to have excerpts of Wagner's *Parsifal* played for the pope in his apartments. At the time of the request, Nazi exterminations on Soviet territory were widely known and reported. Under such circumstances, the pope's demand for this private concert by a German orchestra amazed me; it later appeared that the concert did not take place.

Questions surfaced that had never occurred to me previously: What had been the pope's attitude to Nazi Germany? How did he react to the extermination of the Jews? Were bishops all over occupied Europe told to help the Jews? Would I have been hidden if my parents had not accepted my baptism? (My father had to write to the head nun of the seminary that he permitted the baptism, and promised to have me educated as a Catholic after the war.)

I decided then and there that once the dissertation was completed, I would return to Bonn and examine the files dealing with diplomatic relations between Germany and the Vatican from March 1939 (Pius XII's election) to the end of the war. And so it was: during the teaching break between the two semesters of 1964, I returned to Bonn.

———

The files regarding the Vatican were organized in chronological order (as all the others), and I systematically went through the first five volumes of documents covering the immediate prewar and war years until September 1943. Most of the material had never been published and even if the German diplomats at the Vatican did embellish some reports, the documents gave a fascinating and complex picture of relations that, far from always remaining smooth, were nonetheless never antagonistic on either side.

In early July 1943, the former highest-ranking official of the Wilhelmstrasse, State Secretary Ernst von Weizsäcker, replaced long-serving ambassador to the Vatican Diego von Bergen. The new envoy arrived at a critical juncture, as Mussolini was about to be ousted by his own Fascist Grand Council and arrested on order of the king. Marshall Pietro Badoglio would be appointed head of government. In the meantime, on the Eastern Front, the Soviet army had definitively seized the initiative and was rapidly pushing ahead following its victories in Stalingrad, Orel, and Kursk.

After his initial audience with the pope, Weizsäcker conveyed Pius's fear of Communism to Ribbentrop and pointed to the tacit convergence of attitudes it created regarding the Red menace. The summer went by and, in September 1943, the Anglo-American forces, after occupying Sicily, landed in southern Italy: Badoglio surrendered. Within hours, the Germans, who had troops at the ready, occupied Italy down to the line held by the Allies. About a month later, the rounding up and deportation of the Jews of Rome and of all German-occupied Italy started.

I asked for file number 6 covering the crucial period from September 1943 to February 1944, that of the deportations and thus of the German reports about the reactions of the Vatican.

The file had disappeared; it was never found. The file that followed (number 7), which covered the period between February and June 1944, when the Allies occupied Rome, was in its
place. By then most Jews who could be caught had been caught.
Two essential German documents dating from the deportations
period that had been used in the Nuremberg trials were known:
Weizsäcker's cable about the possibility of a papal protest against
the deportation of the Jews of Rome, followed by the ambassador's message informing Berlin that no such protest would take
place. Some additional bits and pieces from that period surfaced
here and there; basically, that was it. The overall German documentation for these decisive months was gone.

## 2

Back in Geneva, I wrote short comments about the documents I had
gathered. The starting point of my arguments, based on the German archival materials, but also on published American and British
documents, as well as on those of the World Jewish Congress and
other Jewish sources to be found in Jerusalem, in the Central Zionist Archives, was simple and, as far as I could see, incontrovertible:
From the beginning of the campaign against the Soviet Union and
on, the Vatican was well-informed about the German extermination of civilians and particularly that of the Jews, from Catholic and
other religious sources and from its own missions in the Eastern
territories. Soon such information reached the press, and could not
be kept under wraps in any case. Later, information about the sys-
tematic extermination of the Jews regularly reached the pope. Yet
Pius XII abstained from any reaction, even when the Jews of Rome
were deported, "under his own windows."

The question debated ever since has been: What explains that silence? Pacelli's personal liking for the German people (from his days as nuncio in Munich and Berlin) may have been a factor, but a marginal one; his fear of bringing Nazi retribution against the church in Germany certainly became an important consideration. Traditional Christian anti-Semitism also played a role. The pope's main reason, however — one that haunted the Vatican since the end of the First World War and Pacelli personally since his confrontation with the Munich Communists while he was nuncio in Bavaria, in 1919, and that had turned into quasi-panic after Stalingrad — appeared to be a fear that Bolshevism would spread into Central Europe. The Wehrmacht had become the last bulwark against the Red menace, and weakening that bulwark by an open denunciation of German policies had, in my view, ceased to be an option for Pius XII, if it ever was one.

I took excerpts of the documents to Paris, to a well-known publisher to whom I had been recommended: Jerôme Lindon, owner and hands-on director of the Éditions de Minuit. He had published Samuel Beckett and other prestigious names of recent literature, as well as hard-hitting left-oriented political books such as the hugely successful *La question* (*The Question*) that the (Jewish) Communist Henri Alleg had written about French interrogation methods during the Algerian war.

Lindon was enthusiastic. He promised to turn the book into a best seller, offered to work with me on the final version, and couldn't wait to have the full manuscript in hand. It was only after leaving his office that I understood my mistake: the work of a Jewish author critical of the pope, brought out by a notorious Jewish leftist publisher, would look ideologically motivated and thus be easily dismissed.

I wrote a letter full of regrets to Lindon and received a sting-ing answer, ending with the words, *"Je suis content de vous avoir connu jeune. Vous irez loin"* (I am glad to have met you young. You will go far). But here I was, in need of a non-Jewish, nonleftist publisher and without anybody in sight. By chance, Elie Wiesel, who had published *Night* and more to great acclaim, was in Paris; I decided to consult him. As I mentioned, I knew him from his days as Paris correspondent of the Israeli evening paper *Yediot Ahronot*. I had met him again in New York during my work with Goldmann and we'd kept in touch. He generously introduced me to his publisher, Paul Flamand, the owner and director of Édi-tions du Seuil. There could not have been a better choice.

Éditions du Seuil was a left-oriented, nonconformist, Cath-olic publishing house. Among hundreds of titles, Flamand had published the writings of the Jesuit theologian and paleontolo-gist Pierre Teilhard de Chardin, against the explicit opposition of the church. Many years later, he told me the details of that story. When it became known that he would publish Teilhard's complete works, an important Paris Jesuit came to his office and beseeched him to relent. Notwithstanding the pressure, Flamand, a practicing Catholic, didn't budge, although he was being threatened with excommunication. The openly angry and disappointed Jesuit took his leave. A few seconds later, the door of Flamand's office opened, the Jesuit's head appeared, and he blurted out, "Forget all I told you" and was gone.

Flamand didn't waste any time. After seeing the documents I brought, he left for Rome to meet with the highly influential Msgr Agostino Casaroli. I had one side of the story, he pointed out: the German documents. In order to restore the balance, I needed access to the Vatican archives on those same issues. As Flamand wrote to me from Rome, he didn't receive a straightforward refusal. The Vatican officials wanted to see and study the material I had; they would then prepare a detailed response and discuss it with me. The net result of this strategy would have been to delay indefinitely the publication of my book, to eventually publish bits and pieces of my documentation, in short to undermine the whole enterprise. Flamand also perceived it that way. We decided to forge ahead on our own.

We chose an extremely careful tripartite editing of the comments: I had written the basic text; Flamand, together with a journalist from *Le Monde* and a friend, Jacques Nobécourt — who had just published a general study on the Vatican during the war, *Le Vicaire et l'histoire* (The Deputy and History) — went over my comments and suggested, here and there, some "softening" of style by introducing a few "perhaps" or "possiblys," instead of straightforward affirmations. This outside perspective was extremely helpful and never turned into censorship. Finally — and this looked to us like the ultimate protection against any potential accusation of willful partisanship — a moderate and conciliatory afterword was added, written by Alfred Grosser, a converted Jew, specialist of recent German history and professor at Sciences Po; mainly, he contributed a regular and influential column to the Catholic daily *La Croix*. Thus protected on all sides, my *Pie XII et le IIIe Reich: Une documentation* was published in November 1964.

The topic was already being fiercely debated for a year, as German author Rolf Hochhuth's play *The Deputy* had been staged the world over since early 1963 and had provoked a firestorm of controversy by examining Pius XII's silence in the face of the extermination of European Jewry. I had had no contact with Hochhuth and had actually paid little attention to the play (which I read only later), but from the very outset the ongoing debate spilled over to the reactions that greeted my own book.

Looking back at the publication of *Pius XII*, could I still be sure that no resentment rooted in my Catholic years was underlying the writing of that book? I didn't feel it then and I don't feel it now. I was taken aback by Pius XII's silence, although I understood — at least I think I understood — what may have been its main motivations. I wasn't too astonished by the church's lack of opposition to Nazi Germany and its satellites, and was upset only when facing blunt denials and egregious lies. In that sense, the work on the Vatican, and mainly the debates that followed, did erode something of my emotional distance from the Holocaust, but the work was also facilitated because that erosion was already slowly beginning.

### 3

(Very) favorable and (very) hostile reactions surged on all sides, particularly in France, where the book sold between 50,000 and 60,000 copies within a few weeks. For me, barely starting my academic career, this was both flattering and dangerous. The flattering aspect does not require much explanation: from one day to the next I became well-known and much in demand (as the book was being translated into some fifteen or sixteen languages and made the covers of *L'Express* in France, *Der Spiegel* in Germany, and *Look* in the United States, the last two in 1964 and 1966). The danger was no less obvious: addiction to publicity and easy success.

On the hostile side, the attacks concentrated on several claims: (*a*) Pius's attitude and that of the Vatican toward the

Third Reich were entirely different from the slanted version that I (and the German documents) offered; (*b*) I was deeply ungrateful, as I had been saved by the church; and (*c*) I was a sensationalist, not a serious scholar.

The American Jesuit Robert Graham and the group of Jesuits that would later publish the eleven volumes of Vatican documents pertaining to the Second World War (a valuable but highly selective collection) were my fiercest critics in a series of articles published in *America*, *Osservatore Romano*, and *La Civiltà Cattolica*, as were all possible conservative journalists, Catholic fundamentalists, and even an Israeli writer, Pinchas Lapide. Some Catholic scholars joined the fray, and so did, two years later, the British maverick historian A. J. P. Taylor, who in a sarcastic review in the *New Statesman* wondered why I didn't realize that the Catholic Church was a political institution that, like all political institutions, acted only in line with its interests and nothing else.

Taylor's disparaging article was rather unexpected, and throughout used an intentionally derisive term against me personally, referring to me as "Associate Professor Friedländer" (he got my rank from the brief "About the Author" on the back of the book). I didn't plan to answer, but out of the blue, a spirited defense by Hubert Butler appeared in a major article in the *Irish Times*, in October 1966. Furthermore, Butler sent a sharp reader's letter to the editor of the *New Statesman*. It ended with a flourish: "If thrones and crowns (both single and triple) are one day to be abolished, could we not make a start with professorial chairs? They so often confer upon their occupants a small and snooty arrogance which is more hurtful than the domineering ways of the old-fashioned dynasts."

By sheer coincidence, a namesake of my Irish defender, G. P. Butler of University College London, had his own letter about

Taylor's article published in the *New Statesman* at the same time. "Obviously," Butler's letter concluded, "Mr. Taylor doesn't like *Pius XII and the Third Reich*, but his reasons are drowned by the noise of grinding teeth — and axes."

Apart from liberal and left-wing supporters, I also had firm allies on the Catholic side: the Dominican professor of philosophy at the Swiss Catholic Fribourg University, Jozef M. Bochenski; the professor of philosophy at Warsaw University, Leszek Kolakowski; and especially the dean of the College of Cardinals, the French Cardinal Eugène Tisserant, who wrote to me: "It is important that the truth be known." Upon my request, he allowed me to publish his letter.

One of the letters that pleased me most came from my former girlfriend Maryvonne. She congratulated me about the book and had many kind things to say about our past together. I saw her again in 1966 when she met me after a television program and then, the next day, saw me off at the airport with her son, in uniform by then. She was working as a medical secretary. She had had breast cancer but told me that she was cured. I didn't hear from her anymore thereafter.

The most memorable public debate about Pius XII did not take place during any major television program (although these included *Lectures pour tous* with Pierre Desgraupes in France and a not entirely friendly interview with David Frost — who must have just then started his career — in the UK). It occurred in Geneva at the Cercle de l'Athénée. Hundreds of people packed the hall, sitting on the floor, on windowsills and even on the stage. I was to present my arguments and a local Jesuit (they were not officially allowed in Geneva but were present nonetheless) was to comment; an open debate would follow.

The initial presentations took place without any fireworks, but scarcely had the Jesuit finished commenting on my arguments than Jeanne Hersch, a professor of philosophy at the University of Geneva, a free spirit and a powerful speaker, took hold of the microphone and, hammering every word, declared that my arguments were "crystal clear" and that the pope's silence was outrageous. At that moment all hell broke loose, everybody was shouting and, of course, in Calvinist Geneva, anti-Catholic emotions ran high. I even saw a member of the local Protestant aristocracy, a de Muralt, I think, ominously brandishing an umbrella . . . *O tempora, o mores.*

The two years that followed the publication of *Pius XII* were very intense. We moved to a large apartment on rue de Moillebeau with a magnificent view of the city, the lake — and Mont Blanc. Hagith gave piano lessons but mainly kept busy with the two boys, Eli and David, although an au pair from Israel had been living with us for some time already. I had my seminar, my courses, and my lectures about Pius with all the commotion that surrounded the topic and the constant traveling it demanded.

It is only then that I managed to thoroughly read Raul Hilberg's monumental history of the Holocaust (*The Destruction of the European Jews*, published in 1961), which I had skimmed through two or three years beforehand. I also met the most significant historian of anti-Semitism and of the Shoah there was in France at that time: Léon Poliakov. One can hardly imagine two personalities more different than Hilberg and Poliakov (whereas I knew Poliakov from 1964 on, I met Hilberg only in 1968, in Israel; later, I frequently encountered both, over the decades).

Hilberg presented a dour façade and lectured at a very slow and effective pace, in a sepulchral voice. He looked like a sad man to whom life was being unjust, although, after initial controversies, he was widely recognized and respected as the preeminent historian of the Holocaust. Something of his persona transpired in his autobiography, *The Politics of Memory*.

This being said, for many years to come Hilberg's *Destruction* became the necessary and unsurpassed history of the extermination of the Jews of Europe, the essential reference for any historian of the subject. A few other attempts at presenting a historical synthesis of the events as such had preceded (Léon Poliakov, Gerald Reitlinger, Joseph Billig, Wolfgang Scheffler), but none included the massive documentation and followed the rigorous analytic framework offered by Hilberg. Not that Hilberg's work had been vied for by publishers or acclaimed by a wide readership: it was brought out after many failed attempts by a small Chicago publisher and barely reached a limited and specialized group. It was published in German in 1983, twenty-two years after its initial English edition came out.

Hilberg's volume was not without its deficiences and inner contradictions, of course. While the first few pages listed various anti-Jewish measures taken by the Catholic Church and indicated their similarity to some of the Nazi measures, thus establishing a deep ideological link between centuries-long Christian anti-Judaism and Hitler's anti-Semitic crusade, ideology then disappeared from his study, to be replaced by the quasi-autonomous dynamics of four related bureaucracies (State, Party, Army, Economy) that supposedly determined the fate of European Jews from their initial definition as Jews to their ultimate extermination. Moreover, Hilberg excoriated the leadership of Jewish communities in the Reich and throughout occupied Europe for what he considered as their collaboration with the Nazis, their atavistic subservience, and, all in all, for going along with the passivity of Jewish masses in the face of persecution and death.

In contrast to Hilberg, Poliakov had a sunny personality; he was mostly smiling, friendly, knowledgeable, and generous with information. He was a self-taught historian who, during the war, lived in hiding in France, the country to which he had emigrated from Russia, and who, after the war, worked with the French prosecutor in Nuremberg.

Poliakov's history of the Shoah came out some ten years before Hilberg's magnum opus under the original French title *Le bréviaire de la haine* (*Harvest of Hate*). It encompassed none of Hilberg's massive documentation and was an early attempt at summarizing events that — let us recall — were not central, nor even systematically summarized at the Nuremberg Trial of Major War Criminals. Later, Poliakov published his multivolume history of anti-Semitism from its early Christian beginnings to the 1930s; it remains his enduring work.

I liked Poliakov and we got along well, as we also shared the same ideas about Pius XII. An article of his awoke my interest in that strangest of SS men, Kurt Gerstein, whose story was related to the Vatican issue, albeit tangentially. Poliakov helped me get access to the Gerstein archive in Westphalia and thus to the material necessary for a short biography. I wrote it in 1965–66.

Kurt Gerstein was a devout Protestant who volunteered for the Waffen-SS in 1940 and was posted to its hygiene section. There, in charge of disinfection, he dealt with lethal materials, including Zyklon B pellets, which, in gaseous form, could exterminate human beings in an enclosed space. In July 1942, ordered to deliver Zyklon to Lublin, Gerstein was invited to witness the extermination of a transport of Dutch Jews. From that day on, while he continued to deliver Zyklon to camps, he attempted to inform the world of what was happening.

On the nightly train ride that brought him back from Warsaw to Berlin, after the Lublin mission and the visit to Belsec, Gerstein gave a detailed description of what he had seen to the Swedish diplomat Göran von Otter, a fellow passenger. Von Otter sent a report to Stockholm; it remained under wraps until the end of the war. Gerstein attempted to be heard at the Vatican legation and at the Swiss consulate but was refused access to either place. His friends in the Evangelical Church did not dare to publicize what he told them.

Shortly before the end of the war Gerstein surrendered to the Americans and wrote four essentially identical reports about what he knew and what he had witnessed. These reports were to become significant evidence at the Nuremberg trial. In the meantime, Gerstein was handed over to the French authorities and jailed in Paris as a war criminal. In July 1945, he hanged himself in his cell. The loneliness of Gerstein's action contributed to its failure, deepened his despair, and ultimately led to his suicide.

*4*

Over the years, I returned at times to the issue of Pius XII, particularly in *Nazi Germany and the Jews*. In 2011, however, I decided to add a full-length afterword to the French and German republications, as significant new material had become available that confirmed the thesis presented in 1964. The same arguments became even more convincing after the publication of David Kertzer's path-breaking study on the role played by Eugenio Pacelli (the future Pius XII), then secretary of state, in the relations between Pius XI, Italian fascism, and Nazi Germany.

At the beginning of his career, while he was nuncio in Warsaw after the First World War, Achille Ratti (the future Pius XI) brandished the usual anti-Jewish accusations and slogans of the most conservative Catholicism. Once elected pope, he didn't abandon the ultra-right-wing policies that led to the historic concordat between the Holy See and Mussolini's fascist state in 1929. The appointment of Pacelli as secretary of state helped in keeping that same line; it resulted in a concordat with Nazi Germany in 1933. Within a short time, however, the pope began to perceive the nature of Nazism and his attitude increasingly distanced itself from the outright appeasement policy of his secretary of state. Pacelli helped to formulate the first encyclical that mildly criticized Nazism, without naming it, in 1937. From then on, however, Pius XI's and Pacelli's attitudes toward Hitler's Reich clearly differed. While Pacelli maintained his avoidance of confrontation with Nazi Germany, the pope, increasingly frail, decided to attack Nazi racial anti-Semitism in a special encyclical that would be entitled *Humani generis unitas*, prepared by three Jesuits. It was shown to the pope as he lay dying. Pacelli, once elected pope, suppressed the message that could have encouraged European Catholics to offer some assistance to the hounded Jews. The text of the encyclical was found decades after the events, and published in English in 1997 as *The Hidden Encyclical of Pius XI.*

A few exceptional circumstances also brought up the topic over the years. In 1997, I was awarded an honorary doctorate by the German university of Witten-Herdecke. To my utter amazement, a short time before the ceremony, the cardinal archbishop of Paris and converted Jew, Jean-Marie Lustiger, arrived, privately and with no indication of his status, except for the scarcely visible red ecclesiastical collar of a cardinal. He had come to make the festive introduction of the honoree. Needless to say, I remained speechless when I saw him and understood why he came.

A short time thereafter, the president of Tel Aviv University and I invited the cardinal to a conference on the church and the Jews during the war. The debates were interesting, without adding anything to the theme of Pius XII. The memorable moment came at the end of the conference, when our guest addressed an assembly of some seven hundred students (while outside the hall, Orthodox students were yelling insults). He introduced himself: "My name is Aaron Lustiger [he used the German/Yiddish pronunciation of his name] and I am also called Jean-Marie Lustiger [French pronunciation]." His theme: the compatibility of both identities.

The belief in such compatibility was a guiding principle of Lustiger's life; it did not endear him to some Catholics, nor did it seem acceptable to part of the Jewish religious establishment. The cardinal never wavered on this issue; in 2004, three years before his death, he wrote his own epitaph, the first lines of which read as follows:

> *I was born Jewish.*
> *I received the name*
> *Of my paternal grandfather, Aaron.*
> *Having become Christian*
> *By Faith and by Baptism,*
> *I have remained Jewish*
> *As did the Apostles.*

Paul Flamand was *un grand monsieur.* Was Blanche Knopf, my American publisher, *une grande dame?* I met her in Flamand's office sometime in the course of 1964; she saw the manuscript of *Pius XII* and bought the rights for the American publication under Knopf's Borzoi Books imprint. The sums involved were very modest but, as a beginner, I was happy to have been accepted by such a prestigious publisher. Incidentally, this was, I think, the beginning of my cooperation with Georges Borchardt, the literary agent who represented Seuil in the United States, a cooperation that became a friendship and remains so to this day.

Some time after the American edition was published, Blanche Knopf phoned from Paris: she was staying at the Ritz; could I come for lunch the next day? In order to make it and return in time for my seminar, I had to fly from Geneva to Paris and back, quite an expense for me. I imagined that she wished to discuss my next project or suggest a theme worth pursuing; in other words, I had great expectations. On the following day at noon, I was at the Ritz.

Blanche Knopf duly came down and we moved to the restaurant for a very light lunch, as my host, then about seventy, did not eat heavily at noon, nor did she drink anything but water. We spoke of Thomas Mann, Sartre, and Camus, all of whom she knew well and had published. Then we moved on to Freud, Ilya Ehrenburg, André Gide (all of whom she had also published), and others. After an hour or so, she told me how delighted she was to have talked to me.

A few minutes later, I was on my way back to the airport.

## 5

Sometime during the summer of 1966, we all returned for a brief visit to Tel Aviv. Israel was in the doldrums. The economy was faltering; the young generation was accused of having lost all ideals: it was mired in the everyday, lounged in cafés and bars; it was dubbed the espresso generation. Many Israelis attributed the decline to a weakness in political leadership, to the supposedly inept "old guard" of Mapai who had seized the reins of power from the hands of Ben-Gurion, once he resigned in 1964 to set up his own party: Rafi. Levi Eshkol took over as prime minister and defense minister.

Eshkol, naturally fluent in Hebrew, seemed on occasion to prefer the folksy expressions of his native Yiddish to the pathos of Biblical prose. He was a man of compromise and of peace who had inherited a difficult internal situation and would soon be faced with an external crisis of formidable proportions. In the meantime, the general mood was such that the number of emigrants from Israel was larger than that of immigrants. A popular joke summed it all up: a large sign at Lod (today Ben-Gurion) Airport asked the last person to leave to please turn off the light.

I paid a visit to Shimon, who now occupied a nondescript office on some equally nondescript Tel Aviv street. As secretary general of Rafi, he didn't display the upbeat mood of his former days. He was bitter about the lack of commitment (and work) of his comrade-in-arms Moshe Dayan, who, according to him, hardly concerned himself with the fledgling party. In fact, Rafi would soon rejoin the fold and become part of a center-left coalition dominated by the old Mapai. For Ben-Gurion, there was no political comeback; for Dayan there would be a glorious aftermath, followed by a tragic one. Peres's political life went on with ups and downs: he was a true political survivor — possibly too much so. As I am writing, he is the president of Israel, just about to celebrate his ninetieth birthday.

We spent much time with our friends Sabi Teveth and his wife Ora. It's there that, for the first time, I heard of the Beatles and listened to some of their music (I was late to many things). Like most Israelis to this day, Sabi and Ora regularly organized get-togethers on Friday evenings. You arrived at about ten and joined a sizable number of other guests, usually a rather homogeneous group. One ate, drank, and talked (these conversations were not only loud but often turned into simultaneous and competing monologues until, ultimately, one of the guests — or the host — managed to become the center of attention). You were not supposed to look at your watch before the early morning hours — and then the discussion went on for any length of time at the door of the apartment or by the elevator.

To say that I disliked these Friday evenings would be an understatement, though not because I thought that this verbal free-for-all was uncouth. Not in the least. The reason was much more basic: as I already mentioned, I was extremely shy. Not in a one-to-one conversation, not in the company of three to four close friends and not in structured situations such as teaching, a public lecture, or a television (or radio) interview. But put me at a dinner table of let us say eight people or more and you will hear me speak in monosyllables at best. And in the whirlwind of Israeli Friday evening debates, you wouldn't hear me at all. I never overcame this selective shyness, never understood it really. To this day, it remains the same, except that it bothers me less. I stay silent in social gatherings or speak only to my neighbor and almost never in a general conversation. So be it.

Sabi had become one of the most respected journalists in the country and later he would turn into a very thorough Ben-Gurion biographer. As I already mentioned, he was a true insider of the defense establishment, and its elite belonged to his regular list of Friday night guests. Some members could not be invited together, mainly in later years: you had Shimon on one Friday, and Itzhak and Leah Rabin on another. Although they worked together when Labor was in power, Shimon and Itzhak were competitors for the first place in their party, in the government, and in history; they hated each other, quite openly so, probably to the end.

During one of these occasions, in 1966, Sabi asked me, "Do you know Moshe?" No, I had never met Dayan. A visit was arranged for the following Saturday, at Dayan's home in Zahala (a posh residential area, not far from Tel Aviv, mostly built for high-ranking officers and their families). In those days, apart from being one of the three leaders of Rafi, Dayan, who for a while had been minister of agriculture in Eshkol's government, had become head of a semigovernmental Red Sea fishing company and, quite openly, remained a collector of extramarital affairs and of valuable antiquities wherever he found them, in Israel or elsewhere (his many critics called it robbery). A dashing personality if Israel ever had one, he was known worldwide as the general with the black patch over one eye (he had lost the eye in the Second World War, in a British-led operation in Vichy-occupied Syria).

Much has been written about Dayan, yet grasping his personality remains difficult. Israel Bar's story about the scorpion was inspired by hatred, but it may have contained a tiny grain of truth. Dayan, mostly prudent and rational, could at times be reckless and push for dangerous moves, against all reason. Mainly, he was a loner, a deeply pessimistic man, apparently indifferent to the opinion of others.

Dayan guided us through his truly impressive array of antiquities before we sat down for coffee. We touched upon many issues, but it was his view of the conflict with the Arabs that I've never forgotten. He saw the Palestinian issue as the core of the conflict: as long as the Palestinian problem remained unsolved, the overall conflict would find no solution. At that time (one year before the Six-Day War), the majority of Palestinians lived in the West Bank and in East Jerusalem under Jordanian rule; a further few hundred thousand lived in Israel and a similar number were dispersed in refugee camps in Gaza (which belonged to Egypt) and in Lebanon. The Palestine Liberation Organization (PLO) had just been established in 1964 but at that stage it still played a minor role.

Did Dayan believe that the Palestinian issue could be solved? He did not. His explanation was simple: "Most Palestinians have peasant roots," he said. "We have stolen their land to set up our state. Peasants never forget and never forgive those who live on their stolen land." Did it mean that Israel would forever live by the sword? Dayan thought so, and had previously said as much in a widely known eulogy delivered at the grave of one of his friends, Ro'i Rothberg, killed by Palestinian infiltrators near the Gaza border.

## 6

In the fall semester of 1966 I was guest professor in the Department of Political Science at the Université Française de Montréal. I had never before heard "Joual" (Canadian French) and actually did not know that it existed. Imagine my astonishment when the driver who met me at the airport told me, "*Je vais chauffer mon char*," which in French would mean "I am going to heat my chariot." I soon got used to this seventeenth-century French with its

English components and came to enjoy my Quebecois environment. The separatist movement was gaining in strength and de Gaulle would soon throw fuel on the fire when, at the end of a state visit to Canada, he exclaimed, "*Vive le Québec libre!*"

During the few months I spent in Montreal, I rented a room with all the amenities in one of the villas on Westmound, a kind of golden ghetto, mostly English-speaking, mostly Jewish, quite distant from the "French"-speaking Catholic population. Yet some of these Jewish families were relatively recent immigrants from North Africa, naturally the wealthier ones, who had arrived via Israel or directly from Rabat or Casablanca. They usually were fluent in both English and French.

One of those families invited me for the Rosh Hashanah (Jewish New Year) dinner and, for the first time, I experienced the warmth and the particularly colorful rites of a thoroughly Sephardic community. Flashes of that evening return to me to this day, and I recall a kind of joy that I otherwise did not feel in our celebrations, which were always a little stilted and artificial. Strangely enough, something in me has always resisted learning even the most basic religious texts and rituals. To this day, for instance, I barely know a few words of the Haggadah, the text read during the Seder, the festive dinner on the eve of Passover.

The Montreal students were attentive and likable, but they adamantly refused to read anything in English, which, in political science and in the history of modern international relations, created quite a problem. We managed, and they must have been happy with my teaching, as at the end of my last lecture, they solemnly set a box on my desk. I was supposed to open it, which I did, then lift up its contents and show it to all, which I couldn't do: it was too heavy. The object was a magnificent Eskimo stone sculpture of a fisherman holding a fish. It accompanied me for decades, from one home to another.

In early May 1967, I returned to my native city for the first time since April 1939. A few weeks beforehand, I had received a letter from Czechoslovakia. When I looked at the sender's name I immediately recognized it: Vlasta Hajnerova, my nanny. She had read the review of a book by a Saul Friedländer translated into Czech and saw that the author was born in Prague in 1932. Could this Saul be the child Paul she had taken care of? She got my address from the publisher and wrote. We met. In my eyes she had not changed much.

We walked and walked for two days: she showed me the small house and garden in Bubeneč where I had spent my first three or four years and the apartment building on the Vltava quay to which we moved later on. Manifestly she had no great fondness for my mother, but as far as I could remember, she had been kind to me. She had taught me Czech songs that I still remember and tried to pass on to me something of her pious Catholicism. Did my parents know? I wonder. After we left, she went to work in the family of a German general. A professional nanny can't be too choosy.

This reminds me that for my eightieth birthday, one of the children gave me a magnificent photo album of Prague by Karel Plička, published in 1940. I had seen the book many years beforehand and had tried to find it ever since. Well, here it was with its truly extraordinary array of palaces, churches, bridges, gardens, ancient libraries, and all the beauty of the city. I was puzzled, though, to find some ugly modern office buildings in the midst of the Gothic and Baroque splendor. It did not take long to understand that Nazi censorship had erased the photos of the old Jewish cemetery and of the ancient synagogues — in short of any sign of Judaism in the most Jewish city of Central Europe — and replaced them with drab office buildings.

I had barely returned to Geneva when the crisis began that within three weeks would lead to war between Israel and the neighboring Arab states.

# PART II

## *The Unraveling of a Dream*

# CHAPTER SEVEN

# The Footsteps of the Messiah

From every window, every terrace, every coffee shop, radios screamed in unison Uri Zohar's "*Nasser mechakeh leRabin, ai, ai, ai* . . ." (Nasser waits for Rabin, ai, ai, ai . . .) or launched into Noemy Shemer's elegiac "Yerushalayim shel zahav . . ." ("Jerusalem of Gold . . ."). It was frenzy, an outburst of nationalist elation that knew no bounds.

Much of it was a spontaneous reaction to two weeks of waiting with the darkest forebodings and to the stupendous victory that followed. With the hesitant Eshkol as its prime minister, but with Dayan as newly appointed defense minister in a national union cabinet, Israel struck. In six days, the Israeli forces occupied the Sinai Peninsula, the West Bank of the Jordan River (as King Hussein had joined the anti-Israel coalition), and the Syrian heights overlooking the Sea of Galilee; mainly, it conquered the whole of Jerusalem. Some Israelis were already hearing the footsteps of the Messiah.

The contrast between subdued Geneva and this overheated atmosphere was jarring, but as much as the nationalist elation went against my feelings, the Israeli political attitude appeared reasonable to me at the time. I had just debated at a conference in Geneva with a fiery and eloquent anti-Israel professor from Princeton, Arno Mayer. And, a few days after the end of the war, a "memorable" confrontation took place, this time on French television, between four Israelis and four Palestinians. We were seated in separate studios, as the Palestinians refused to sit together with us. Our group comprised Elie Wiesel, the journalist Yeshayahu Ben-Porat, the Foreign Ministry official David Catarivas, and myself. In the midst of the program, Wiesel and Catarivas left in protest against the Palestinian attitude; Ben-Porat and I battled on.

A few weeks later, sometime in July 1967, we arrived in Israel: I had been offered a one-year guest professorship in history at the Hebrew University in Jerusalem on Talmon's suggestion.

2

A year after our last visit, we discovered a different country. Along with the nationalist outburst, Israel reveled in an entirely new sense of power, almost of "superpower." For Israelis and for many Jews in the Diaspora, this was a previously unknown feeling. Droves of tourists filled the country and its "empire." The economy suddenly turned around and a boom followed the stagnation of previous years. Within a few months, the very sight of the country had changed: everywhere, Arab workers from the occupied territories bustled on thousands of new building sites; on city streets, the smells of new restaurants wafted in the summer heat. In the spring of 1968, on the twentieth anniversary of Israel, the first national television channel was inaugurated. As for peace, it was nowhere in sight. Israel would not move from the occupied territories as long as the Arab countries rejected all negotiation, which they did at the Khartum conference, at the end of 1967.

During the year we spent in Jerusalem, there wasn't the least difficulty in visiting, shopping, or eating in the Old City (the mostly Arab part of Jerusalem), or traveling anywhere else in the occupied territories from Sharm el-Sheikh at the southern tip of the Sinai Peninsula, to the Saint Catherine Monastery in the middle of Sinai, to the souk (the covered market) of Hebron or the slopes of Mount Lebanon. You were received with open arms, business was brisk: the buyers made money (prices were extremely low at the outset), the sellers made even more money. Occupiers and occupied were happily coexisting — or so it seemed.

We loved to stroll in the Arab quarter of the Old City, particularly in the souk. Most of the stalls, taken singly, were not overly impressive, but the jumble of hundreds of them on both sides of the crowded narrow path that led downhill from Jaffa Gate — or across the souk from the Damascus Gate (Shechem Gate in Hebrew) — offered a display of colors and a pungent smell of spices that assailed and overwhelmed the senses and made you slightly dizzy — or rather, dazzled — from the richness of it all.

From the souk, you could follow a side alley and within minutes you reached the Holy Sepulcher. The church with its multiple additions over the centuries had none of the beauty of European cathedrals. Once you entered, you couldn't help being taken aback as monks of diverse and mutually hostile Christian rites pulled you, each to his own corner of the church, to show you "their" burial site of Jesus. You quickly forgot all this awkwardness, however, on the occasion of some of the grand ceremonies, particularly on Easter week. During this first stay, we attended the Holy Fire celebration of the Greek Orthodox Church, and although we got only brief sights of the fire, we were soon surrounded by thousands of burning candles that the throngs of faithful had lit from that holy fire and were holding in an ecstasy of devotion.

If you followed the main path through the souk, down from Jaffa Gate, you reached the Western Wall and, dominating it, the Temple Mount, with its two magnificent mosques, the Dome of the Rock and the Al Aqsa Mosque. In 1967–68, the absence of the vast square cleared years later enhanced the majesty of the Wall; the huge stones arose literally a few feet away from where you stood: they overwhelmed you not so much (as far as we were concerned) by a feeling of holiness but rather by the weight of history they carried.

One of our preferred and most frequent excursions — when the weather allowed it from the autumn on — was the drive from Jerusalem down to Jericho or straight to the Dead Sea for wading in water not ideal for swimming (not for me in any case, even if it was supposed to carry you). The road from Jerusalem to the Dead Sea inspired awe. At first you only saw the dozens of burned-out tanks, armored cars, and trucks of the Jordanian army that dotted both sides of the highway. Very soon, however, a different sight took over. The barren hills that surrounded you in both directions did not look desolate; they arose there, wrapped in an almost unnatural stillness, displaying an austere beauty that did not remind you of any landscape you carried in memory or imagination. It was Ernest Renan, if I am not mistaken, who linked that surreal bareness to the birth of monotheism. And if you traveled down in late afternoon, the mounts of Moav, on the far side of the Dead Sea, turned violet just before becoming a dark barrier on the background of a fading, cloudless sky. But then if you chose Jericho and settled under the pergola of a restaurant, the pita, the hummus with tahini, and the beer tasted better than anywhere else, precisely because you had just undergone such a "spiritual" experience.

And, although nothing much remained of my Catholic adolescence, I nonetheless liked to visit the sites of a story I literally once knew by heart (in the seminary, during the Passion Week, we had to memorize — in Greek — the story of the Last Supper and the events leading to the Crucifixion, according to the Gospel of John).

We had rented an apartment on Aza Street (Gaza Street), a ten-minute drive from campus; we soon got acquainted with our very friendly neighbors and, in short, became true Jerusalemites. Eli, who had turned seven on the eve of our arrival, went to grade school in the fall and, as we spoke Hebrew at home, had no problem in adapting. I assume that we sent three-year-old David to a preschool; I am sure that we didn't just leave him to his own devices.

I often think of my nonchalant attitude in 1967–68 regarding the ongoing national exaltation. As I said, I didn't like the "noise" it made but I have to admit that in my heart of hearts I shared the euphoria. Obviously I did not share the messianic dreams or the sudden devotion to the "whole land of Israel" that well-known leftist writers such as Moshe Shamir and Haim Guri suddenly discovered and proclaimed; but I was not shocked. Nothing shocked me yet. My private euphoria was in the order of things and I didn't hear many voices that warned of inherent dangers.

And yet, that I, who of all people should have understood what occupation does to the occupied and to the occupier, didn't see any "writing on the wall" embarrasses me in hindsight. How didn't I perceive that notwithstanding the economic benefits enjoyed by many Palestinians (the term was not yet commonly used), humiliation was lurking and that it was just a matter of time for humiliation to turn into a thirst for revenge, a need to inflict pain on the occupier by any available means? It would lead to repression that would intensify the anger and turn it into rage. This is, as we know, the disastrous course that events were to follow. The only thing that I perceived soon enough was the danger of a moral degradation that the occupation could foster within Israeli society.

The Six-Day War has turned into a crucial landmark in the history of Israel; it became the end of an epoch and the beginning of a fateful evolution, the outcome of which cannot yet be surmised, particularly today (2015). It isn't only the occupation of Palestinian or other Arab territory that *caused* the change. Rather, the victory of those days activated a deep, preexisting impulse within Jewish history, albeit shared only by a small minority at first: closure to the surrounding world and the nurturing of a fanatical, messianic identity, whether in strictly religious terms or in its extreme nationalist equivalent after the rise of Zionism.

2

We were taken in by a small group of German Jews, mostly living in the Rehavia area of Jerusalem, all more or less linked to the university. This was a remnant of Weimar Germany, presided over by the already mentioned member of the pacifist movement Brit Shalom, the world-famous historian of Jewish mysticism, Gershom Scholem, and his wife Fania.

Why the Scholems invited us to their house as frequent guests, I do not know. Perhaps the master had read and liked my book on Pius XII? I vaguely remember something else: we met the Scholems at Justice Haim Cohen's home and, over tea, I asked Scholem whether he knew the real identity of Thomas Mann's Chaim Breisacher, the crazy Munich Jew portrayed in *Doktor Faustus*. Of course Scholem knew, and he happily started describing the revolutionary mystic and indeed crazy Jew, Oskar Goldberg. I had probably passed the test that I had unintentionally set for myself. The Scholems' door opened.

You entered a small apartment on Alharizi Street, with book-lined walls on all sides. And here were the Scholems. You couldn't look at them without smiling to yourself. While Fania was small and chubby, Gershom was tall, thin, slightly stooped from talking to people shorter than he was, with a somewhat triangular face and a long, pointed nose. Large ears widely spread sideways framed it all. I don't know whether he could move these remarkable ears at will, but it wouldn't have surprised me.

Scholem had strong likes and dislikes; Fania followed suit. Beyond specific individuals, his dislikes extended to entire domains: sociology and Freudian analysis, for example. As I had just completed my Geneva analysis with what I then considered a measure of success, I expressed my disagreement regarding that issue (I had no desire to fight on two fronts and in any case had nothing much to say about sociology). I don't recall how Scholem reacted; had there been a discussion I would have remembered it. What followed either immediately or within a few minutes was the story he loved to tell: how, in 1916, he fooled the head of one of the military draft commissions in Berlin, the psychoanalyst Karl Abraham, by simulating schizophrenia, and thus escaped the draft.

Yet, strangely enough, Scholem took Jungian concepts seriously and regularly participated in the annual Eranos conferences in Ascona, which were of a decidedly Jungian hue. All in all, he harbored strange ideas at times. When Philip Roth's brilliant and hilarious *Portnoy's Complaint* was published, Scholem wrote a letter to *Haaretz*, warning that the book would trigger anti-Semitism in the States and beyond.

Although I was flattered to be included in Scholem's circle, I didn't feel at ease in it. I was impressed by the kind of German scholarship that appeared to me so much deeper, so much more *gründlich* than my own patchwork learning. At times, among the Scholems, Simons, Samburskis, and other "*Yekkes*," I felt like an impostor who would one day be unmasked. It's a feeling that has surfaced from time to time, from before that year in Jerusalem and to the present day.

Some of Scholem's blind spots frankly annoyed me. I was irritated by his flaunting in conversation and in writing the story of his faked schizophrenia; it even appeared in his memoirs. He knew as well as I did that the main anti-Semitic argument used in Germany during the First World War and afterward was that Jews shirked their duty and escaped the draft by using one dirty trick or another. In reality there was no statistical difference of any significance between the military service of Jewish and non-Jewish Germans. Of course, in the 1960s nobody in Germany or elsewhere would criticize Scholem for this story, but I found that stressing it and being openly proud of it was in bad taste, to put it mildly. Or was I wrong after all?

## 3

At the university, I gave a lecture course on the history of international relations between the two world wars and a graduate seminar on Nazism in which I dealt extensively with Nazi anti-Semitism and some aspects of the Holocaust.

At that time — notwithstanding the strongly increased awareness of the Holocaust in Israeli society (beyond the community of survivors) as a result of the Eichmann trial in 1961 and of the prewar "waiting period" of May–early June 1967, which awakened many dormant fears of extermination, the Hebrew University did relatively little to encourage the teaching of the subject. One researcher and teacher of the history of the Shoah in the department of contemporary Jewry, Shaul Esh, died in 1968 and was not replaced for quite some time. One full-fledged professor of contemporary Jewish history, Shmuel Ettinger, dealt intensively with modern anti-Semitism, but not with Nazi anti-Semitism as such. One couldn't dismiss the impression that the Shoah was not *salonfähig* (socially acceptable) in a serious scholarly institution such as the Hebrew University.

It took me some time to understand that the reticence regarding open "academic acceptance" of the study of the extermination came from the same German-Jewish scholarly elite that had taken us in: the Scholems and their group. I realized, during our stay in Jerusalem, that the institution that dealt with the history of German Jewry, in Jerusalem, London, and New York, the Leo Baeck Institute, did not research or publish anything belonging to the Nazi period; this would change only in 1985. In short, the German Jews who could have been considered the mentors of the Hebrew University well into the sixties were unable (or unwilling) to recognize that much of German culture and society, their cradle and their intellectual compass, had also been the cradle of Nazism. They were torn. In the early sixties, Scholem declared that there had never been a "German-Jewish symbiosis," but he took this back later on. Wasn't he in many ways a typical product of that symbiosis?

Thus, the study of the Shoah was left to the memorial and documentation center Yad Vashem, established in 1953 but kept mostly at arm's length by the academic world. The Israeli scholars soon to become recognized names in the study of the Holocaust (Yisrael Gutman, Yehuda Bauer, Dov Kulka, and others) were still working on their doctorates or were very junior faculty on the morrow of the Six-Day War, as they all had resumed their studies at a relatively late age.

I can't recall with any certainty when I decided that if I were asked to return to Jerusalem, my history seminar would deal essentially with European fascism, with Nazism, as well as with modern anti-Semitism and the Holocaust. After writing the Gerstein biography and after my intensive involvement with the issues swirling around Pius XII's attitude during the war, I knew that notwithstanding my dwindling but still existent emotional distance from the Shoah, it would be the domain to which I would devote my main scholarly efforts, at least for a few years. Little did I know that the history of the Holocaust would not only become the focus of my academic interest for some time but would in fact come to virtually dominate my entire scholarly life.

The Jerusalem seminar on Nazism was a graduate seminar, and I had a full house of exceptionally motivated and bright students. I felt close to them, as I felt close to the country I had returned to. It was the enthusiasm of new beginnings. I have to admit that although I remember some splendid graduate seminars in Geneva, Tel Aviv, and UCLA, this Jerusalem première remains somehow engraved in my mind. Apart from four or five of the students, I've since forgotten the names of the participants, but I can still recall their faces, their attentiveness, and their eagerness to learn, and this shortly after most of them had returned from the nerve-racking waiting period in their units and then from the war.

Raul Hilberg came to Israel sometime at the end of 1967 or in early 1968 and was shunned by Yad Vashem (he was not allowed access to its archives, if my memory is correct). As I previously mentioned, in *The Destruction of the European Jews*, Hilberg accused the Jewish Councils (the Jewish leadership in each community under German occupation) of becoming instruments of the Germans in the process of persecution leading to extermination; he also attributed to Jews in general atavistic attitudes that facilitated their own annihilation. Later, Hilberg nuanced his judgment but never retracted his overall assertions. For Yad Vashem of the 1960s, this was too much and Hilberg was excommunicated, but only for a while.

One scholar was excommunicated forever: Hannah Arendt. Widely known and respected from the early fifties onward for her very original though utterly idiosyncratic book, *The Origins of Totalitarianism*, Arendt, who covered the Eichmann trial for the *New Yorker*, adopted Hilberg's criticism of the Jewish Councils (she simply "adopted" Hilberg's material, as she was totally ignorant of the history of the relations of Jewish communal leadership with local or national authorities, according to the Columbia Jewish historian Yosef Haim Yerushalmi). But in her sensational *Eichmann in Jerusalem*, she managed to add a high dose of sarcasm about Jewish leadership to Hilberg's theses — for example, calling the elderly leader of German Jewry, Rabbi Leo Baeck, "the Jewish Führer" — thereby deeply hurting many Israelis and Jews far and wide, particularly her former German-Jewish friends in Jerusalem. Scholem wrote to her that she lacked any "love for the Jewish people." She never set foot in Israel again.

In those days, Yad Vashem considered itself as the depository of some sort of "orthodoxy" regarding the Shoah; that orthodoxy found its quintessential expression in the law establishing Yad Vashem as the Martyrs' and Heroes' Remembrance Authority and in the designation of the yearly memorial day for the victims of the Shoah, Yom Hazikaron Lashoah Velagevurah (Remembrance Day for Catastrophe and Heroism). Israel in those times could not accept the catastrophe without giving an equal place in its national memory to heroism, which, historically, was of course a mythical construct. Although the designations remained the same, Israeli consciousness evolved from the Eichmann trial on and so did Yad Vashem's horizons, albeit more slowly.

I invited Hilberg to my seminar and although I do not remember the issues we discussed with him, it would be a fair guess to suggest that his criticism of the councils and his assessment of collective Jewish attitudes were among our main topics. The historian of "German ideology," George L. Mosse, was another guest, and I am almost sure that I also asked him to present his own iconoclastic views: the impact of German *völkisch* (nationalist, racist) ideology, in its early twentieth-century guise, on some important trends within Zionism. In any case, I wanted to keep the seminar open to controversy. It also led to a baffling experience.

I wanted the students to see Leni Riefenstahl's Nazi propaganda film *Triumph of the Will*, public screenings of which were not permitted in Israel. It wasn't easy tracking down a copy, but finally I received three separate nonsubtitled reels from the Kibbutz of Ghetto Fighters. The only appropriate hall for the screening was one of the largest halls in the university, and, as I had put a notice in our building, the news spread and on the day and hour of the presentation some four hundred students sat waiting.

The film arrived after a great delay and could not be viewed before the screening. As the right sequence of the reels was not indicated, we set them haphazardly. The first reel had "lost" the entire beginning of the film and opened with the end of "day one" of the Nuremberg rally of 1934: Hitler leaving the immense field as schoolchildren holding flowers in their hands shout "Heil!" Throughout, noise and laughter did not cease and most of the audience must have wondered about the whole idea of showing throngs of excited Nazi children.

The second reel started with the assembly of high party officials inside a covered hall, cheering the leaders who, one after another, proclaim the achievements of their twenty months in power: a series of short speeches in expectation of the address by the Führer. Then Hitler speaks, in a low voice at first, moving to a crescendo of incantations, exhortations, promises, and threats (the rally took place a few weeks after the murder of the brownshirts, the SA leadership). Although almost nobody in the audience understood German, silence fell and lasted for the duration of Hitler's speech and the setting of the third reel.

The last sequence opened with the central ceremony of the rally, during which Hitler addresses the tens of thousands of men of his massed battalions and the half million or so of faithful followers present in the stands. The speech leads to the "blood flag" ritual. Hitler walks slowly past the flag bearers of the battalions, touches their flags with the "blood flag" of the "martyrs" killed during the failed Nazi putsch of 1923, each time staring straight at the flag bearer, that is, into the camera, while one hears the muted sounds of the hallowed military song "Ich hatt' einen Kameraden" and of the party hymn, the "Horst Wessel Lied." There, the reel abruptly stopped. It took a while for the audience to get up and start moving out, exchanging a few words in low voices. They were, it seems, troubled and pensive.

The strange impact of Riefenstahl's film on a few hundred Israeli students led to intensive discussions in our seminar, and I remember adding Gustave Le Bon's *The Crowd* to the readings, as well as some excerpts on propaganda from Hitler's *Mein Kampf*. It also convinced me of the significance of an initiative I was considering for some time: a study of Nazi anti-Semitism from the angle of collective psychology, as a kind of collective psychosis. Obviously, I was influenced by psychoanalysis, by my treatment and by my readings. It resulted first in *L'Antisémitisme Nazi*, published by Seuil in 1971, then, a few years later, in *History and Psychoanalysis: An Essay on the Possibilities and Limits of Psychohistory* (1975). The two studies led me on a road I should not have taken; they were simplistic.

Why did I get sidetracked for a while? The amount of psychoanalytic literature I had read during my therapy gave me — or so I thought — enough wherewithal to turn in that direction; the conviction that behind anti-Semitic ideology an obsession, a cluster of delusional beliefs lurked which seemed to justify the attempt. My major mistake, as that of much psychohistory, resided in the simplistic move of psychoanalytic concepts from the individual field to the collective one. Moreover, after a while I recognized that the spreading of an obsession to a sizable population depended on a vast array of social factors that, in turn, molded the psychic structure of the obsession as such. Thus, whatever insights psychohistory could offer, they had to be part of a complex sociological analysis to avoid any reductionist kind of interpretation. I had learned my lesson.

In any case, as we were leaving Israel, in the early summer of 1968, I had a more immediate project.

At the end of the semester, the dean of social sciences, the sociologist Shmuel Eisenstadt, asked me to return after the coming year in Geneva and tacitly offered (before the regular nomination procedure) a full professorship in history and international relations, if I agreed to reestablish and chair the Department of International Relations that had been closed several years beforehand. Half of my appointment would be in international relations, the second half in history. It was understood that I could keep my position at the Geneva institute and teach there from April to July every year (the second semester there, equivalent to only a quarter in Jerusalem). Whether this arrangement was temporary or permanent was not spelled out; thus, it could be interpreted in both ways. I accepted, and Freymond, to whom I communicated the proposal, also accepted.

A few weeks after our departure, I started writing a book-length essay, *Réflexions sur l'avenir d'Israel* (Reflections on the future of Israel), while Hagith and I spent a month at the Rockefeller Foundation's Villa Serbelloni in Bellagio on Lake Como, in northern Italy.

In 1968, an American couple, the Marshalls, was in charge of the villa. Mr. Marshall, a genial personality, had written apparently well-known cookbooks, while Mrs. Marshall was a "connoisseur" of Italian paintings and something of a snob.

Our small group included the American poet Louise Glück; Stanley Hoffman, a professor of international relations at Harvard, and his wife Inge; the playwright Arthur Kopit and his wife; and a historian of religion from Notre Dame University whose name escapes me. On the first Sunday, Mrs. Marshall explained in great detail how to get to mass in Bellagio, though in vain, as we were all Jews (the historian of religion was a converted Jew, but I doubt that he went to mass). In August, shortly before the end of our stay, we anxiously followed the news of the Soviet invasion of Prague.

For the first time since 1969, the year of its publication, I have now read again *Réflexions sur l'avenir d'Israel*; I must have continued to write it through the end of 1968, as I refer to events of that autumn. I remained essentially an advocate of the official Israeli position. Yet I had doubts about the open-ended prolongation of a full-scale occupation, not that I thought of the Palestinians' rights to their own state, but because of the dangerous impact the domination of a vast and potentially hostile population would have upon Israeli society. Thus, I suggested the establishment of an "autonomous Palestinian entity" (in those very words) in which all internal matters would be in the hands of the Palestinians while Israel would keep military control until peace with the Arab world was achieved. As for Jerusalem, I suggested keeping the unified city as the capital of Israel, while the small area of the holy places could be internationalized or, alternatively, while the Muslim holy places could be put under Jordanian authority and considered as a foreign enclave.

Did I believe that these measures were steps on the way to general peace? Explicitly not, even in the long run: thus, the "autonomy" and the exterritorial status of the Muslim holy places were, in my view, the best possible arrangement within an indefinite waiting period, with the probability of further wars. All of this was neither very audacious nor very original, even at the time (it was in fact close to Dayan's position). As for my pseudo-moral concerns, they were identical (in my book) to those of a group of soldiers, mostly kibbutz members, brought together by the left-wing intellectual Avraham Schapira, with the assistance of the writer Amos Oz, for a series of conversations on the war and its aftermath; they were published under the Hebrew title *Siah Lohamim* (Fighters' Conversations, which in its English version became *The Seventh Day*). I quoted it at length in *Réflexions*.

I didn't keep the letters I received about *Réflexions*, except for one; it inaugurated my friendly relations with Claude Lanzmann, at the time (and to this day) editor in chief of *Les Temps Modernes*, the periodical founded by Jean-Paul Sartre and Simone de Beauvoir. "Dear Sir," Claude wrote in February 1969, "Your book isn't amusing at all. But it is truthful [*il est vrai*] and I wish to express my full agreement. Rarely did I so fully agree with anybody on the issue of Israel." According to Claude, Simone de Beauvoir also read the book and was very impressed by my analysis. They wished the three of us could have lunch together on the occasion of one of my trips to Paris. I didn't follow up as far as the lunch was concerned and never met Simone de Beauvoir (nor do I remember meeting Sartre, except maybe briefly in 1973), but my relations with Claude hold to this day, although I didn't see him for some years. I shall come back to him.

A conversation I had upon our return to Geneva with Yakov Herzog, Eshkol's closest adviser, who was attending some meeting in Switzerland, reinforced my pessimism about peace prospects. Herzog got in touch with me to discuss what I had written about his father, the chief rabbi of Palestine, in my book on the pope, and his (failed) attempts to meet with Pius XII and plead with him for the handing over to Jewish institutions of hidden Jewish children who had been converted to Catholicism. Herzog, his father's secretary at the time, added some details that have since slipped my mind. But I did not forget the part of the conversation that dealt with peace negotiations between Israel and the Arab states.

According to Herzog, there could eventually be peace with each of the Arab countries if Israel declared its readiness to give back all the territories conquered during the war (this had briefly been Israel's position regarding Egypt and Syria — not Jordan — immediately after the end of the fighting, before the government decided on "defensible borders"). But then, Herzog added, the fate of Jerusalem would be brought up and everything would fall apart.

Herzog was almost right: a change of relations with some Arab countries demanded another war and the giving up of territory occupied during the Six-Day War, while an arrangement with the Palestinians and acceptance of their demand to turn East Jerusalem into the capital of their state remains hanging in midair.

## 5

On our return to Europe, in the fall of 1968, I realized how much a part of public opinion, mainly on the left, was becoming hostile to Israel. The Vietnam War, increasingly loathsome to many, fed a preexisting, anti-imperialist stance, particularly in the academic world. Israel as such and, since 1967, the Israeli occupation of densely populated Arab territories, became prime examples of Western domination: anti-Zionism and anti-Americanism turned into one and the same ideology. In France, for example, Maxime Rodinson's *Israel, fait colonial?* (*Israel: A Colonial-Settler State?*) was widely read. Rodinson, a well-known anthropologist, was Jewish, as were many leaders of the Western anti-Zionist campaign.

At Lycée Henri IV, in 1947–48, one of my closest friends, one year ahead of me, had been an Egyptian Communist, Samir

Amin. He helped me to leave the lycée without drawing attention, on the day I had to reach the Gare de Lyon (the Communists, following the Soviet Union, were in favor of the UN partition plan and the creation of a Jewish state). I hadn't seen Samir since then but knew that he had become a well-known Marxist theoretician of the anti-imperialist struggle.

Sometime at the end of 1968 or in early 1969, the Geneva institute students' association invited Amin for a lecture. I was in the audience, delighted to see my old friend. When the time for questions arrived, I raised my hand and was called on by my name. "Dear Samir, I am so delighted to see you here," I began, then asked my question. "Sir," he answered, without the slightest sign of recognition. Obviously he had recognized me, but wouldn't it be shameful on his part to admit that he knew a stooge of imperialism, or even worse, let it be known that we had been friends? Samir was tremendously applauded at the end of his thoroughly political presentation, and he continued to ignore me. We didn't exchange a further word. At the institute, a friend of several years, an Egyptian law professor, stopped speaking to me.

In moving between Jerusalem and Geneva, I missed the excitement of the student movement. Some demonstrations took place at the University of Geneva, but were modest in scope. After all, this was Switzerland. At the time, I did not perceive the importance of the cultural changes that the events generated in Western society in general, nor did I realize the importance of the changes that would follow in the academic world. What I perceived, though, was the provocative and extremist aspect of some of the demonstrations (the bullying of teachers and so on); the little I knew of it didn't attract me.

Mainly, I soon became disappointed by the dogmatism of the extreme left, by what I considered their total misunderstanding of Nazism and fascism, tags they applied so easily to the existing democratic systems, either out of ignorance or in bad faith; by their naive infatuation with Mao or Che Guevara; and by their rabid hatred of Israel, which at times sounded like anti-Semitism. As for the outbursts of wanton violence that sporadically shook Germany and Italy then and in later years, they appeared abhorrent to me. The German philosopher Jürgen Habermas was right in calling leftist extremism "*Linksfaschismus*" (left fascism). Much later, I encountered remnants of these ideological zealots who mostly called themselves Trotskyites, but were nothing less than purebred Stalinists.

# CHAPTER EIGHT

# Hubris

In the early fall of 1969, I was back in Jerusalem. During the year just spent in Geneva, I had attended to my courses, given some talks about the newly published *Réflexions*, and continued planning the reopening of the Department of International Relations that I was expected to chair upon my return to the Hebrew University.

Easier planned than done. I could rely on assistance from four old-timers of the defunct former department: two professors of international law and two in the history of international relations. There was no new faculty, there were no assistants, there was nothing. When enrollment opened, eight hundred students, mainly undergraduates at that stage, descended on the new department. It was a true deluge, as befitted the land of the Bible, but the tiny and fragile ark rose and fell dangerously on the stormy waters, under the "guidance" of a rather inexperienced captain. We survived. Temporary adjunct faculty was appointed within weeks: some stayed, others had to go. It didn't win me many friends. Yet, within approximately two years, the department was running according to the usual routine of academic life.

How I managed at the time I do not remember clearly; the obvious answer would be: in 1969, I was a mere thirty-seven. I had to deal with all the problems of the new department in Jerusalem and with an entirely different academic setting once I returned to Geneva, in April of each year. In fact, I soon had to advise graduate students and tackle administrative problems at both ends throughout the academic year. Teaching the history of international relations was the same in Geneva and in Jerusalem, but the graduate seminars were entirely different: Nazi anti-Semitism in one place and the Cuban Missile Crisis in the other.

During my first regular year in Jerusalem, Hagith, pregnant with our daughter, stayed in Geneva with the boys. I joined them in April and again took up my teaching at the institute. In June 1970, Michal was born and a few months later, we all returned to Israel.

*l*

The family was now *au complet*, if I may say. Hagith and I had never discussed how many children we wished for but, tacitly, we felt that three was the right number. As I mentioned previously, a child represented some sort of revenge for me, and this irrational, instinctive reaction persisted until Michal's birth. There was an old female pediatrician in Tel Aviv, Dr. Aharonova, who had written the textbook of a former generation; I found it at my in-laws' home and used to quote it: "Two children like the number of the parents, and one to strengthen the community." What I quoted ironically, even before Eli was born, became, ironically, our family.

Was Hagith right to reproach me, in later years, that she never saw me on all fours with one of the kids riding on my back?

I didn't have this kind of playful, natural, easygoing attitude: as a father I was reserved, in the way my father had been with me (much less so, however). I knew that he loved me, although he generally seemed distant, except for the last day of our life together (in the hospital in Montluçon). And I think that the children knew how much I loved them, notwithstanding my relative shyness and my yearly absence for two to three months, in Geneva. They would join me there when school was over and we would spend the summer together and return together to Jerusalem or, quite often in fact, I would return to Jerusalem when my own "school year" was over.

In Jerusalem we moved from one rented apartment to the next. Eventually, we decided to build a house on a plot in the Talbyeh district that my father-in-law had acquired well before the Six-Day War for a very modest sum. In the euphoria of the postwar months we turned to an Arab contractor from East Jerusalem. He would excavate the ground and build the foundations according to the plans of a Tel Aviv architect, a friend of ours.

The contractor received a rather hefty down payment, and, indeed, the excavations were soon completed. But that was it: the foundations were never laid. Our contractor had lost the money playing poker and, soon thereafter, he died of cancer. We took a contractor from Jewish Jerusalem and Hagith became the supervisor of daily progress from that moment on until we moved into the house, four years later.

2

In Geneva, the question soon arose: What should be done with our apartment while we were in Jerusalem, during the autumn, winter, and early spring, year after year? The monthly rent was due whether we resided there or not. I arranged with the institute the subleasing of the apartment to guest professors, who happened to be mainly Americans. Thus, in the fall of 1972 our first "tenants" arrived: George Kennan and his wife.

For those who would not remember George Kennan's name, he was for all intents and purposes the architect of the American policy of containment in confronting the Soviet Union in the cold war. His policy recommendations became the basis of the Truman Doctrine and of the Marshall Plan. As head of the Policy Planning Staff of the State Department during the late forties, later ambassador to Moscow and to Yugoslavia, and a lifelong student of the Soviet Union and of international affairs more generally, Kennan was possibly the most important professional and scholarly voice in American foreign policy before the Henry Kissinger era.

The Kennans were supposed to arrive at the apartment by 3 p.m. on a given day in late September 1972 to leave us enough time for explaining the basics and catching our own plane to Israel. A few minutes before three, no Kennans were in sight. We were getting nervous. Shortly after the hour, a ring at the door: here they were, very tall, blue-eyed, with a severe mien; that's how I imagined typical WASPs. Their explanation of the slight delay confirmed my intuition: they had not taken a taxi from the airport to our address, less than a mile away. Notwithstanding their multiple suitcases, they had taken a bus to the central bus station in town and, from there, another bus to our house.

Two months went by and on December 3, the Kennans left for Paris; they had transferred the apartment to the American delegate to a disarmament conference, Paul Nitze, and his wife, and left us a handwritten letter that I have kept. After telling of the arrangements with the maid, Kennan moved to the books:

*I was delighted to find in your library certain books that were of value to me in connection with my own work: namely, Bülow's memoirs, those of Hohenlohe, the book on the Rothschilds, Chastenet's history of the III République. I have used them all and I think you will find them in their accustomed places. We have been very happy here and are most grateful to you and Mrs. Friedländer for letting us use the flat.*

*Very sincerely,*
*George Kennan*

Then, a PS: "Mrs. Friedländer might like to know that the vacuum cleaner, which needed medical attention, was repaired at the nearby shopping center."

How nice and civilized!

Unfortunately, George Kennan was no great friend of Jews, either before or during the world war, as I learned when I read his memoirs.

*3*

The Hebrew University, a full-fledged member of which I had now become, was a proud institution. Established in 1925, it aspired to become the university of the Jewish people. From its original site, Mount Scopus, it overlooked the whole city of Jerusalem on one side and the Judean Hills descending toward the Dead Sea on the other. It would be hard to imagine a more august and inspiring location. After the war of 1948 and the division of

Jerusalem, the university buildings on Mount Scopus remained an empty enclave within Jordanian-controlled territory, reached only sporadically and under strict supervision for basic maintenance purposes. In 1967, after the Israeli occupation of the whole of Jerusalem, access to Mount Scopus was free again.

While Haifa could take pride in its Institute of Technology, and Rehovoth (south of Tel Aviv) in its Research Institute in the Sciences, while Tel Aviv was setting up a still fledgling university, Jerusalem remained, in the early 1970s — and in its own opinion — the guardian of excellence in Israeli higher learning. Truly important from the outset and throughout the first two decades of the state's history was the Hebrew University's role as a bastion of liberalism in opposition to the wanton supremacy of state interests preached by Ben-Gurion. Later, it was there that quite a number of voices arose against the extreme nationalism that followed the Six-Day War, particularly in regard to the occupied territories and the fate of the Palestinians more generally.

"Tell your friend Talmon that we will not suffer such attacks for long without responding." This was Israel Galili's ominous message, delivered to me on one of our occasional meetings. Yakov Talmon was back in Jerusalem from a one-year stay in Princeton. For some time since his return in 1969, he was publishing long and eloquent articles in *Haaretz* against the policy of occupation. As a matter of fact, the government waited passively — and contentedly — for the Arab states to make a first step toward peace, knowing well that they wouldn't take it. And, if immobility was the rule of the game, why not start setting up some strategically located settlements in the West Bank and, as a bonus, some historically (Biblically) significant ones, according to their location?

Israel Galili was a strange bird. He was minister without portfolio in Golda Meir's government and possibly its most influential member. I knew him from Goldmann days and, for some reason, he chose me to convey to Talmon and others the "official" reaction to my wayward colleagues' publications criticizing the occupation policy. I stopped meeting him after he presented me with a riddle: "Do you know," he asked me, "what the definition of our conflict with the Palestinians is?" As I silently conveyed my ignorance, he proceeded: "It is the agrarian question." And after another puzzled look on my part: "That is: who will be first in pushing the other's head into the ground!" Only much later did I hear that this was how the Bolsheviks defined their struggle against the Mensheviks.

Eshkol, in comparison, had been a Menshevik of sorts. He could have accepted some compromise agreement with the Arab states, but he died in early 1969 and was replaced by Golda Meir, a very different kind of leader, a stone-hard "Bolshevik."

It would be a mistake to perceive Israeli settlement policies in the occupied territories as one single swoop from its beginning to the present. In the fall of 1967, Eshkol accepted the settling of Gush Etzion, south of Jerusalem, on the site of the former Kibbutz Kfar Etzion, destroyed by the Jordanian army during the 1948 war; more precisely put, Eshkol did not oppose the national religious initiative, given that the location of the new settlement (camouflaged at first as a military outpost) was included in the outline of new defensible borders, later known as the Allon Plan (named after the vice prime minister Yigal Allon, who had authored it), a sine qua non condition for any peace agreement.

I am telling all of this in order to describe common thinking during the first two or three years following the war, a thinking that I accepted. The pre-1967 borders were indeed indefensible, and if Israel hadn't struck preemptively and destroyed the Egyptian air force, the course of the war would have been lengthier and more painful. During these early postwar years what I and others started questioning was not the principle of defensible borders but, under Golda Meir's watch, the refusal to respond to any positive initiative coming from the other side.

In 1970, an "attrition war" started along the Suez Canal: the Egyptians shelled Israeli positions and exacted a toll in Israeli lives, while Israel retaliated by bombing Egyptian cities along the waterway: Port Said, Ismailia, and Suez.

I mentioned previously how unsettling it was to move from dormant Geneva to the nationalist excitement of post–Six-Day War Israel. During the war of attrition along the canal, traveling in the opposite direction, from Israel to Geneva, was even more unsettling. The Israeli press published the names of the soldiers killed almost daily along the canal on front pages, at first also publishing their photos. I had just looked at the names and pictures of soldiers killed the previous day on the plane to Geneva, in the spring of 1970. After landing I bought the *Tribune de Genève*. The front page carried a banner headline: "Neuf filouteries d'auberge" (Nine restaurant swindles).

That same year, Nasser succumbed to a heart attack. He was replaced by a fellow "Free Officer," Anwar Sadat, little known by the masses of Egyptians and even less so outside of his country. On the face of it, nothing much had changed.

## 4

In early 1971, Sadat proposed a first step toward a truce along the canal by reciprocal demilitarization of a mutually agreed-upon zone on both sides. Meir said no. A group of colleagues under the aegis of Dan Patinkin, a celebrated professor of economics, met in the apartment we rented on Magnes Square, and we sent a cable of protest to the prime minister (it became known as the Patinkin cable). We were excoriated by all possible right-wingers and also, to my astonishment, by Haim Herzog, Yakov Herzog's brother. Haim's outburst reminded me of the saying attributed to his mother, the wife of the chief rabbi of Palestine, who once told my in-laws, their neighbors in Jerusalem before 1948: "I have two sons. One, Yakov, has a brilliant mind; the other, Haim, is very good-looking." Yakov died in the 1970s and, in due time, Haim Herzog became president of Israel.

I started participating regularly in public meetings against the occupation and often expressed myself rather bluntly. Here and there my words found an echo. On January 26, 1972, I received the following letter:

> *Professor Friedlander, as an Arab student may I extol your brief speech which you delivered last week in Weiss auditorium. Your insight in the future is right. May all your efforts for spreading out the ideas of justice be blest. Thanking you and with best regards, I remain yours sincerely,*
>
> *Selim I. Khoury*

Two years after the Patinkin cable, in early 1973, I had my own confrontation with Golda Meir. It demands some background details.

In the 1950s, Albert Einstein and Bertrand Russell met in Pugwash, a small town in Nova Scotia, and initiated a series of periodic encounters between American and Soviet nuclear scientists, a sort of informal communication channel, to ease tensions between the two nuclear superpowers locked in the cold war. The Pugwash conferences were born. Over time, the organization became internationally all-inclusive, and countries involved in conflicts used the venue to exchange ideas with their opponents; moreover, the delegations came to comprise academics of various backgrounds who represented their governments but were allowed some leeway to explore various possibilities.

Shalheveth Freier, whose job, it may be remembered, I inherited at the Defense Ministry, headed the Israeli Pugwash group. Shalheveth had remained brilliant and eccentric; in 1970 he offered to appoint me to the Israeli delegation: I gladly accepted, as I liked and respected him and the four or five other members of the group. Our contacts with the Egyptian delegation were reasonably good and even the relations with the Soviet delegation, headed at that time by Yevgeni Primakov, were cordial (the Soviet Union had broken off its diplomatic relations with Israel after the Six-Day War). Naturally, we were on friendly terms with the U.S. delegation, one of whose main members was Bill Polk, the director of the Adlai Stevenson Institute of International Affairs in Chicago.

Sometime in early 1973, Polk called me at home in Jerusalem and told me that he had succeeded in organizing a meeting, under the auspices of Pugwash, among an Egyptian, a Russian, himself as chair, and — this was the breakthrough — a Palestinian (a Palestinian professor living in the States, but a Palestinian nonetheless), who agreed to meet with an Israeli. He asked me to be the Israeli representative at that very confidential gathering. I agreed immediately, as our lack of initiative regarding the Palestinian issue — even at Pugwash — increasingly bothered me; but, I told Polk, I had to ask for an official authorization and would call him back.

I reached Mordechai Gazit, director general of the prime minister's office, and asked him to get me the authorization. Within half an hour or so, Gazit returned my call: "Shaul," he said, "the prime minister wants to see you." "When?" "Now."

Golda Meir was our "Iron Lady." The Ukrainian-born, Milwaukee-raised, chain-smoking, first-generation leader of the new state was a formidable presence, "the only man in the cabinet," as the quip went. She had the basic, immutable belief of those early Zionist political figures in the Jews' exclusive historic rights to a state in Palestine, and she was ready to fight for those rights with a fierce determination that she hammered in with a heavy American accent. We met and she launched into a diatribe about the nonexistence of a Palestinian people and told me in no uncertain terms that I was not permitted to attend the Chicago meeting if a so-called Palestinian was present. There was clearly no point in trying to argue with her. I informed Polk and that put an end to this initiative.

5

Hubris characterized the Israeli attitude toward the Arab world (Palestinians included), a foolish sense of superiority and hyperconfidence. This was often acknowledged later on, after the deluge, but I am not sure that it has changed in the long run. In the early seventies, it was particularly visible among some politicians, and even more so in the army. The victory in the Six-Day

War had convinced the population and the army that stemmed from it (Israel, from its beginnings, had introduced compulsory military service for both men and women, with some exceptions) that Zahal (the Hebrew acronym for the Israel Defense Forces) could crush any Arab army or coalition, if they ever dared to attack. Even my friend Teveth contributed to this dangerous complacency with a book that inordinately praised the leaders and feats of the armored division during the six days: *The Tanks of Tammuz*.

I remember sayings current before that time and used even more frequently after the six days. One was attributed to a well-known military figure that showed contempt both for the Arabs and for the "Oriental" Jews who were mostly relegated to the lowest positions in the army (kitchen, drivers, foot soldiers, etc.): "When I want to know what the Arabs plan to do (in a given battlefield situation), I ask my driver [of course an Oriental Jew] what he would do."

While a general sense of superiority in regard to the Arabs became widely shared after 1967, it was not only, in my opinion, the cumulative effect of the victories of 1948, 1956, and 1967 but mainly the deeper reaction of a people that had suffered from a long history of humiliations, weakness, and — just a few years earlier — an attempt at total extermination. This specific Israeli pathology stemmed at first from Diaspora history and from the Zionist reaction to it: "You, the Diaspora Jews, went like sheep to slaughter; we, the proud youth of Eretz Israel, will show you what self-defense and strength mean." Now, the stereotype of the European Diaspora Jew had yielded, as symbol of inferiority, to that of the Oriental Jew, often identified with the indistinct mass of "Arabs."

# CHAPTER NINE

# Expiation

On Yom Kippur (the Day of Atonement), October 6, 1973, Jerusalem, like all of the country, was silent, a silence somehow rendered even deeper by the luminous and mellow weather of a crisp autumn day. Our daughter Michal was three and a half years old by then; the five of us lived in a rented apartment, as the house we were building was still "almost" ready. This time, we camped on Metudela Street amidst ever more furniture, desperately eager to move to our permanent home. Within two weeks the academic year would start again. I could only hope that the students of the forthcoming graduate seminar would be as good as those of the previous one, on European fascism, which I'd taught from October 1972 to February 1973.

At three on that afternoon, something unthinkable happened: the silence of Yom Kippur was shattered by the scream of a jet fighter flying low over the city. Seconds later sirens started howling. We moved to the staircase where, one after another, our neighbors joined us, all of them stunned and trying to make sense of what was going on. Nobody knew. We went back to the apartment and switched on the television: the Syrians had attacked in the north, the Egyptians in the south. The surprise was complete.

Toward evening, upon listening first to Dayan and somewhat later to Golda Meir, the possibility of catastrophe dawned on us: the Syrians controlled part of the Golan Heights and the Egyptians had crossed the Suez Canal and were moving into the Sinai. The defense line along the waterway had simply been overrun. For several days we didn't know how bad the situation was, how panicky Dayan, still the defense minister, had become, and how disheartening was the impact of his doomsday predictions for members of the government and for some senior officers. Lou Kedar, Golda Meir's longtime assistant and close friend, mentioned later that at some point during these first days of the war, Golda contemplated suicide.

On the ninth, an Israeli counterattack in the Sinai failed miserably: the tanks were easy targets for the massive numbers of antitank missiles carried by Egyptian infantry and the planes were paralyzed by the equally unexpected number of antiaircraft missiles, both supplied by the Soviet Union. Israel considered asking for a cease-fire; the tentative request was flatly rejected by Egypt.

Although the situation in the north had stabilized within three days, it was only on the night of October 15 that Israeli forces, led by Ariel Sharon, seized the strategic initiative in the south by crossing the canal and encircling the Egyptian Third Army. On both sides, the rate of attrition of equipment and ammunition soon led to a Soviet airlift, particularly to Syria, quickly followed by an American one to Israel.

When you traveled from Jerusalem down to Tel Aviv and reached the plain near Lod Airport, the sight was impressive:

while one huge Galaxy military cargo plane descended toward the runway, another one was already approaching (this, incidentally, followed President Nixon's explicit orders, notwithstanding reluctance from the State Department and the Pentagon). Despite my growing alienation from the policies of Meir's government, in such a moment of extreme danger, an instinctive identification with the country took over, and together with other colleagues, I signed an appeal for solidarity addressed to universities all over the West.

In mid-October, the Foreign Ministry sent me to France to help get public opinion on the side of Israel. I was asked to meet both with some key journalists and with various intellectuals to explain how Israel viewed the Egyptian-Syrian aggression and the uncompromising attitude of the Arab world. Before beginning my rounds, I needed some sustenance and, albeit feeling slightly guilty about self-indulgence in such hard times, on the second evening of my stay in Paris I went to hear *Parsifal* at the opera (I should have mentioned previously that I love classical music and am a "selective" Wagner fan, with *Parsifal* at the top of my list). I don't remember who sang or who conducted on that evening in Paris, but I clearly recall my elation: the performance was outstanding and I think that this was the best *Parsifal* I'd ever attended. The slight feeling of guilt may have added something to my enthusiasm.

I did not feel any guilt in seeing, a few days later, Claude Lanzmann's *Pourquoi Israel*. It was the right film at the right time. As for my mission, I accomplished it as well as I could: I was cordially received by Jean Daniel, for example, the editor in chief of the weekly *Nouvel Observateur*; yet, by then, an influential daily such as *Le Monde* remained firmly critical of Israel, due to its left-leaning tendency and to the hostility of the head of its Middle

Eastern desk, Eric Rouleau, an Egyptian Jew, toward the Jewish state. All in all, the results of my efforts were mixed.

*l*

Militarily, Israel turned the early chaos into a victory of sorts, but the toll in lives was enormous: 2,500 soldiers had been killed and 7,000 badly wounded. Two students of my 1972–73 seminar (attended by some fifteen graduates) had been killed: Shaul Shalev and Avi Shmueli. Shalev was a tank commander killed by a direct hit in the early days of war in the Sinai, whereas Avi, who was also my assistant, died slowly; he had been burned in his jeep in the Sinai and brought back to the Tel Hashomer hospital near Tel Aviv. I visited him there and saw only a hugely inflated body covered with bandages. Wherever skin was visible, it was black. It took many days for Avi to die. He was buried in the military part of the vast Givat Shaul cemetery on one of the hills of Jerusalem.

Since my return to Jerusalem in 1969, I had met at times with General Israel Tal ("Talik" to his friends), whom I had first encountered, as usual, at the Teveths'. When he came to Jerusalem, he would occasionally visit me at the university; we talked about his various academic interests and also about current Israeli politics. Tal, who had commanded the armored forces on the Egyptian front during the Six-Day War, would become the "father" of the Israeli tank, the very advanced Merkava, which he designed and the production of which he organized and supervised in later years.

During the Yom Kippur War, Tal was deputy chief of staff and, on the morrow of the war, briefly in charge of the southern front. He had a precise knowledge of the events and considered Dayan eminently responsible for many of the initial mistakes; in fact, he hated him. Could it be that this intense hostility impaired Tal's objectivity? Be that as it may, he told me that Dayan had become so irrational that he had ordered missiles armed with nuclear warheads to be readied. An article later published in *Time* magazine confirmed the story but attributed the decision to both Golda Meir and Moshe Dayan.

It seems, in fact, from testimonies gathered in 2008 by the historian of the Israeli bomb, Avner Cohen, and published on the fortieth anniversary of the war (October 2013), that Tal's version was correct. During a cabinet meeting on October 7, Shalheveth Freier — who had been appointed head of the Israeli Atomic Energy Commission in 1971 — was summoned by Dayan. The defense minister met Shalheveth outside the cabinet room and, giving the impression that Golda Meir had agreed, asked him to order the positioning of missiles with nuclear warheads for a "demonstration option" (a nuclear blast). The same testimony indicates that when, somewhat later on that day, Dayan submitted his plan to the cabinet, he was rebuffed by Deputy Prime Minister Yigal Allon and by Minister Israel Galili. Golda Meir simply told Dayan "to forget it."*

Quite pessimistic attitudes regarding the future of Israel and the significance of the war surfaced in Europe and in the States. In

---

* Avner Cohen, "When Israel Stepped Back from the Brink," *International Herald Tribune*, October 4, 2013, p. 8. Cohen's article was published in Hebrew in *Haaretz*.

a letter of November 26, a colleague from the department, the Sovietologist Nissan Oren, who was spending a year in Princeton, sent me some of his observations:

> *I keep contact with such people as George Kennan (who is no Jew lover), Bill Bundy who is the Director of the Council on Foreign Relations, various Sovietologists and the like ... To cheer you up: I have here at the Center two colleagues from Lebanon who tell me every day that we must be strong because Lebanon would not survive more than a week unless Syria is kept down. On the other hand, the Princeton Jewish professors who are of the left remain remote and act like swine. The Arabs here say we have had our political Stalingrad, which ... is probably right.*
>
> *... Our friend Hans Morgenthau [a well-known Jewish professor of international relations at the University of Chicago] was on TV for a full hour last night. What he said was in effect that this is the beginning of the end of the Jewish state. I was quite mad not so much with his analysis as with his attitude. He acted up as a minor prophet. He was sorry for the Jews in Israel but there was little or nothing that could be done ...*

In France, a few weeks later, Eric Rouleau published an article accusing Israel of perpetrating a "Dreyfus Affair" by having transferred the general initially in command of the southern front, Shmuel Gonen, to a position of lesser responsibility. What should Israel have done? Leave in place an officer manifestly incapable of mastering the situation? You had to send to the south your most experienced commanders, which was done. The din of nasty stupidities such as Rouleau's relentless criticism was sometimes hard to take.

## 2

In this postapocalyptic atmosphere I organized a conference to mark the official opening of the Leonard Davis Institute of International Relations at the Hebrew University. As director of the new institute, I chose the theme for the conference: the strategy of small states in an international crisis.

Notwithstanding the circumstances, all the invited foreign scholars agreed to attend: Hans Morgenthau (nonetheless), Thomas Schelling from Harvard, Alastair Buchan from London, Bernard and Fawn Brodie from UCLA, and others. Golda Meir attended the lectures and debates on the first day, Dayan on the following one. While Meir's interventions were limited to informal remarks here and there, Dayan gave a lecture in which he tried to explain the dilemmas facing Israel on the eve of Yom Kippur. All in all it was a tense and fascinating event, attended by hundreds.

The conference took place in January or February 1974. After it ended we invited the foreign participants for a two-day tour of northern Israel. The institute had rented a minibus and put all our guests aboard. As we drove in the rapidly falling evening darkness along the Sea of Galilee, flashes started illuminating the eastern sky, as if coming from the Golan Heights, followed by powerful rumblings. I sat in a front seat next to Fawn Brodie; we didn't pay much attention to the outside scene as we shared views on psychohistory. The other guests, though, had noticed everything, and since an "attrition war" between Israel and Syria still raged on, all bets were open as to the significance of the ominous flashes. Some argued for mortar fire while others heard the pounding of heavier guns. In short, what could be more fascinating for specialists in strategic studies than driving near a live gun battle? Alas, it was simply a powerful storm, all thunder and lightning.

## 3

Years went by, but for me the Yom Kippur events didn't fade from memory, as was the case for many Israelis. I had my own reasons for that, apart from the sadness of it all. I have mentioned that during my three years in the army, I was posted in Intelligence 2, which had vastly changed and expanded since and ultimately became Unit 8200, the Israeli NSA. In my time, in the early 1950s, one of the young officers in the unit was Lieutenant Joel Ben-Porat. Ben-Porat stayed in the army and made it to colonel, if I am not mistaken; he became the commander of either the whole unit or a crucial part of it. Days or weeks before Yom Kippur, he intercepted information that clearly indicated the Egyptians' intention to attack.

The general heading military intelligence, Eli Zeira, was certain that the Egyptians were merely getting ready for large-scale maneuvers and nothing else. He convinced Dayan and the entire cabinet that there was no need to mobilize the reserves. Ben-Porat knew that his information conveyed a very different scenario, yet Zeira's second in command refused time and again to forward his warnings. Finally, Ben-Porat managed to call Zeira's home on a Shabbat, but the chief dismissed his message.

After the events, Ben-Porat became obsessed with what had happened and could have been avoided if his information had been believed. He became a crusader of sorts, spoke to various people, and on Yom Kippur anniversaries wrote articles in the papers alluding to whatever he was allowed to publish. He came several times to visit me in Jerusalem, as he knew that I had a better understanding than many of what he was saying over and over again. Parts of Ben-Porat's story were recently (2014) published in Israel, as protocols of the postwar investigation commission were made public. Did it bring him some peace of mind? I can only hope so, but given his frustration and his anger, I doubt it.

While Ben-Porat focused mainly on the deficiencies of the military and political system that became accountable for the initial catastrophe of the war, others, much closer to me, asked far more fundamental questions about Israeli society and the undercurrents that threatened its very texture as a democratic entity. I mainly think of my close friend Uriel Tal, the historian of Jewish thought and Christian-Jewish relations in pre-Nazi Germany.

Uri was unusually sensitive, with a tendency to depression. He was religious but the most open and tolerant religious person I knew. His thorough knowledge of Jewish thought allowed him to be among the first Israelis to perceive and expose the deep religious roots of the political movement that arose on the morrow of Yom Kippur: Gush Emunim (the Bloc of the Faithful).

Gush Emunim openly aimed at tightening Israel's grip over the West Bank, the occupied Palestinian territories west of the Jordan. It became one of the most vocal, active, and dangerous ingredients on the Israeli political scene at that time. The movement's messianic fervor, its total disregard for the Palestinians, its relentless drive for establishing ever more new settlements in the occupied territories, made of it an example of "authentic Zionism" in the eyes of many and seemed to offer a new credo to the tens of thousands of Israelis dispirited by the war and losing all faith in the traditional political establishment.

Uri had also lost all confidence. He perceived how the crisis of Yom Kippur fostered what he came to consider as some sort of

Israeli fascism. We had a heart-to-heart conversation regarding the future of the country during a long taxi drive from Manhattan to JFK Airport after both of us had participated in a conference on the historiography of the Holocaust, in March 1975. Uri had moved from the Hebrew University to Tel Aviv University and I was soon to follow. I entirely agreed with his interpretation of the events, and both of us witnessed, to our dismay, how Mapai, still the leading party in a coalition of the moderate left called Avoda (Labor), was giving in to the demands of Gush Emunim and assorted ultra-right-wing pressure groups.

Although she had won the elections, Golda Meir resigned in early 1974 and Itzhak Rabin became prime minister, with Shimon Peres as defense minister. To my profound disappointment, Shimon was the driving force within the government for cooperating with the fanatics of Gush Emunim in the establishment of new settlements. I had to admit — notwithstanding my previous admiration for him — that, at this juncture, Shimon appeared to me as a sheer political opportunist.

### 4

I expressed some of my thoughts about possibilities of peace between Israel, the Arab countries, and the Palestinians in a dialogue with two Egyptian Marxists, organized and moderated by the French journalist and author Jean Lacouture. Lacouture told me that my partners to the dialogue were close to the Palestinians and had authored several texts under a common pseudonym: Mahmud Hussein. In the summer of 1974, we met in Paris for a series of conversations in which I expressed my support for the establishment of a Palestinian state next to Israel (i.e., in the

West Bank and the Gaza Strip), the return of a significant number of refugees and compensation for the others, as well as the division of Jerusalem, the Arab part of which would become the capital of the Palestinian state. The rather conventional views I expressed in *Réflexions* in 1968 had certainly changed. The book came out later that same year under the title *Arabes et Israéliens: un premier dialogue*. It was translated into English and Hebrew.

Upon the publication in Israel, the students' newspaper at the Hebrew University called me a traitor, and one of my colleagues and a longtime friend, Yehoshafat Harkabi (chief of Israeli military intelligence in the early sixties), told Hagith that talking to Mahmud Hussein was akin to talking to Himmler. A few years later, though, Harkabi became an eloquent apostle of negotiations and compromise. I didn't know (and Lacouture had not told me) that one of the two Egyptians who went under the name of Adel Rifaat was actually a Jew converted to Islam: Eddie Levi. The first to publicize this fact was Egypt's most important paper, *Al Ahram*. It didn't change anything as far as I was concerned but made me look like a fool in the eyes of many.

How, in fact, did I view the chances of peace offered by the evolving situation? The last lines of the afterword that I wrote in 1975 for the American edition of the *Dialogue* sum it up rather clearly, with a major omission, however:

> *At the beginning of the dialogue I mentioned the explosion of collective hatred against Israel that shook the Arab world on the eve of the Six-Day War. Now we are facing a kind of polarization: on the one hand, we notice growing signs of moderation among some Arabs but, on the other, positions of extreme hatred are intensifying and solidifying within an important "rejection front." No one can tell which of these two*

*currents will prevail, and this is, in the end, the fundamental*
*uncertainty that gnaws at our hope for a settlement. Even*
*within the limited context of this dialogue, this uncertainty*
*casts its shadow on its positive elements.**

I had forgotten to mention one essential element: our own contribution to that situation.

The spring of 1975 was difficult.

My duodenal ulcer bled for the fourth time — and massively so. I underwent surgery at the Hadassah hospital in Jerusalem, and a postsurgery infection kept me there for three weeks or more. When I finally got home and started recuperating, the university served me with an unexpected ultimatum: either Jerusalem full time, or else . . . I decided to keep Geneva and turned to Tel Aviv University. Would they accept the part-time arrangement?

My friend Uri became my very energetic lobbyist. He convinced the rector, while the head of the School of History, Zwi Yawetz, was all for it in any case. Once back from my sabbatical, in the fall of 1976, I would start teaching in the Department of History in Tel Aviv, and during the last quarter of each year I would move to Geneva. This time there was no limitation to the arrangement.

As we continued to live in Jerusalem, finally in our own house, I became a wanderer among three cities: Jerusalem, Tel Aviv, and Geneva. I soon adapted to Tel Aviv University and,

---

* Saul Friedländer and Mahmoud Hussein, *Arabs and Israelis: A Dialogue*, Holmes & Meier, New York, 1975, pp. 216–17.

once again, experienced the enthusiasm of new beginnings. Quite different from the Hebrew University, the Tel Aviv campus was an urban one, entirely integrated into a city that fed it with its own energy and drive. It appeared to me as a university much more open to all, in contrast to the snobbishness of Jerusalem. By and large, however, the students were the same, with the same smattering of military uniforms among an attentive audience, reminding one that this was Israel, barely three years after the Yom Kippur War.

# CHAPTER TEN

# The Mount of the Blessing

I never felt entirely at ease in our Jerusalem house, into which we moved in early 1974. Somebody once told me: "You look like a stranger in your own home." It was partly true. The house itself was quite an achievement: right from the entry, you saw the dining room, the vast living room, and the garden as one continuous space; works by excellent Israeli painters, discreet furniture, and a Beckstein grand piano defined the living room. Hagith truly had an eye for design, and had produced impressive results.

The house comprised two separate and identical parts which both could be accessed through the common garden. My in-laws, to whom Hagith was extremely close and devoted, came to live in the other part; their proximity was a great help, and I had agreed to it. Yet as far as I was concerned, their constant presence also created problems I should have foreseen.

In more general terms, such a grand house may have been too much for me. Until then we had rented, in Geneva and in Israel; this was my first *home*, since childhood. Perhaps I couldn't feel completely at home anywhere. Hence my slight — yet apparently noticeable — discomfort.

And yet it was the house where I spent most of my life in Israel, where I saw my children grow, graduate from high school, thrice over, at five-year intervals; where I had a glimpse of, then met, their dates. It was where they congregated with their friends (mostly in the basement), where we celebrated the boys' bar mitzvahs and Michal's bat mitzvah, where Eli and Michal (Eli's Michal) were married, where we had house concerts in which our little Michal would soon participate, and where we (Hagith was the master of ceremonies and the superchef) frequently entertained our friends from home and many a guest from afar. And it's there that I read *Mireille, l'abeille* (Mireille the bee — in French the two words rhyme) to Thom, my first grandson (David and Fabienne's son), when they came visiting from Paris. But all of this was still hidden in the future as we entered the house in February 1974.

*2*

My domain was the study, contiguous to the living room but separate from it. My books had arrived from Geneva and, half consciously, I reconstructed the private and secluded space that had been my father's study in Prague.

I loved the presence of books, not stacked in any library but in *my* library: I loved to sit, empty-minded, just vaguely contemplating, among *my* books. I never had — and don't have — a hobby: I was not interested in sports or cooking or collecting tin soldiers. My main pastime was reading and so it remains to this day. It would be pointless to follow the meandering of my taste in literature; in that domain, very little remains stable outside of the core that I mentioned previously: Flaubert, Proust, Kafka,

Dostoevsky, and Thomas Mann, at times. In short, my basic staple was and is ultraconventional.

There were exceptions, but not particularly original ones: Malcolm Lowry's *Under the Volcano*, Djuna Barnes's *Nightwood*, James Joyce's *Dubliners*, Italo Svevo's *Confessions of Zeno*, and, of course, the three Roths, Henry, Joseph, and Philip (just to be clear, I am alluding to *Call It Sleep* in the first case and *Radetzky March* in the second; as for the third Roth, I particularly liked his early books, *Goodbye, Columbus* and *Portnoy's Complaint*, and still enjoy his generally ironic, iconoclastic view of American Jews and American society more generally).

You may be astonished that I mention *Dubliners* and not *Ulysses*; it shows my simplistic taste, or rather what I really loved: I used to read aloud the last paragraph of "The Dead" to whoever, in the family, was ready to listen or else to myself.

Simultaneously, I read or started reading and abandoned whatever novels, biographies, memoirs, diaries that I sampled rather haphazardly, according to reviews and rumors. I also devoured every new Le Carré and, over the years, any P. D. James I laid my hands on. Unfortunately, in both cases, their earliest books were their best.

Literature was and is a necessity but, in terms of time, it remained marginal to other domains — apart from the strictly professional reading — from literary criticism to the history of ideas, theories of history, the history of philosophy, and the like. I say history of philosophy and not philosophy as such, as I have but limited ability for abstract reasoning (it already was the case, decades beforehand, with science and mathematics in particular).

Closer to home, I systematically perused the publications of the *Annales* school and over the years came to know personally most of its main representatives. I liked the work of these French historians but could not apply their concepts and methods to my domain. There was no way to use the *longue durée* in conceptualizing the history of the Shoah, an event-dominated period par excellence. Much had to be rethought in the history I was dealing with, but it demanded approaches of a very different kind that I first conceived of in 1974–75 but that would come to fruition only from the 1990s onward.

Let me add at this point that although I personally liked Le Roy Ladurie, Furet, Besançon, and others, I was perplexed by their political move from the Communist Party after the war to extreme conservative positions in the following decades. Why not stop midway, at social democracy for example? In fact, it wasn't a peculiarity of *Annales* historians but rather one of the French and other intellectuals of their generation and of the following one, whose onetime Maoists became the sharpest critics of the gods they had once adored. I never quite understood the need to move from one extreme to the other. This possibly was some psychological trait, a "closed mind," as it was tagged at some stage. Here in the States, you would find the same move from the far left to the far right when following the trajectory of the *Commentary* group, for example, among the many neoconservatives of the first generation.

A fascinating personification of such a total change of sides was the excellent historian of the French Communist Party, herself a high-ranking member of that party after the war, Annie Kriegel; she became a truly obdurate right-winger not only in regard to French politics but also concerning Israeli policies. Incidentally, when my dialogue with Mahmud Hussein was published, she declared that I should be shot. I didn't take that fatwa very seriously.

Many years beforehand, in 1966, I had met Pierre Nora, who belonged to this cohort of French historians without adopting the same kind of bipolar extremism. We became friends. In 2014, we participated together in a ceremony and a debate at Tel Aviv University, where we shared the Dan David prize in history. The charming Anne Sinclair, Pierre's companion, also came: I had met her in the 1980s when she arrived in Israel with a TV crew to report on the political situation under Begin; I said what I deemed necessary. I don't know whether it was ever broadcast.

I often ponder about the splendid series of volumes that Pierre conceived, commented on, and edited: *Les lieux de mémoire* (*Realms of Memory*), those sites that a nation keeps revering and which supposedly become, over the years, the only remaining foundations of national identity. There is actually one sentence from the introduction to *Les lieux de mémoire* that perfectly defines Pierre's project: "There are *lieux de mémoire*, realms of memory, because there are no longer *milieux de mémoire*, real environments of memory."

When the first volume, *La République*, was published, in 1984, I wrote the review for *Le Figaro*. It was very positive but I wondered nonetheless whether different communities, even within a homogeneous nation such as France, didn't have different realms of memory, together with remaining *milieux de mémoire*, sites of living memory, beyond the official and ritualized ones. The framework can hardly apply to more heterogeneous national entities such as the United States. In a country so diverse, where even these days (2014) flying the Confederate flag is passionately defended by many throughout the South, the choice of generally recognized sites of memory, to say nothing of the many remaining environments of memory clung to by dozens of different ethnic and religious groups, would be impossible. In any case, this achievement opened the doors of the Académie française to Pierre.

We went on living in Jerusalem and I drove down to Tel Aviv two or three days a week. The new house wasn't the only reason for this slightly tiring arrangement. We had Jerusalemite friends, most of whom did not belong to my fields at the university, so that the ostracism that some of my former colleagues (including the Scholems) maintained against us for my rejection of the Hebrew University in favor of Tel Aviv and Geneva did not have an impact on our everyday life. Our small group was quite homogeneous as far as politics were concerned. Some were even more critical than I, others slightly less so; all in all, we were left of center regarding main issues.

Hagith and I also felt real attachment to the city as such. Every day, for years, I took a walk of about an hour, always along the same route and usually alone. I went down our street, Pinsker Street, along a small public garden on the right side and the lush grounds and trees of some institution on the left; I crossed Keren Hayesod, passed the Montefiore windmill, and proceeded down the Yemin Moshe stairs and over Gei-Hinnom (Gehenom) valley. Yemin Moshe is one of the most picturesque and ancient residential areas of Jewish Jerusalem, with an elegant guesthouse for a chosen few, mostly foreign visitors, a music center, and villas built during the Ottoman period; the view from Yemin Moshe encompasses the western walls of the Old City and part of the hills descending toward the Dead Sea.

From Gei-Hinnom, I followed the road ascending Mount Zion and crossed over to the Old City, usually through the gate facing the last part of the Armenian quarter, just before one reaches the first houses of the newly rebuilt Jewish quarter. From there alleys descend toward the Western Wall. I rarely stopped at the Wall, but usually crossed the square in front of it and climbed back to the Jewish quarter, then followed the path home.

Nowadays, on occasional visits about forty years later, I do not venture into the Arab part of the Old City anymore. The danger of getting attacked is real. Mainly, however, I cannot bear the hate-filled looks that follow you if you are identified as an Israeli, nor can I stand the sight of gun-toting settlers, easily recognized by their knitted yarmulkes, strutting down the alleys. As for Jewish Jerusalem, it has much changed over time, populated as it is by an overwhelming mass of Orthodox and ultra-Orthodox Jews.

## 2

We spent the sabbatical of 1975–76 in Geneva. For all of us, this was, I think, a happy period. In October 1975, Eli was admitted into tenth grade at Collège (high school) Jean-Jacques Rousseau, the best in the city, with Jean Calvin. As he had remained bilingual, there was no problem of adaptation. David, also bilingual, moved to the equivalent of junior high, and Michal (this was the biggest school event) entered first grade in a school very close to where we lived and, within a few weeks, babbled only in French. For the boys there were ski outings later in the year with all the excitement of a few days in the "wild," the fondues, the new friends, and whatnot.

Some three years beforehand, a major confrontation with Eli had taken place. Over time, the boys had read a lot in French, from the children's book series *Babar*, *Tintin*, and *Astérix*, to tearjerkers such as Hector Malot's *Sans famille*, most of Jules Verne, and so on. At some stage in the early 1970s, it occurred to me that it was high time for Eli to read Victor Hugo's *Les misérables*. He said no. It became a matter of paternal authority against filial rebellion. Nothing helped: Eli refused to read *Les misérables*. Why, I never figured out, nor did he, probably. Finally, I gave in. I had no choice, the less so that I had never read *Les misérables* myself...

It is at about that same time that I took Eli for a first visit to Paris. We saw the well-known tourist sites and my own lycée, of course; we visited museums, as Eli was a passionate drawer and painter. We were flying back from Orly and as usual, we arrived very early for a flight that moreover was delayed, so we went to the airport cinema and saw *The Green Berets* with John Wayne. I love to remember that as something special. Generally, I loved to see films with the children, even after years.

It is during those months that, for the first time, I decided to write down the memories of my childhood and wartime adolescence. Why then? Hadn't I shown a measure of indifference regarding my personal past for many years? I had embraced the history of the Shoah as my professional domain — which, in itself, indicated a growing sensitivity to the collective past — but, precisely, the "detached" dealing with the collective fate had probably become a way of pushing back too close a contact with personal memories.

I don't know what produced the change. Could it have been the rejection that I felt when the Hebrew University confronted me with its ultimatum, or the ostracism that I mentioned once I chose Tel Aviv? It sounds ridiculous, but such seemingly

inconsequential events can be invisible triggers of dispropor-
tionate emotional reactions. This is the only explanation I can
offer and it is but partly convincing, as my first attempts at writing that story were as "distant" from the personal past as ever. I
had tried repeatedly — and repeatedly failed.

The same scene surged forward each time as a necessary
beginning. I had been brought to the seminary in Montluçon
sometime in early September 1942. At first, I hated the place, still
empty during summer vacations; I hated the nuns, the catechism
they imposed on me, the disgusting food. I decided to run away.
I knew, probably from overheard conversations, that my parents
were hiding for a few days in the hospital of the town, before
leaving for Lyons and starting their trek to the Swiss border. I
waited near the main gate of the seminary until nobody was in
sight, slipped out, and was on my way to the hospital.

In my early attempts, I described the scene time and again
in one page or so, found it unsatisfactory, and tore up each successive draft. And yet no other beginning came to my mind.
I had even found a title for the book that says it all: *Le portail*
(The Gate).

After a number of unsuccessful attempts, I decided on dras-
tic measures: I left Geneva for a self-imposed retreat in nearby
Annecy, in a hotel on the lakeshore (I probably imagined that
the lake of Annecy would provide better inspiration than Lac
Léman). And, lo and behold, my fortnight-long seclusion seemed
to work: I started writing. Back in Geneva, I rapidly completed
a first draft of the memoir and sent it to Flamand. The gist of
his response was an elegant rejection: "Interesting but lacks all
feeling." According to him, I had produced a lifeless narration of
events. I instantly recognized that Flamand was right but I didn't
believe I could do any better.

I then suggested turning the memoir into a conversation that, so I thought, would help me overcome my emotional paralysis. I asked Claude Lanzmann if he would agree to be my "interviewer." He accepted. We had become good friends and saw each other frequently when he was in Jerusalem. Claude was not exactly easygoing; later on, he would not take criticism or contradiction with a smile. I had no reason or desire to criticize him, so we got along smoothly. Yet, after making all the arrangements for the dialogue, I stalled. This wasn't the right way.

A few months went by. In the meantime I had received a letter from a former friend of seminary days. He had been ordained and was a monk in Sept-Fons, a Trappist abbey on the Loire River. In *When Memory Comes*, I have told the story of my visit to Georges A., of our spontaneous and entirely natural reconnection and of our exchange of memories about "Les Samuels." When I returned to Geneva, I realized that we had discussed much, except what preceded the seminary: my life in Prague, in Paris, in Néris, as well as his life in Toulon from where he came. I started a long letter that I never sent: in addressing Georges, I had found my voice.

It is during these feverish months that I decided to locate the road probably followed by my parents to cross the Swiss border. From a letter my father had sent to Madame de Lépinay, I knew that after their arrest they were kept in Saint-Gingolph for a day or so. For the first time, I drove to Saint-Gingolph. But, I thought, that couldn't have been the crossing point, as this little town had but one street, following the lake, with the French and Swiss border police and customs stations right in the middle of it. It didn't take me long to discover Novel, a hamlet well above Saint-Gingolph, in the mountains; my parents had most plausibly reached it, but I didn't know what happened then. Did their guide take them along some forest lane that would lead to Switzerland around and beyond Saint-Gingolph? At the time of writing, I had no answer; I only knew that they had been arrested. Now, I know the course of events, having read Swiss and French police documents at the end of the 1990s.

The group of fifteen Jews, including several couples with small children, indeed reached Novel, and from there descended to Saint-Gingolph. At around three in the morning they all started walking along that one street which, at this hour of the night, was empty of border guards on both sides; they reached the Swiss side of the stretch. By a fateful coincidence, some youngsters coming out of a bar spotted them and called the police. The entire group was arrested. The next morning, parents with small children were allowed to stay in Switzerland (a very brief exception), while my parents and another couple without a child were kept overnight and, on the following day, delivered to the French police in Saint-Gingolph, then sent to the French camp of Rivesaltes, followed by Drancy, followed by Auschwitz.

In writing down the various aspects of my years in Montluçon I relied on the very vivid memories I had kept of that period, on letters my parents had written between September and November 1942, and on a few letters I wrote mainly after mid-1944 to Madame de Lépinay or to my grandmother in Sweden. All these letters had been returned to me over the years. Nonetheless, once again, a few details became clear only long after the memoir had been published in 1978.

Thus I was told, years later, that my uncles' delegate, Mr. Rosemblat (who was to become my temporary guardian until I could be reunited with one of my uncles), twice came up against a straightforward denial of my being at the seminary. Only the third time, after he showed a written order from the district *préfet* (governor) to have the seminary searched by the police, was I released. I wondered why the nuns had behaved in a way that didn't fit with their generally meek spirit. Was it to ensure that I pursued my Catholic path?

Once more, years went by until the answer became clear. A researcher discovered in French archives an instruction sent by Pius XII soon after the end of the war to the bishops of previously occupied countries (via the nuncios): Jewish children hidden in Catholic institutions were not to be released if they had been baptized and if their parents were not alive anymore; even hidden children who had not yet been baptized should not be released if the parents had not returned. Baptism, let's remember, is a sacrament that cannot be annulled: once a Christian, forever a Christian; hence this problematic compromise. The nuns of Montluçon had to obey their bishop and the pope.

In late 1977, my manuscript was ready. A year later, the book came out, first in French at Seuil, as usual. Did the writing of these memoirs, their publication, and their warm reception in various countries induce some sort of catharsis? Not really. Yet a move, a transformation, had accelerated. It led to a shift in priorities: from then on, the wartime past increasingly dominated my thinking. Nonetheless, it would take a difficult stay in Berlin in the mid-eighties and some fierce debates in those same years for the switch to be complete.

The publication of the memoirs in Germany in 1978 or 1979 earned me an award, the Andreas Gryphius Prize in literature. The prize had gone to many authors I didn't know; the previous year it had been awarded to Siegfried Lenz for his novel *Deutschstunde* (*The German Lesson*); that looked safe enough to me. The ceremony took place in Düsseldorf and, as usual, a book signing followed. With each signature, I inscribed the name of the person buying the book. It all proceeded without a hitch until I asked the name of a lady whose turn had come: "Von Papen," she said. "Von Papen?" I asked, somewhat taken aback. "Yes," she answered. I hesitated for a few seconds, then signed and added the usual formula: "With best wishes." Was Franz von Papen possibly the lady's father? He was the politician who convinced President Paul von Hindenburg to appoint Hitler as chancellor, on January 30, 1933.

## 3

In early 1977 Rabin was forced to resign for a flimsy reason; general elections followed in May. The results stunned everybody, including the winners: Menachem Begin's Likud was victorious and Begin was appointed prime minister. A sea change had put an end to the traditional primacy of the center-left in Israeli politics. Over the years, as I mentioned, Israel's new leader had managed to draw to his side the underprivileged "Oriental" Jews to whom he appealed and whose dignity he restored. But now, the settlements' expansion into Palestinian territory would become the sacred mission of the new government.

This wasn't the end of surprises. Today, the events of the late 1970s look hardly real in view of the following decades, and yet they shook us and many others the world over: Anwar Sadat's peace initiative, his journey to Israel, his speech to the Knesset, Begin's brief hesitation, the birth of the Peace Now movement in Israel, the peace treaty with Egypt, later with Jordan. Returning the Sinai to Egypt, however, gave Begin's government the credit and the time to tighten its grip on the Palestinians by accelerating the settlement policy and even to mention the possibility of annexing the West Bank (Judea and Samaria, as the region was called by the true believers and their hundreds of thousands of passive supporters). Nonetheless, although I immediately understood the motives behind Begin's "generosity," I preciously keep a group photograph in which I stand alongside Sadat, Begin, Goldmann, Mendès-France, Simha Flapan, and a few other members of the Israeli left. My smile is genuine.

In 1979, the Supreme Court ordered the government to evacuate the Elon Moreh settlers (Elon Moreh was a particularly "activist" group of settlers) from land they had confiscated illegally from its Palestinian owners. The Begin government refused to comply.

It so happened that just as the conflict between the government and the Supreme Court was taking place, a minor incident occurred: a rampage by high school youngsters in the southern city of Beersheba. Israeli television Channel One was airing a daily prime-time political debate on current controversial events after the main evening news. I was invited to participate in a discussion on "Law and Order." I would represent the left and would face the ultra-right-wing activist Eldad Scheib. The chairman of the national lawyers' association, whose name I forget, represented the so-called center. Yakov Achimeir, a somewhat right-wing television personality, moderated the debate. No one expected this top-rated political program to remain focused for long on the rampage of high school students in Beersheba.

When asked to give my opinion on what should be done with the unruly youngsters, I answered that in a country in which the government refuses to obey a decision of the Supreme Court, what kind of respect for the law could one expect from high school kids? The temperature shot up. Scheib went after the leftists and from high school discipline the discussion moved to government and the Supreme Court. When my turn came again, I decided to up the ante and said that if the government pushed its illegal behavior to the point of annexing the West Bank, as many voices on the right demanded, I would favor civil disobedience, such as refusing to serve on reserve duty in the annexed territories. I added that I knew that such civil disobedience would incur punishment under the law and that such punishment should be taken into account.

The reaction was immediate: Achimeir turned his back on me and didn't address me again, even after the end of the program. When I came home, Hagith, who usually shared my views regarding "our" policies, told me that I was crazy to speak that way when Eli was doing his military service; my father-in-law, a very mild man who, as may be remembered, lived in the other part of the house, had come over and added, "Next time we will be wiser..." The worst, though, was the complete silence of the phone.

The following day was overcast and rainy: typical Jerusalem winter weather. In our house the humidity penetrated into the vast living room, equipped with entirely insufficient central heating. I huddled by the fireplace but managed only to produce more smoke than fire. Silence remained unbroken as the hours went by. In the early afternoon, fifteen-year-old David came back from school. *"Aba"* ('Dad' in Hebrew), "you look sad. What's wrong?" "Well, you know, I expressed views yesterday that nobody seems to agree with." David put an arm around my shoulders: *"Aba,"* he said, "with you all the way."


In 1982, the Lebanon War, initiated and manipulated by Defense Minister Ariel Sharon, broke out. Begin had become a puppet in Sharon's hands, and soon the moderate segment of public opinion understood that the wily minister had lied about the goals of the operation. Refusal to obey the summons started here and there among the reservists called up to fight in Lebanon and landed them in jail. The opposition to the war grew. Our son David was also in Lebanon. Toward the end of that unjustifiable campaign, Lebanese militiamen, "allies" of Israel, massacred hundreds of Palestinians in the refugee camps at Sabra and Shatila. Along with four hundred thousand other Israelis, I protested against the horror on Kings of Israel (today "Rabin") Square in Tel Aviv.

Uri Tal, my friend Uri, increasingly depressed, took his life.

## 4

Let me backtrack to early 1978. I had been invited to spend a semester in the Department of International Relations at MIT. The chair, Eugene Skolnikoff, added a modest fellowship to my sabbatical money and asked me, in return, to teach a seminar, possibly a faculty seminar, on a topic of my choice. This was tempting, although I knew that it would be time-consuming. I had just completed my memoir; it was to come out in France in the fall of that same year. I had no new project in mind but was toying with the idea of writing a small essay about representations of apocalypse in the contemporary Western imagination; I suggested it as the theme for the seminar. A somewhat puzzled Skolnikoff agreed.

I will not forget the first days of my stay. For some reason — probably to check the house we had rented in Belmont, to get a car, and to prepare the basics — I arrived alone, in the early days of January. Hagith, David, and Michal (Eli remained in Jerusalem to prepare for the final high school exams) stayed in New York and would join me two or three days later. The weather was grayish but not too cold. I rented a car in Cambridge and drove to the house on Center Street, Belmont; it seemed perfect. I left the car in front of the entrance and, tired from all the traveling, went to sleep. In the meantime, light snow had started falling.

When I woke up and looked outside, I couldn't see a thing, except for a veil of snow, blown in all directions by heavy gusts of wind. The car had disappeared and the front door was blocked. In short, I had arrived just in time to experience the worst snowstorm on record in Massachusetts history, during which all life stopped. The governor declared a state of emergency; the famous Route 128 which ran around the greater Boston area was unusable and, for the first time ever, Harvard closed its doors. The National Guard was called in to help police, firefighters, and snow-removing personnel. The mess lasted for a few days and, of course, Hagith and the children had to stay in New York.

I wasn't too worried, as I had bought some basic food en route to the house. Moreover, a nice young couple lived on the top floor, so that we got organized together. Ultimately, the snow stopped, the entrance was cleared, the car reappeared, the family arrived, and life returned to normal.

At MIT, the seminar began. The topic seemed to be of interest. In any case, I had never been in charge of such a galaxy of participants, who all presented papers and attended regularly. Thus, for several weeks I enjoyed the presence of discussants such as Frank Kermode, the literary scholar from Cambridge (UK); Phil Morrison, an astrophysicist from MIT; Gerald Holton, physicist and historian of science from Harvard; Frank and Fritzie Manuel, the biographers of Newton and historians of utopias from Brandeis; the American historian Leo Marx;

Gene Skolnikoff; and a few other equally eminent scholars. The seminar eventually led to a volume of essays edited by three of us and entitled *Visions of Apocalypse: End or Rebirth?*, published in 1985.

During that period, I traveled several times to New York to decide between two publishers interested in acquiring the English version of my memoir. I opted for Farrar, Straus and Giroux, where I encountered a forthright acceptance of the text as it was, with its various time frames and other aspects I didn't want to change. I met Roger Straus only once and very briefly, but found a perfect interlocutor in Aaron Asher, the literary director. Aaron was highly cultivated, very quick, very sensitive, and, as I discovered later, also an excellent pianist. His only problem was that he couldn't work contentedly with the same publisher for any length of time, so that, for my next book — not the MIT volume but *Reflections of Nazism* — I moved with him to Harper and Row, later renamed HarperCollins, where I remained after he left. I will return to the main themes of *Reflections of Nazism* in the next part of the book.

After Roger Straus and Aaron Asher gave me the good news, I rushed down to tell Hagith before boarding the Amtrak back to Boston. At that time, Farrar, Straus was located on Union Square, and Union Square had its problems. I noticed that in the middle of the square there were two pay phone booths. I went straight to one of them, inserted the coins, and started dialing when I heard a man's voice behind me: "Get off that phone." With a tilt of the head I indicated that the booth next to me was not in use. "Get off that phone!" The voice had become threatening; I turned around: the man behind me was holding a knife. I didn't ask for any explanation, dropped the phone, and walked very quickly away, quite shaken. The reason for the threat was obvious: drugs. The man was waiting for a call at the booth from which I had started to dial. He would have used the knife and nobody would have dared to stop him. This too was New York in the late seventies.

Apart from such minor incidents, our stay was pleasant in more ways than one: we saw plays at the Brattle Theatre in Cambridge and went to concerts at Symphony Hall in Boston. Yet our most memorable musical experience occurred sometime in the early spring at Harvard's Memorial Hall, where we attended a chamber music concert performed by Harvard students. The last piece on the program was Beethoven's *Archduke* Trio. We knew that the performance would be good, but right from the outset, as the cello joined the other two instruments, both Hagith and I stared in disbelief, probably as astonished as many in the audience; the cello player belonged to another sphere. He was a student named Yo-Yo Ma. We had never heard of him.

Otherwise, there were several movie theaters in Belmont or nearby. It is to one of these theaters that I took David to see *Close Encounters of the Third Kind*. For us it remains unforgettable. And, with David, I read Saint-Exupéry's *Vol de nuit* for his French class, while both children were acquiring flawless English. Only the house cat caused problems: to demonstrate its loyalty and gratitude for the good food, it would from time to time present us with a bird still half-alive held firmly in its jaws. We left in the summer, Hagith and the children back to Israel and I to Paris to get ready for the publication, in September, of the French original of my memoir, *Quand vient le souvenir*.

Incidentally, during the stay in Cambridge I got acquainted and then very friendly with one of the truly brilliant young graduates of the Harvard Department of Jewish Studies, the budding public intellectual, Leon Wieseltier. I hope he won't mind the reappearance of words from this very distant past. Already then he was a master of the hard-hitting style that characterizes him to this day. "Dear Saul," Leon wrote in December 1978, "At last the verdict is in, and it is good: I have been elected a Junior Fellow at Harvard. For three years I will enjoy all the blandishments of membership in that deplorably elitist institution. It means that at last I will not have to worry about the material conditions of my work." Leon also mentioned some articles he was writing and that he would send me. Then: "Now I am about to begin a long and decidedly severe piece on Edward Said's new book [*Orientalism*] and on the excesses of the Palestinian position generally. That too I will send you . . ."

Wieseltier's position regarding the Palestinian issue was more pessimistic than mine. In 1979 he wrote to me: "They really do want everything. I don't believe they will ever concede legitimacy to a Jewish state. In short, for all the obstacles presented by our side, the Palestinians present obstacles sevenfold. I think that people of our political persuasion must take care to perceive the Palestinians clearly and not invent our adversaries."

Would Leon or would I ultimately be right?

In early 1983, a phone call informed me that I had been awarded the Israel Prize in history. The Israel Prize is the highest distinction granted in Israel to an Israeli; it is awarded yearly in a ceremony that takes place on the evening of Independence Day, the national holiday, in the presence of the president (Itzhak Navon in my case). The novelist Aharon Appelfeld, the political writer Haim Hefer, and the composer and singer Noemy Shemer ("Jerusalem of Gold") were awarded the prize along with me.

That I received the prize astonished me, be it for political reasons. I could have refused to accept it as a form of protest against the war in Lebanon and the settlements. I chose an easier way: on the morning of that Independence Day, I joined a group of like-minded demonstrators at Har Habracha (the Mount of the Blessing), in the occupied West Bank, on the site of a planned new settlement. In the evening, I went to receive the prize. To be publicly embraced remained vital, after symbolically expressing my opposition to the ongoing policies.

Among the sacred topics in Israeli self-perception, I particularly disliked the myth of the Sabra, of the new Jewish man and the new Jewish woman (as opposed to the Diaspora Jew), a myth celebrated in particular in a vast literature of the 1940s and 1950s. The most exalted figures of this cult were the fighters of the Palmach, the elite units of the Haganah that, indeed, contributed greatly to the military successes before and during the War of Independence. This generation of fighters, writers, and keepers of the flame considered themselves and were accepted as the crème de la crème of Israeli society, its aristocracy, somewhat like the ghetto fighters after the Shoah: the comparison was often made and the distinction between these heroes and the ordinary Jews of those and later times was almost instinctively kept. "Post-Zionism" was still a few years away.

I started a critical discussion about myths of national memory, and specifically of Israeli national memory in my graduate seminar in Tel Aviv. The reception among the participants was mixed, as could be expected, and so it was in the large undergraduate lecture courses labeled as "an introduction to twentieth-century

Western culture," whenever I critically alluded to Israeli culture and its myths.

In 1979, following the publication of my memoir in Hebrew, the then journalist (later historian) Idith Zertal brought up the subject of Israeli culture and Zionist mythology in a wide-ranging interview with me for *Haaretz*. I don't remember how I answered Idith's questions but, for good reason, I remember speaking of the "intellectual superficiality of the Palmach generation." Nothing much happened, except that our neighbor from across the street, Haim Guri, one of the main poets of that generation, stopped talking to me. I regretted it, but that was to be expected, wasn't it?

A few months later, the same Guri organized a large reception in his home to celebrate the publication of a new volume of his poems. To our astonishment, we were invited. We crossed the street, climbed the stairs, entered the apartment, and followed the chatter to the living room. Lo and behold, dozens of the best and brightest of the Palmach generation stood there. We were entrapped ... Nobody seemed to pay attention; nobody talked to us.

Guri was "introduced" and started speaking. He sat on the floor and the guests sat around him. Slowly, almost languidly, he pointed to one after the other among his attending friends and reminisced about how they met, what they did over the years, and so on. Some forty minutes into this, Guri stopped. Silence. Then, turning toward me, hand outstretched, finger pointed, he literally yelled: "As for Friedländer, we will settle accounts with him!" It was an exorcism: *Vade retro, Satana*! (Get thee behind me, Satan!) We didn't wait. Out we went, down the stairs, across the street, back to the safety of our house.

––––––––

I couldn't remain indifferent to the catastrophic evolution of the political situation in Israel during the 1980s. Itzhak Shamir had replaced a Menachem Begin exhausted by the disastrous evolution of the Lebanon War. An older saying could have perfectly applied to the diminutive Shamir: "He is even smaller than he looks." Shamir was a dangerous fanatic, opposed to all compromise and to the tiniest move toward peace. One couldn't keep silent.

For the first and last time of my life, I addressed a mass demonstration of Peace Now, in front of the prime minister's (Shamir's) office, organized in the memory of Emil Grunzweig, a Peace Now activist murdered on that spot by a right-wing fanatic. I hurled (not my style) Cromwell's words to the Rump Parliament into the Jerusalem night: "You have sat here too long for any good you have been doing . . . In the name of God, go!" It didn't unseat Shamir.

At the end of the 1980s, during Shamir's last year in office, I summed up my view of the situation in Israel in a letter to Leon Wieseltier:

> *Unfortunately, articles, petitions, speeches do not help anymore and, as you see, nothing will sway Shamir, as long as the US won't move. No need to add, the US won't move. The elections in Israel will, as you know, lead more or less to the present division of the country into equal camps with a possible shift to the right. So, what should be done? You may know that some years ago, I spoke of the possibility of civil disobedience and, believe me, I studied my Rawls very well. The trouble is that in the present situation this may legitimize the argument of Gush Emunim and others that they too act according to the dictates of their conscience. I am really at a*

*loss and, I must admit, terribly depressed by what I see and
even more by what I foresee. Needless to say, all that Peace
Now does is fine but, to me, this has become something
of a ritual which alleviates our conscience without leading
anywhere.*

The elections of 1992 did bring a change but the hope that did arise was brutally smashed. I will return to it.

## 5

Nahum Goldmann died in Europe in August 1982 and was buried in Jerusalem, on Mount Herzl, along with all major Zionist leaders. The decision had encountered strong initial opposition. Begin's government resisted having Goldmann buried on that hallowed spot and, even worse, the leadership of the Jewish Agency (the institution that Goldmann chaired for years and to which some of its leaders at the time of his death owed their careers) supported the government's position. As a former Goldmann secretary, I was asked to express my opinion on the evening news. I didn't hesitate to call it a shame — one more — for the government of Israel and mainly for the leaders of the Jewish Agency. Even as I write about this, so long after the events, I still feel some of the anger of those days.

I don't know what brought about the official change of decision, but a Mount Herzl burial was finally allowed. Very few Israelis were present at the funeral; neither the government nor the Jewish Agency sent any representatives. Most of those who came belonged to the diplomatic corps and to a delegation that arrived specially from West Germany. Goldmann's widow Alice and his two sons, Michael and Guido, attended, as did Michael's son, Goldmann's grandson.

Michael, who lived in Paris, had married an African-American woman; they divorced a few years later. The boy — who must have been ten or eleven at the time of the funeral — suddenly stood there alone, as everybody was leaving, and looked utterly lost (an aide arrived shortly afterward to lead him away). That moment of "abandonment" of the little black grandson, standing in dismay on the dusty path of the cemetery, looked like a Fellini ending to Nahum Goldmann's saga.

# PART III

*Germany*

CHAPTER ELEVEN

# The Inability to Mourn*

In *The Tin Drum*, novelist Günter Grass tells of clubs in West Germany in the 1950s in which people ate onions to be capable of shedding tears. The metaphor was not wrong. Most Germans in those years wanted first and foremost to forget how much they had felt, each in his or her own way, part and parcel of the Third Reich, at least until the last year of the war. They constructed a mythic story of the past and desperately wanted to believe in it.

I remember stopping over in Hamburg, on my way to Sweden in 1956; the railway station bookstores were filled with the cheap productions of one Heinz Konsalik singing the praise of the Wehrmacht soldiers fighting heroically on the Eastern Front, without ever mentioning the criminal side of the coin. As I indicated previously, change occurred during the sixties, but it was followed by ups and downs that didn't find some sort of resolution before the late eighties. I tried to understand that moving scene from Geneva or Jerusalem and on the occasion of brief visits to Germany.

---

* In homage to Alexander and Margarethe Mitscherlich

In the early 1970s, I caught a glimpse of weird mutations in the representation of the Nazi years, both in Germany and elsewhere in Western Europe. A strange sort of countermemory of the Third Reich was appearing: in Germany it was dubbed the Hitler Wave (*die Hitlerwelle*), in France the retro fashion (*la mode rétro*), in Italy something else. It was the strangeness of it all that caught my attention and led me to write, almost as an afterthought, a book-length essay published in French in 1983 as *Reflets du Nazisme*; it became *Reflections of Nazism: An Essay on Kitsch and Death* in its English version. I mentioned it in the previous chapter.

Grasping what was going on was not easy: the Hitler years had become an object of public fascination expressed with utter moral relativism and some playful, postmodern aesthetics. Remember Albert Speer's wildly successful memoirs, Joachim Fest's unusually eloquent and best-selling biography of Hitler and the ensuing film, and Hans-Jürgen Syberberg's aesthetic reworking of history in his film *Hitler, ein Film aus Deutschland* (*Our Hitler* in the States). The death camps inspired Liliana Cavani's sadomasochistic film *The Night Porter*; French collaboration found its noncommital interpretation in Louis Malle's *Lacombe Lucien*, and so on.

In my *Reflections*, I attempted to grasp the essence of that mood and of that fascination. I perceived the new representation as a playful free-for-all, beyond good and evil. More specifically, I recognized in the new productions the very use of some of the components that so effectively ensured Nazism's hold on millions of Germans and other Europeans: syrupy sentimentality (kitsch) mixed with the exaltation triggered by total destruction and mass death. The German edition of my essay put the emphasis on this insight by changing the title to *Kitsch und Tod. Der Widerschein des Nazismus* (Kitsch and Death: The Reflection of Nazism).

The book didn't find much echo in France. The time of such questions hadn't yet arrived. *Le Roi des Aulnes* (*The Ogre*), a novel by Michel Tournier, one of the icons of French literature in his day, illustrated my argument with its eroticization and mythification of Nazi young boys in one of their leadership schools; it didn't seem to bother anybody and, in 1970, Tournier's novel received the Goncourt Prize, the highest literary prize in France. My book led to interesting, at times tense debates in Germany and garnered a warm reception in Israel. As for the American world, the Hitler Wave had not reached its shores in any significant manner.

I never thought of applying the concepts I used to analyze the Hitler Wave and its antecedents to renditions of the Shoah during the sixties and seventies. It simply didn't occur to me. It so happened, however, that just before I started working on *Reflections*, NBC produced the miniseries *Holocaust* in 1977, which could be perceived as a mixture of kitsch and death. Despite its worthlessness in artistic terms, that Hollywood production revolutionized Western awareness of the Holocaust: millions in the United States and in Europe — particularly in Germany — became aware of the extermination for the first time. Kitsch and death, or in other words, cheap sentimentality and extreme violence, penetrated as never before the imagination of vast Western audiences.

The intention of the NBC production was essentially commercial (following the success of ABC's *Roots*, a docudrama about slavery). The subtext of some of the productions of the Hitler Wave was different: it was ideological in the widest sense of the word, and here and there offered a muted echo of emotions from another era. At a loss for a more adequate term, I called this reinterpretation of Nazism a "new discourse," and, in the introduction to *Reflections*, I tried to convey the gist of the underlying problem: "Is the attention fixated on this past only a gratuitous reverie, the attraction of spectacle, exorcism, or the result of a need to understand? Or is it, again and still, an expression of profound fears and, on the part of some, of mute yearnings as well?"

Although this "new discourse" was mainly a German and West European phenomenon (France and Italy), its ambiguous message also emerged in a puzzling novella, published in 1981, by the brilliant, world-renowned British and Jewish intellectual George Steiner under the title *The Portage to San Cristobal of AH*. Powerfully written, Steiner's text tells of a ninety-year-old Hitler, alive and hidden in the Amazonian jungle, captured by a group of Israeli agents and transported toward the coast to be shipped to Israel to stand trial. Ultimately, AH's trial takes place in the jungle: the prosecutor, the leader of the group, Lieber, presents with deep feeling Hitler's quintessential crime, the extermination of the Jews. But it is Hitler who has the last word (literally: his answer ends in midsentence and with it the novella ends); it seems to turn the table on his Jewish accusers. Somehow, the satanic dimension was back and AH's eloquence appeared overwhelming.

I knew Steiner well as, for years, he taught English and comparative literature at Geneva University and we often met either at the brasserie Candolle, opposite the main university building, where Lenin used to spend much time, or at our apartment. In August 1981, as he was home in Cambridge, I wrote to him about *Portage*:

*Our discussion in Geneva may not have conveyed to you how puzzled and, in a way, ill at ease I was about some aspects of the book; ill at ease but also spellbound by the extraordinary brilliance and the uncanny power of the piece. My immediate problem is the following: I cannot avoid discussing your book in my forthcoming essay on the "Metamorphosis of Nazism" [the early title of Reflections], as I am trying to interpret, among other things, some new images of Hitler and a new discourse about the Jews. Doubtlessly, your final pages, that is the famous Hitler speech which you leave without any answer belongs to some of the major categories of arguments I wish to analyze . . .*

Steiner wrote back:

*A work of art is a work of art and must stand on its own feet. To this day many ask "whether Milton is of Satan's party" and why Dostoevsky gave Christ no single word in reply to the Grand Inquisitor. God knows, I am not comparing myself with these titans, but I think such debates often misunderstand how art works, how fiction allows the anarchic play of ideas and metaphors. Lieber's speech may be the most intense thing yet written on the Holocaust . . . AH's speech is NO answer, no possible answer, but an explosion of language out of the Hell that Lieber recounts. Both texts, and whatever else is memorable in the story, are meant to force mind and soul to face the terrible mystery of the limitless potentials of human speech . . .*

Was I becoming too much of a moralist?

———

No, I wasn't too much of a moralist. In some cases, my comments may have been entirely wrong but in others, regarding Syberberg's *Our Hitler* for example, I felt intuitively that exploiting to the hilt the aesthetics of Hitler's pageants, creating quasi-mystical comments to accompany the Wagnerian sound track of Nazi ceremonies meant adding layers of "enchantment" intended to reevoke the fascination of yesteryear. I said this to Syberberg, whom I met several times, until, once in Hamburg, he snapped back at me, *"Aber es war ja faszinierend!"* (But it was truly fascinating!)

Syberberg was never too keen on hiding his anti-Semitism. Our first encounter took place at the cinematheque in Jerusalem where he came to present an extract of his Hitler film. Both the writer Amos Elon and I immediately criticized his aesthetic endeavors, and our critical comments went on during the dinner that followed until Syberberg exploded: "What I am presenting is art, while the Jews are making money with Auschwitz!" He was probably alluding to the NBC miniseries, but "the Jews are making money" rang a familiar bell.

It took some years to get the full picture, once Syberberg published his political diatribe *Vom Unglück und Glück der Kunst in Deutschland nach dem letzten Kriege* (On the Misfortune and Fortune of Art in Germany after the Last War), in 1990. Here is a tiny sample that Ian Buruma translated in an article published in the *New York Review of Books* on December 20, 1990: "The Jewish interpretation of the world," Syberberg wrote,

> *followed upon the Christian, just as the Christian one followed Roman and Greek culture. So now Jewish analyses, images, definitions of art, science, sociology, literature, politics, the information media, dominate. Marx and Freud are*

*the pillars that mark the road from East to West. Neither are*
*imaginable without Jewishness. Their systems are defined by*
*it. The axis USA-Israel guarantees the parameters. That is*
*the way people think now, the way they feel, act and dissemi-*
*nate information. We live in the Jewish epoch of European*
*cultural history. And we can only wait, at the pinnacle of our*
*technological power, for our last judgment at the edge of the*
*apocalypse . . . So, that's the way it looks, for all of us, suf-*
*focating in unprecedented technological prosperity, without*
*spirit, without meaning . . . Those who want to have good*
*careers go along with Jews and Leftists [and] the race of supe-*
*rior men* [Rasse der Herrenmenschen] *has been seduced,*
*the land of poets and thinkers has become the fat booty of cor-*
*ruption, of business, of lazy comfort.*

I am about to plunge deeper into German issues and, during the
1980s, I spent much time in Germany. Thus, it may be the right
place to say a word about "my German Question," as the historian Peter Gay would have put it and as I remember it from that
period.

In the first chapter of this book, I briefly mentioned the place
of my German Jewish background in the emergence of a "poly-
morphous" identity. In my childhood memoir I referred to two
contradictory and coexisting attitudes to Germany and a German environment: familiarity and fear. Both were still very
much present in the years I am dealing with now and are easily understood: familiarity inherited from early childhood, fear
from later years. In short, I felt simultaneously very much at ease
and constantly on edge, not without good reason on occasion, as
will become amply clear further on.

Throughout those years, I particularly hated the unavoidable contact with people old enough to have been active adults in Nazi Germany and about whom you knew that they had been "brown" to a degree; they now turned into syrupy do-gooders regarding Jews and Israel. My reticence led at times to the comment (naturally made behind my back): *"Er ist ja schwer belastet"* (He is quite heavily burdened).

It took years before I felt somewhat more at ease in Germany; yet eventually I almost did. My two Berlin grandchildren, Yonatan and Benjamin, could not imagine anything else.

2

Heightened public awareness of the Shoah was, as mentioned, a paradoxical result of the NBC miniseries; it led, almost immediately, to debates and to new historical work that marked the beginning of an exponential growth of sustained scholarly attention to the subject. In 1983 the then president of the École des Hautes Études en Sciences Sociales, François Furet, asked me to organize an international conference on the history of the Shoah in Paris. Soon thereafter, in May 1984, a much larger international historical conference — the first ever held in Germany on this theme — was convened in Stuttgart.

The mayor of Stuttgart, Manfred Rommel, formally opened the meeting. The academic conveners, the historians Eberhard Jäckel and Jürgen Rohwer, followed, and then came my turn with a lecture addressing the issue that at the time divided historians of Nazi Germany between "intentionalists" and "functionalists" (opposite categories formulated by the British historian Tim Mason to analyze the political dynamics of Nazi Germany).

I later regretted having chosen such abstract concepts regarding the Shoah; over the years, these distinctions disappeared.

At the time, though, the opposition between the two approaches went much deeper than appeared at first glance. In my lecture, I criticized the functionalist position as strongly as I could and tried to argue for a moderate intentionalism that took into account the impact of circumstances, but nonetheless interpreted the extermination policy as the outcome of an extreme ideology of Jew hatred and of Hitler's active role. In short, it considered the extermination the outcome of a willful policy, of an "intention." To cross the threshold from persecution and even massacres into total extermination, Hilberg declared on that occasion, Hitler's go-ahead was necessary.

Two of the most recognized German historians of the Third Reich, Hans Mommsen and Martin Broszat, were staunch advocates of "functionalism," and although Eberhard Jäckel did not share their approach, they set the tone — or so it seemed to me — for a "German position" at the conference.

Functionalism stressed the centrality of independent institutional processes, the constant rivalries between the "grandees" of the system and their agencies creating what Mommsen called "cumulative radicalization." This led quite naturally to the conclusion that the policies of extermination were the unforeseen consequence of a blind dynamism turning into murderous activities unintended at the outset, that nobody could control anymore, and for which nobody carried specific responsibility. Thus, the extermination of millions disappeared in a dense institutional fog.

Mommsen's lecture at the conference explicitly mentioned the fog covering intentions, decisions, and responsibilities, which thereby excluded the possibility of resistance. Martin Broszat did not give a lecture, but in his remarks he defined my criticism and that of others as an "Israeli" (he avoided saying Jewish) perception of this history, in contrast to a "German" one. He expressed thereby the underlying unease that could be felt throughout the meeting between the most vocal German scholars on the one hand and most of the Jewish ones on the other. A few years later, that opposition would turn into a more personal confrontation between Broszat and myself.

My relations with Hans Mommsen remained friendly throughout: we corresponded and met oftentimes over many years, although we disagreed in our interpretation of Nazi policies. Thus, in January 1985, I wrote to Hans at some length about his essay on Hitler in the series *National-Sozialismus im Unterricht* (National Socialism in Instruction), which he had sent me. After summing up our fundamental disagreement, I criticized the functionalist interpretation by addressing one aspect of the text in more concrete terms:

> *The chapter on foreign policy is as lucid as the others, but if you reread it carefully, you may notice that even when one takes into account that Hitler had no overall plan, that he left many issues open, that he was a master in exploiting opportunities created by others, you will not find one decision on any of the major issues you discuss or, in fact, on any other one in this field (and please refer to your own text), which was not taken by him.*
>
> *Ribbentrop's opinions on how to handle Great Britain were not taken into account, as, much later on, his military experts' opinions on how to carry on the war were dismissed if they were not in agreement with his own views. If one started reading your text with this chapter, one could hardly be in agreement with the thesis presented at the outset.*

*Let me add a further word about the absence of resistance stemming from the chaotic aspects of the system and from the lack of clear decisions. As you know, I was very puzzled by this argument . . . I think you should reconsider this last point, as some of the most criminal orders were very clearly given: the Kommissarbefehl [the order to shoot all Soviet political commissars], for example, and as the criminal activities on the Eastern Front and in Poland, among many other places, were visible to many and could have elicited protests at any level whatsoever, if people had dared to protest.*

*Finally, the euthanasia program did create the resistance that you are looking for — as you yourself mention — within the same chaotic structure, for the very simple reason that, in this matter, the average German was directly hit by the impact of the atrocities. I am afraid that the explanation for the lack of resistance is simple: fear, indifference to the fate of out-groups and particularly that of more or less despised groups like the Jews, the faith in the essential worthiness of the system, of its Führer and of the Volksgemeinschaft [the racial community], and this almost to the end. The absence of any clear decision-making process seems to me a very minor matter and more of a rationalization than anything else.*

*My dear Hans, I am sure we will be arguing about these matters for many years to come. The trouble is that for those who were born during that time, on whichever side they may have been born, these remain the only issues they really argue about, mostly with themselves, whatever else they may be doing with their lives . . .*

And, indeed, we continued to argue.

In 1983, I saw part of Claude Lanzmann's film *Shoah* (the elaboration of which I had followed for years). It would be shown in full in 1985. Thirty years beforehand, *Night and Fog* had been entirely based on the filming of the sites and artifacts of persecution and extermination. Although, in the fifties, the narration did not mention the word "Jew" even once, in good Communist fashion (both the screenwriter Jean Cayrol and the director Alain Resnais were Communists), the viewer knew that the film dealt in great part with the extermination of the Jews, if only by looking at the names on the death lists of Auschwitz displayed in one of the film's sequences. Lanzmann's film systematically avoided any presentation of visual remnants of the Shoah and was entirely built around narratives of memory, the memory of Jewish survivors, of Poles, and of a few Germans, some of them unaware of being filmed by a hidden camera. We have, on the one hand, artifacts and documents; on the other, only the words of the witnesses.

Lanzmann fought vigorously for the absolute primacy of the witness (vigorously is an understatement). I admired Claude's work, a segment of which I described in *When Memory Comes* (based on what he had told me). Yet exclusive reliance on witnessing is not a position that the historian can accept.

These contrary approaches were turning the representation of the Shoah into a complex domain that, to me, became no less important than straightforward documentary history. Here was an apparent dichotomy that would inform and challenge my own work for years to come. The basic question was: How could one achieve a representation of the Shoah that would integrate both aspects as intertwined yet independent elements? It would take me many years to figure out a potential solution and build a historical narrative that would include both dimensions without the one being just a prop of the other, or, more specifically, without the witness merely illustrating documentary evidence.


Representation of the Shoah meant memory of the Shoah. What form would this memory take, within and beyond the memory of the Hitler years? This issue was never purely theoretical or artistic; it was, as we saw in Syberberg's case, ideological. In its ideological dimension, it involved Germans and Jews on the one hand and turned into an internal German debate on the other.

The German–Jewish debate became explicit around the pivotal mid-eighties. Thus, in 1984, the German filmmaker Edgar Reitz brought out a remarkable television series, the first part of a trilogy, entitled *Heimat*. It described the everyday life of the inhabitants of Schabbach, a fictional village in the Hunsrück, Reitz's own homeland (*Heimat*) in the west of Germany. The villagers, whose life in the first series was chronicled from the end of the First World War to the 1960s, lived their traditional existence throughout the years of the Third Reich, practically untouched by the political upheaval of 1933–45. A few words here and there vaguely alluded to the crimes of the regime. It was the arrival of the Americans, and of modernization in their wake, that destroyed the agelong traditions and, in Reitz's eyes, represented the true catastrophe.

In and of itself, Reitz's message would have been problematic enough, but his declaration in a major interview that the series was meant to restore German memory stolen by Hollywood's *Holocaust* turned it into a "manifesto." A year after the screening of Reitz's *Heimat*, Lanzmann's *Shoah* reached television screens and theaters.

As we shall see, this "confrontation" of memories was about to turn into an intra-German issue during the highly tense debates of the years 1985 to 1987; they took place almost exclusively in the Federal Republic but with a wide echo throughout the Western intellectual world.

The intense scrutiny of anything related to the Third Reich that characterized the late 1970s and early 1980s, particularly after the NBC film, led to serious controversies and to some that were less so. Thus, shortly before the Stuttgart conference, a morning news anchor at Kol Israel (the Israeli radio station) woke me up at home in Jerusalem with a real sensation: Hitler's secret diary had been discovered, it was handwritten, it apparently did not mention the extermination of the Jews! What did I have to say about such an extraordinary event? I was told moreover that the diary was in a safe in Zurich, and that the world-known Oxford historian, Sir Hugh Trevor-Roper, had authenticated the manuscript, particularly its handwriting.

In my opinion, this sounded weird: Hitler spoke, dictated his speeches, had dictated *Mein Kampf*, but did not leave any lengthy handwritten texts. This was probably a fake. The interviewer didn't believe me: after all, the world-famous Oxford historian . . . The Israeli reporter was not alone in setting his faith in Trevor-Roper. The German magazine *Stern*, followed by the London *Sunday Times*, used him as the expert and bought the rights to the diary for a huge sum. Some German colleagues declared their readiness to give up teaching and to travel delivering lectures about Hitler's message from hell. Alas, it was a fake.

One of the funniest byproducts of this farcical embarrassment was a British cartoon (I don't remember in which newspaper) that showed an exhausted Hitler sitting between two mounds of manuscripts and furiously writing when an adjutant informs him that the war is lost. "Don't disturb me with such nonsense," the Führer answers, "I'm writing my diary!"

4

During the early 1980s, I made frequent trips to Berlin as a member of the committee set up to choose the first director of the newly established Center for the Study of Anti-Semitism at the Technical University. After rather lengthy deliberations we agreed on the American candidate, Herbert Strauss. On one of these trips, I met a publisher whom Roger Straus (no relation, as far as I know) had strongly recommended: Wolf Jobst Siedler.

The flamboyant Siedler tried to convince me to write a history of German–Jewish relations throughout the nineteenth and twentieth centuries (at first he suggested starting even earlier); I turned the offer down from lack of sufficient expertise regarding the early period. Siedler nonetheless succeeded in persuading me to moderate a television discussion about the Jews in Prussia, on the seven hundredth anniversary of Prussia, in 1982 (to this day, I don't know how this date was calculated).

The one-hour discussion would supposedly be no problem, as the participants, all well-acquainted with the topic, had merely to be kept in line. Siedler did invite the historians Fritz Stern and Reinhard Rürup, the director of the German broadcasting authority and former ambassador to Israel, Klaus Schütz, and — to my great pleasure — Nahum Goldmann. When on the eve of the event I arrived in Berlin from Geneva, I found a message: Nahum Goldmann, too ill to participate, would be replaced by Gershom

Scholem, who was in Berlin as fellow of the Wissenschaftskolleg (the Institute of Advanced Study) that had just opened its doors.

The last-minute replacement worried me: I felt sorry about Goldmann's illness, and Scholem's participation unsettled me, as it may be remembered that he and Fania had stopped talking to us once I decided to leave the Hebrew University for Tel Aviv. But it was too late to opt out. We all met an hour or so before the beginning of the program to discuss various technical matters. Slightly late, the Scholems arrived and we greeted each other courteously. As I had done with the other participants, I asked Scholem to step aside for a minute to discuss what he would like me to include in my introduction. I knew how to present his scholarship, I told him, but "was there anything else?" "If you are so kind, sir" — it was as formal as that — "maybe you could say that I just received the Pour le Mérite" (the highest German civilian award but, until the end of the Second World War, also the highest military award, and best known as such). At that moment, I simply could not help myself: "The Pour le Mérite? For military services rendered to Germany?" I previously mentioned how much I disliked Scholem's story about his fake schizophrenia to avoid the draft. He smiled. The evening proceeded peacefully.

## 5

In the early 1980s, the Federal Republic appeared to move to the right. A significant segment of the German population opted for an explicit conservatism, a rolling back of the student rebellion of the 1960s and 1970s. This *Wende* (turn), as it was called, carried here and there a whiff of national self-affirmation that had been present in the past but hadn't dared express itself.

Whether as a result of the rightward drift of German politics or of the painful fortieth anniversary of "the German Catastrophe" of May 1945, there was nervousness in the Federal Republic from the very beginning of 1985. The German liberal weekly, *Die Zeit*, asked me to contribute a short article to the series it was publishing on the occasion of that symbolically loaded year. I don't remember the gist of my text but I clearly recall some of the other articles.

Thus, Golo Mann, the eldest of Thomas Mann's children and a well-known conservative historian, protested in his article against "commemorations that reopen old wounds." He wondered whether any Frenchman would have had the idea of commemorating Napoleon's defeat, forty years after Waterloo. The recurrent theme of articles, speeches, and books coming from the right was clear: Enough! After forty years, the time had come to draw a line. Some authors, such as Andreas Hillgruber, were more aggressive, arguing, for example, that, on balance, the crimes of the Allies — of the Soviets in particular — and the criminal plans regarding the future of a defeated Germany, discussed even before the Western Allies knew of Auschwitz, proved an equivalence of evil.

Resentment from that political direction also swirled around the outcry, in the United States, regarding a meeting between President Ronald Reagan and Chancellor Helmuth Kohl in the military cemetery of Bitburg, where both German and American soldiers were buried, once tombs of Waffen-SS were discovered alongside those of the Wehrmacht. What was meant to be a symbol of reconciliation turned into a source of further bitterness.

Did this represent the attitude of a majority of Germans? I do not believe so. I rather think that the greater part of the population identified with the words of its president, Richard von

Weizsäcker, in his eloquent and dignified address to the nation, on May 8, 1985, about historical responsibility. It echoed far and wide and for me it amply counterbalanced the demands for drawing a final line behind the past.

During the summer of that same year, another debate highlighted the Jewish issue as such. The director of the Frankfurt city theater intended to open the season with Rainer Werner Fassbinder's play *The City, Garbage and Death*, in which "the rich Jew" played a central and unsavory role. On the opening evening, leaders of the Frankfurt Jewish community occupied the stage and compelled the theater to cancel the performance. It is in that somewhat tense atmosphere that I arrived at the Wissenschaftskolleg at the end of September 1985.

# CHAPTER TWELVE

# Berlin

I knew some Berlin sites well before seeing the city for the first time, in 1981 or 1982. The trouble was that once I became a frequent visitor and then a six-month resident in 1985–86, I couldn't help associating what I knew of Nazi Berlin with sites I recognized. On balance though, I like the city for its mixture of industrial buildings and vast areas of natural beauty. In my private ranking, Paris comes first, then New York, followed by Berlin. I am a big-city person, and in that category, Prague, Jerusalem, or Geneva can scarcely compete; nor can Los Angeles, in any traditional category.

The end of my stay in Berlin in 1985–86 was painful for me and potentially embarrassing for others. Thus, I have never mentioned some of it publicly to avoid bringing up a misunderstanding that — albeit thirty years old by now — could be hurtful to people for whom I keep much esteem. As a result, I was in a quandary regarding the present chapter: for more than a year I remained undecided and "stuck," although the four or five people I asked for advice all suggested there was no reason for skipping such an "old story." I finally decided to go ahead.

The Kolleg, an institute for advanced study, partly imitates the Princeton model. Most of its fellows are invited for one year and given much leeway to work on their various projects while receiving the equivalent of their habitual salary. There are a few permanent fellows but they mostly deal with major institutional decisions and the choice of new fellows.

In 1985, the rector was Peter Wapnewski, a medieval German literature scholar who had written about the Jewish minstrel Süsskind von Trimberg (the only one there was, I guess). Wapnewski, in his sixties by then, had an engaging personality, which did help in dealing with a very diverse group of fellows. The second in command, the much younger Wolf Lepenies, a sociologist with a literary bent who had written on *Melancholia and Society*, among other books, looked more down-to-earth than the chief; while W.'s future was probably behind him, L. could expect a long way ahead.

Among the fellows (or second-year fellows), you could not miss the vivacious Nike Wagner, Richard Wagner's great-granddaughter, whose resemblance to her great-grandmother Cosima was almost eerie; she didn't share her politics, though, and had some of the sharpness and the wit of the fascinating Viennese Jew, Catholic convert, monarchist, and editor of *Die Fackel* (The Torch), Karl Kraus, to whom she had devoted a major study. She also wrote about her own famous family with great emphasis on her father Wieland, who redeemed Bayreuth after the war.

When a former fellow came through Berlin, he or she was heartily invited to share the Kolleg's excellent meals; if the former fellow lived in Berlin and was Jacob Taubes, he considered himself a quasi-permanent guest, despite Wapnewski's silent anger. Taubes was a man of vast erudition, eccentric behavior, and unusual success with women. He ranked quite high on a list of evil people kept by Scholem, possibly because of the widespread belief that he had driven his first wife, Susan, to suicide.

The main building of the Kolleg, a mansion among many in leafy, opulent, quiet, dignified Grunewald, stood on a sharp bend of the Wallotstrasse. On that bend, Walther Rathenau's open car had to slow down on a fateful day in June 1922, allowing a group of right-wing extremists to shoot and kill the Jewish foreign minister of the Weimar Republic, "the Jewish sow" (*die Judensau*), as they called him. Another "historical site," close to the Kolleg, was the dainty Grunewald railway station, which was no longer in use. From that station, some of the Berlin Jews had been shipped to Lodz between the fall of 1941 and mid-1943, and from Lodz to Chelmno, where they were exterminated in gas vans.

Throughout the autumn of 1985, I kept busy preparing a conference about German memory of the Holocaust, writing some short articles and afterwords for the new German and American editions of *Kitsch*, discovering Berlin architecture and museums, and attending several meetings of a seminar on Carl Schmitt at the Free University.

Carl Schmitt was, with Heidegger, one of the most prominent intellectuals of Nazi Germany and a party member since 1933. His influence as a political theorist was considerable under Weimar, during the Third Reich up to the beginning of the war, and no less so after the war (and to this day). He was still alive during my stay in Berlin. His fierce anti-Semitism exploded sky-high in the 1930s and one of his frequent visitors in the postwar years reported a comment (apparently known to many): "The best thing Hitler ever did was to exterminate the Jews." I don't know if the rabbi's son, Jacob Taubes, was aware of Schmitt's infamous declaration, but he couldn't ignore the man's virulent and open anti-Semitism during the Nazi years. Such trifles didn't deter Taubes, nor his assistant, Werner Sombart's son, Nikolaus. (The economic historian Werner Sombart was famous for his work on Jews and capitalism, which gave the Nazis some of their ideas in this domain.) They stoked the Schmitt enthusiasm in their highly successful seminar at the Free University.

Why did I attend a few sessions? I wasn't particularly interested in Schmitt as such, but my steady interest in the evolution of German attitudes to the Third Reich must have given me the idea that the students' reactions would be meaningful in that regard. That is how I explained it at the time, in a letter to Ellen Kennedy, a professor of political science at the University of Pennsylvania: "I am very interested in the Carl Schmitt reception in Germany today. It links up, in my opinion, with many other discrete phenomena which possibly are not without significance."

Throngs of students filled the seminar room, but their comments enlightened me less than Taubes's and Sombart's pontificating, a somewhat bizarre spectacle. The following year Schmitt died and Taubes wrote an eloquent necrology for the *Frankfurter Allgemeine Zeitung*. It was this mixture of contradictory traits that ultimately gave a distinct flavor to Taubes's personality. Incidentally, my friend Uri Tal (Taubes) was a cousin of his.

Sometime during the early days of my stay, Amos Elon came by and suggested we cross to the East to see a performance of Bertolt Brecht and Kurt Weill's *Mahagonny*. We were allowed through at Checkpoint Charlie; our Israeli passports led to a very thorough search and multiple phone calls before we got the clearance. The performance was impressive; the aftermath, less so. We decided to have a bite — for the sake of experience — at some restaurant close to the theater. To this day, I remember the utterly depressing atmosphere of this "restaurant," more like a cafeteria in Israel's austerity days in the early fifties. I don't think that anybody watched us, although Amos was in touch with political figures on both sides and wrote about Germany and Berlin. When we had crossed back, I felt relief.

I tried to invite some East German intellectuals to the conference I was preparing but without success, although the collapse of the regime was close. I remember in particular the exchange of letters with a writer whose books I much admired, particularly her *Patterns of Childhood* (*Kindheitsmuster*): Christa Wolf. From her answer to the invitation, I clearly understood that she would have liked to participate but was not permitted to. She conveyed this in a veiled language, but to me the meaning was clear enough. A few years later, as Wolf spent some time in Los Angeles, she confirmed it.

From the outset, Wapnewski liked the idea of a conference on the German memory of the Shoah and agreed to finance the costs and host the meeting at the Kolleg.


The conference that took place in mid-February 1986 gathered historians who were or had been fellows at the Kolleg and some others (Heinrich A. Winkler, Wolfgang Schieder, Hans Mommsen, Rudolf Vierhaus, Lutz Niethammer), a psychologist from Goettingen, and the major German philosopher and public intellectual Jürgen Habermas. My Tel Aviv and UCLA friend Amos Funkenstein, to whom I shall return, attended and so did a very remarkable historian and political scientist whom I had met shortly beforehand and who remains a friend to this day: Dan Diner. During the discussions, the hall was packed with fellows and guests.

An intrinsically elusive, though decisive, issue kept coming back: What did Germans know of the extermination as it was happening? Two entirely opposite answers emerged. A professor of philosophy at the Free University, Margarethe von Brentano, declared without hesitation that she, a student in Munich during the war and other students like her, knew at the time that the Jews were being exterminated. To this unambiguous statement, Wapnewski objected strenuously: "I was a soldier on the Eastern Front for three years and throughout this entire period I didn't hear anything regarding the fate of the Jews." He then added a troubling detail: "The only comment about the Jews came with the distribution of some greenish and quite disgusting soap that was soon called *Judenseife* (Jew soap). Why? I didn't know." Could it be that Wapnewski had never heard the widespread rumor that the fat of killed Jews was used to manufacture soap? Could it be that he never wondered or asked why the disgusting soap was given such a weird designation?

Today we know that a majority of adult Germans were aware of the extermination by mid-1943 at the latest. A flood of information came back to the Reich from the East in letters sent by thousands and thousands of soldiers, Nazi officials of all ranks, camp guards, and even journalists; what letters had not done, home leave did. Moreover, throughout 1942, Hitler alluded to the extermination in no less than five speeches; his hints were clearly interpreted by the Nazi press, while the Gestapo was attempting to squash the "rumors." Incidentally, a widespread reaction to the Allied bombings throughout Germany, as reported in the public opinion surveys of the SS Security Service, was the best proof of common knowledge: "the bombings are a retaliation for what we did to the Jews." Either Wapnewski had forgotten all of that or he had opted for silence.

The conference was a success and I was quite proud of it. My stay in Berlin would have ended on a high note had it ended right then, but two or three weeks remained . . .

## 2

I met Ernst Nolte during one of his frequent visits to the Kolleg. I had read his early work, *The Three Faces of Fascism*, a highly original, albeit controversial, book that I assigned in my Geneva courses in the 1970s, without seeing in it the extreme theses that my friend George Mosse had criticized in a sharp review.

I didn't read Nolte's further publications, except for an article entitled "The Third Reich Seen from the Perspective of the 1980s" that had been published at the beginning of 1985 in a collective volume edited by one H. W. Koch, in England. The article was shocking in many ways, as it peddled some of the common apologetic arguments about Nazi Germany and the extermination of the Jews. Why, notwithstanding my hypersensitivity on this issue, did I consider this piece as some kind of passing aberration, I don't know. When Nolte invited me to give a lecture in his seminar at the Free University, I accepted.

The lecture took place in a friendly atmosphere, so that I saw no reason, somewhat later, to find an excuse for refusing another invitation, this time to a family dinner. Peter Demetz, a professor of German literature from Yale and a fellow at the Kolleg, was also invited. Alexander and Gesinne Schwan, two political scientists from the Free University, completed the group of guests.

The evening started pleasantly and the conversation focused on the hot topic of the day: a corruption scandal in the granting of building permits that involved members of the Berlin Senate.

As we sat down for dinner, I felt almost completely at ease: the article in Koch's volume was probably an aberration indeed. Soup was served, and in the momentary silence, Nolte turned to me.

"Herr Friedländer, what is it actually to be a Jew? Is it a matter of religion or of biology?"

I sensed early signs of danger and tried to defuse them by mentioning Ben-Gurion's decision, soon after the establishment of Israel, to ask some thirty Jewish scholars how they would define Jewishness; he received thirty different answers and decided to keep them under lock and key.

Nolte was not so easily put off and repeated his question. I then told him, still in as much of a matter-of-fact way as I could, that the Knesset had debated the issue and, in order to assuage the religious parties, members of the governing coalition, had accepted the traditional religious definition: whoever is born of a Jewish mother is a Jew.

"Then," said Nolte, "it is ultimately a matter of biology."

"Not really. Anybody can convert to Judaism and become a full-fledged Jew."

The silence that had descended on the dining room did not last long.

"Herr Friedländer, you cannot deny that there is something like world Jewry [*Weltjudentum*]."

"How so?"

"Well, isn't there a World Jewish Congress?"

I tried to explain why and when the World Jewish Congress had been established. It didn't help; nor did the fact that I had been secretary to the president of the World Jewish Congress bolster my authority. The sniping continued.

"Didn't Weizmann declare, in September 1939, that world Jewry would fight on the side of Great Britain against Germany?"

"Herr Nolte, I hoped that you wouldn't bring up the weird arguments that you presented in your article of last year. Indeed, Weizmann declared that Jews would fight against Nazi Germany. Not that this Zionist leader in any way represented Jews of different countries, but given the way the Third Reich was hounding the Jews and given the nature of the regime, he assumed quite rightly that Jews, wherever they lived, would be on the side of Great Britain."

"But, Herr Friedländer, didn't it mean that World Jewry was thereby at war with Germany and thus that Hitler could consider the Jews as enemies and intern them in concentration camps as prisoners of war, as the Americans did with the Japanese?"

So it went. Everybody was silent around us. Nolte was red in the face and I was pale, or perhaps it was the other way around. The soup was cold. My host carefully added, "Concentration camps, not extermination camps." The entire situation was becoming unbearable, but Nolte was far from done.

"Did you know, Herr Friedländer, that Kurt Tucholsky wrote in the 1920s that he wished the German bourgeoisie would die from gas?"

"Herr Nolte, where do you read such insanities?"

"I find them, for example, in Wilhelm Stäglich's *Der Auschwitz Mythos* [The Auschwitz Myth]."

"You use neo-Nazi literature as your source?"

"Of course. I find in it many unknown facts; then I go back to the references and check whether the facts are correct. Soon I shall bring out a book where many things, unsaid up to now, will come to light."

"What you have 'discovered,' in a nutshell, is that soon after Adolf Hitler stated in *Mein Kampf*, 'Had some tens of thousands of Hebrews died by gas, the war would have turned out differently,' the Jew Tucholsky was wishing a similar fate to the German bourgeoisie."

"That is correct."

For me, this was it. I got up and asked for a taxi. Demetz got up with me; the Schwans remained. At the door, I told Nolte that where I came from, one did not invite people for dinner in order to insult them. In the taxi, I asked Demetz whether the Tucholsky quote was correct. "In part," he said, "but entirely out of context." Tucholsky, a converted Jew and a brilliant satirist of German society, was a staunch left-wing pacifist. When, under national conservative pressure, the Reichstag, in the late 1920s, started debating the building of a cruiser for the German navy, a furious Tucholsky addressed the German nationalist middle class: "If you want war again, you will have it and die by gas" (as so many soldiers did during the Great War).

As we were being driven back to our homes, I physically trembled. The trembling subsided eventually but sharp anxiety — of the kind I had not experienced since the early Geneva days — kept me miserably awake throughout the night. I wished for one thing only: to leave Berlin and Germany as quickly as I could. But this was far from the end.

During the last days of the stay, *Die Zeit* asked me about my Berlin experience. The interview lasted for two hours or more; the journalist turned it into a short excerpt of tidbits that were not inaccurate, but entirely out of context. In my conversation with him I mentioned all the good things I had experienced, my impressions of the Kolleg, the city, the conference, its theme and the discussions that took place; none of this was published. I also mentioned some of the views a well-known historian was peddling around (I didn't indicate a name but quickly after publication, Nolte announced that he was the unnamed historian). Finally, I alluded to the dissonance between my perception of some sites or situations and that of truly excellent people who simply did not share my specific sensitivity or historical awareness, again without any attribution. What I referred to was the following incident.

A few days after the Nolte evening, I was invited for dinner at the Lepenieses' (Wolf and his wife Annette), together with Wapnewski, his wife Gabrielle, and Nike Wagner. I should mention here that at the end of the conference, Lepenies's words to me were particularly warm and kind. The dinner was very pleasant: excellent food, splendid wine, and lively conversation. I surely had nothing to complain about and was merely slightly astonished by the fact that the host served an outstanding 1943 white wine as aperitif and that, toward the end of the dinner, for whatever reason, Wapnewski started quoting the words and humming the tune of an apparently well-known hit of the 1970s, "*Theo, wir fahr'n nach Lodz* . . ." (Theo, we travel to Lodz . . .). On the spot, I merely wondered about the fact that both the 1943 wine and traveling to Lodz from Grunewald (where we were) didn't ring a bell, except for me. I didn't say a word, as it would have ruined an evening that, by itself, was very enjoyable and that the hosts meant to be so.

The episode, as minute as it was, continued to bother me, and whereas I assumed that traveling to Lodz couldn't mean a thing for anybody except me, serving a 1943 wine could have been avoided. But then, I thought, how remarkable it was that "we" and "they" — the best among them — still have such different perceptions of dates, sites, events, or such different memories of them. That was all, nothing much in fact.

I take full responsibility for the two missteps that followed and, although I have mulled over all of this again and again for years, my only excuse is my own oversensitivity, probably aggravated by Nolte. First, I confided in a couple, among the fellows, who had become good friends; I told them about the evening and added how baffled I remained by the difference of perception between Jews and Germans over those years. Then — and this was my most egregious blunder — I repeated these remarks in the lengthy interview I gave to the *Die Zeit* journalist, naturally without mentioning any names. Unfortunately, this became one of his choice tidbits. A few days later, in early March 1986, I left Berlin.

Sometime in May, I met an acquaintance in Geneva who told me that he had just read an interview I had given to *Die Zeit* during my stay in Berlin. A glance at the paper sufficed to make me cringe. The article was a caricature of the interview, and I immediately sensed the turmoil it would cause if people at the Kolleg were to discover the identity of the hosts. Too late: the "culprits" were identified and all hell broke loose.

I wrote desperate letters to Wapnewski and to Lepenies to explain what I meant and to repeat that I felt only friendship toward them and deep contrition for any offense I could have caused. I was called a liar, among other things, one who had invented facts and so on. It stuck with some of the fellows, at least for a while.

After a while, Wapnewski turned around and sent me a conciliatory letter; it took longer for Lepenies to let go (in the meantime he succeeded Wapnewski as rector of the Kolleg), but some years later our relations became friendly again and he introduced me very warmly when I came to Berlin to present the first volume of *Nazi Germany and the Jews*, in 1996. That is why I hesitated for so long over whether to mention this unfortunate event here. As already said, thirty years will have gone by if and when the memoir is published. In any case, the responsibility for this entire incident is mine.

For me, at the time, this episode became an ongoing torture: how could I have wronged my German hosts, people that I liked and respected, in such a dumb way? Couldn't I keep my feelings to myself and hold my mouth shut? It took about three years, the move to Los Angeles, and an intervening series of new problems to partly (only partly) lessen the brooding about my final days at the Kolleg.

The Nolte story was different: it had a public and resounding afterlife.

## *3*

In *Antwort an meine Kritiker* [Answer to my Critics], Nolte accuses me of starting the "historians' controversy." This wasn't the case. Nolte was disinvited from a German intellectuals' debate about to take place in Frankfurt in the spring of 1986, once the text of the speech he was about to give there became known. It included some of the items he had served me (the speech was probably circulated among the participants). No sooner had Nolte been disinvited than the *Frankfurter Allgemeine Zeitung* published his speech. The controversy started.

In the articles and books he brought out then and later, Nolte shifted the debate to what indeed became his main mantra over the years: the comparability between Bolshevism and Nazism. The additional twist he concocted was the historical priority of Bolshevik exterminations: the Gulag, according to Nolte's notorious formula, was "the original," whereas Auschwitz was "the copy." Later, in his *Der europäische Bürgerkrieg* (The European Civil War), he came to portray Hitler as the protector of the European bourgeoisie against the threat represented by Bolshevism. The question of course arises: Why exterminate the Jews to protect the European bourgeoisie against Bolshevism? The answer had been offered by Nazi propaganda from the outset: the Jews were the initiators and the carriers of Bolshevism. Nolte, however, was careful enough not to use this argument.

Whereas the comparability or noncomparability of the Nazi and Bolshevik exterminations became the quintessential issue in the "historians' controversy," what I had been served at the dinner was something quite different: provocative questions about the Jews as such and about issues relating to them. Bolshevism was not even mentioned. As the anti-Jewish dimension of our discussion was not known, it became only implicitly apparent in Nolte's Nazism versus Bolshevism arguments. The controversy ultimately became an internal political confrontation between left-leaning German intellectuals and conservative ones, dressed up as a scholarly historical debate, during a brief period just preceding the unification of Germany.

It started slowly. Over the spring of 1986, no large-scale response to Nolte's article appeared: with a few exceptions such as Heinrich Winkler, left-liberal historians were mute, while Nolte garnered quite vocal support from the conservative side. Finally, in July, *Die Zeit* published Jürgen Habermas's counterblast under the title "Eine Art Schadensabwicklung" ("A Kind of Settlement of Damages"). I was in Geneva when Habermas's article appeared; for me, reading and rereading it was an immense relief, although my other Berlin problems continued to weigh on me more than ever. Habermas's voice represented a clarion call, soon followed by those of liberal German historians suddenly intervening — and massively so. By the end of 1986, the "historians' controversy" was calming down, although to this day it still flickers on, mainly in Europe.

*4*

My Berlin experience had a profound impact on the further course of my life. In the next chapter I will tell why at first I refused the appointment to the Chair in the History of the Holocaust at UCLA after teaching there for a semester in 1982–83. But in 1986, following Berlin, I had no hesitation anymore.

I wrote to the UCLA dean of humanities that, after thinking it over, I was interested in the position. In early 1987, I was invited for a "job talk" and, following the ritual meetings and quizzes, plus the necessary confirmations at all levels of the University of California system, I was appointed as the first permanent incumbent of the UCLA "1939 Club" Chair in the History of the Holocaust.

My German concerns were far from over. During my stay at the Kolleg, I had read an article that Martin Broszat had published in the highbrow monthly *Merkur*; its title: "Ein Plädoyer für die Historisierung des Nationalsozialismus" (A Plea for the Historicization of National Socialism); its date of publication: May 1985. In short, it belonged to the salvo of books and articles demanding

a change of approach to the historical representation and interpretation of the Third Reich, forty years after its demise.

In concrete terms, Broszat pleaded for a cancellation of the
limitations imposed by the dates 1933 and 1945 on German history and a reinsertion of those twelve years within the wider
framework of German economic and social developments in the
twentieth century; in short, he pleaded for a distinction between
the initiatives taken by the Nazi leadership of the Reich and the
everyday life of the immense majority of Germans, practically
untouched, according to him, by Nazi ideology and propaganda.
This looked like Edgar Reitz's *Heimat* on a historiographical
level, and it was, most probably, the perception many Germans
still had of their recent history, forty years after the fall of the
Reich. The word "Auschwitz" did not appear in Broszat's essay,
nor did any reference to Nazi crimes as a dimension to be "his-
toricized," given that Broszat implicitly considered them as
belonging to the thin political layer at the top.

I didn't like Broszat's "Plea" and responded in a lecture at
the University of Essen, upon Dan Diner's invitation. The lecture was published in German and English. It came to Broszat's
attention. He felt challenged and suggested an exchange of letters between us — three letters each — that would be published
in the periodical of Munich's Institute of Contemporary History,
*Vierteljahrshefte für Zeitgeschichte* (Quarterly Journal of Contemporary History), the most widely read professional publication
by historians of the Third Reich. I accepted.

As far as I could judge, Broszat allowed the subtext of his
position to emerge toward the end of his first letter (he started the
exchange and I would end it): the memory that the victims (the
Jews) and their descendants kept of the Third Reich demanded
respect, he wrote, and could eventually contribute to our

understanding; yet, it was a "mythical memory" that constituted a "coarsening [*vergröbend*] obstacle for a more rational German historiography." This was, in its very bluntness, an astonishing statement. Broszat considered the subjectivity of the victims "and of their descendants" — in short of Jews — whenever and wherever they spoke of Nazism, as leading to fictitious renderings of this history. I had no choice but to ask him, in my response, whether he did not think that former members of the Hitler Youth generation (like himself) weren't also carrying a burdened subjectivity in their perception of those years. The exchange was published in early 1988.

As at that same time I had started teaching at UCLA, I invited Broszat — who was on an American lecture tour — to come to Los Angeles and present his ideas to the faculty and the graduate students of the history department. The debate that took place in early 1989 was memorable both on the spot and even more from hindsight: Broszat argued that resistance against an oppression like the Nazi one was impossible and that Germans in their great majority rather opted for *Resistenz* (impermeability, immunity) in the face of the regime's propaganda and ideology; it allowed the bulk of the nation to remain untouched by the regime's blandishments and, until very late, ignorant of its crimes. A few months after Broszat's lecture, the population of East Germany rose against the Communist regime and brought it down.

Later on the day of Broszat's visit, I showed him the craziness of the Venice boardwalk, while his wife and daughter were lured to Disneyland. Our conversation became friendly; he told me about some of his experiences with the right-wing historians of the sixties, such as Gerhard Ritter, and of his worries about the future of the institute. We had found the human level at which much could be understood and taken in stride. A few months later, Broszat died of cancer. I wrote the obituary for *Die Zeit*. Nobody knew then that he had been a Nazi Party member.

My stay in Berlin had convinced me to turn entirely to the history of the Holocaust. The debate with Broszat pointed to some of the questions I needed to deal with. What mattered immediately was getting rid of the feelings of guilt that the incident at the Kolleg had triggered and redirecting my life toward new aims in teaching and writing.

# PART IV

*America*

# CHAPTER THIRTEEN

# A Sense of Exile?

In the summer of 1987, my twenty-six years as student and teacher in Geneva came to an end. I haven't written enough about our everyday life there: the friends we made, the vacations we spent in some of the most beautiful areas in the world, the white Fendant wine and the fondue bourguignonne that I loved, as well as the bistros where you could find the best of both.

When you live long enough in a place like Geneva, you discover hideouts not too far away that are off the tourists' track; thus, sometime in the late 1960s, the two boys, Hagith, and I ventured into the Jura mountains, above Neuchâtel, the Franches-Montagnes, where yet untamed horses roam in freedom and tiny towns surprise you when you follow some valley you had never heard of. That's how we arrived in Sainte-Ursanne, to an inn whose name I forget; there you really ate the best cheese fondue ever, while the house parrot (or was it a blackbird?) whistled the entire march from *The Bridge on the River Kwai*.

Years later, I was driving alone from Geneva to Basel, sometime in the fall. I took a roundabout way via Château d'Oex and Gstaad, and toward evening, as I entered the foothills of the Berner Oberland Alps, the copper, red, and gold of the surrounding forests suddenly overwhelmed me with a sense of exhilaration, while Jessye Norman's magnificent voice in Richard Strauss's *Four Last Songs* merged with the shimmering colors of the landscape. I never forgot that moment of pure bliss.

Thus, after a difficult early period, Geneva had become a haven, a peaceful retreat, despite the usual problems with this or that colleague or this or that doctoral student (in short, the usual vagaries of academic life). Nonetheless, the stay couldn't last once I decided to concentrate on the history of the Holocaust; my teaching had to be as close as possible to the intended writing. Moreover, the institute as such was changing.

Small institutions flourish or wither according to the quality and efficacy of their leadership. Freymond had retired in the late seventies and the directors who succeeded him kept the institute afloat, but did not innovate. I left during that lackluster transition period. A few years later, the institute entered — and radically so — into a remarkable new phase.

The quaint charm of Hautes Études Internationales (or HEI as it was called in short), typified by the villa on the lake, gave way to a "new realism" represented by impressive structures of glass and steel built inland, close to the United Nations. The traditional courses were replaced, in great part, by teaching adapted to the challenges of a global international scene. Under the guidance of my former doctoral student Philippe Burrin, the brilliant historian of "the fascist drift" in France, of *France under the Germans* and *Nazi Anti-Semitism*, the institute rushed into the twenty-first century, while I remained fixated on the first half of the twentieth. In that sense, the appointment at UCLA made things easier.

My first visit to UCLA had taken place over ten years before my definitive appointment. In 1975 or 1976, I had been invited to discuss *History and Psychoanalysis* in the Department of History and *Arabs and Israelis* in Political Science as well as with a Jewish students' organization. On that last occasion, a question came up that had often crossed my mind and bothered me considerably. "Why is it," one of the students asked, "that someone who survived the Shoah as you did, has become so 'dovish' toward the Arabs? Generally, Jews who survived the Shoah take a hard line about the Israeli-Arab conflict."

It was true, in most cases. And I knew that by teaching, speaking, or writing about the Shoah I was reinforcing the nationalism of those Jews, in Israel or in the Diaspora, whose motto, Never again!, was misused to reject any compromise or, worse, who used the Shoah as a pretext for harsh anti-Palestinian measures. To avoid any misunderstanding, I argued on every possible occasion that the only lesson one could draw from the Shoah was precisely the imperative: stand against injustice, against wanton persecution, against the refusal to recognize the humanity and the rights of "the others."

It is, incidentally, what I declared in the opening lecture I gave to the hundreds of scholars assembled at the Hebrew University for the tenth International Congress of Jewish Studies in August 1989. As I specifically mentioned our attitude to the Palestinians, many silent, angry faces greeted me at the end. A few days later, though, the president of the Congress and preeminent historian of rabbinic thought, Ephraim Urbach, told me of his complete agreement.

In the fall of 1982, I was invited to return to the history department at UCLA to teach for a semester as visiting professor within the framework of the newly established Chair in the History of the Holocaust (no permanent appointment had yet been made). Amos Funkenstein initiated the invitation.

Funkenstein was quite an unusual person: a historian at Tel Aviv University and UCLA, a philosopher and mathematician, and an erudite interpreter of Jewish thought — in short a polymath par excellence. According to Carlo Ginzburg, a mutual friend, Amos shared a striking resemblance with Franz Kafka; it was so indeed, but you had to imagine Kafka with a permanent cigarette at the corner of his lips, twisting and twirling a nonexistent sidelock when deep in thought (the remnant of an Orthodox childhood) and springing into action after any public lecture to ask a first question that would often put the lecturer in some difficulty.

Amos shared my thinking about the political situation in Israel; like Uri Tal, he was more blunt than I in his use of historical comparisons. Thus, in an interview in *Haaretz*, he compared our way of treating the Palestinians to Nazi policies against the Jews in the thirties. I didn't agree with the comparison, as I knew that "Nazi" immediately evoked "extermination" for most readers, who saw no difference between Nazi persecution of the Jews in the 1930s and Nazi extermination policies in the 1940s.

This first extended stay in Los Angeles left a mixed impression. I migrated from one noisy apartment to the next. I even landed once in a building mostly occupied by undergraduates; I learned what partying meant, soundwise. A few weeks after my arrival, I finally discovered a quiet abode in a hotel on Wilshire Boulevard renting apartments by the week, the month, or the year. The weather was mild, most colleagues friendly and welcoming, students — serious enough.

Yet, facing a large class of undergraduates, I soon understood that I belonged to another world. When I made a joke, nobody laughed; sometimes, as I spoke seriously, everybody burst out laughing. Our associations were thoroughly different; or was it my accent that at times they considered funny? All in all, however, we got along well. Nonetheless, although I liked UCLA and the Department of History, I didn't accept the offer to become the permanent incumbent of the Holocaust history chair, preferring to return to Tel Aviv and Geneva. As I told, the stay in Berlin changed all that.

The mildly negative impression that I had kept of Los Angeles turned into culture shock once I realized, in early 1988, that I had arrived for good, for over half a year every year. As I write this, I am reminded of my friend George Mosse, an heir to the Berlin German-Jewish media empire Mosse-Ullstein, who managed to flee the Reich in 1933, telling in his memoirs of his reaction when, on his way to teach at the University of Iowa, his first appointment, he descended from the bus onto the main street of Iowa City: he started crying.

Well, I didn't cry, but I seriously wondered whether I hadn't made a bad mistake. Regarding the work to which I wanted to devote the following years, I was in the right place; but would I be able to live in that place? For a while I considered the possibility of leaving. I confided in the new chair of the department, the outstanding scholar and unerringly elegant American historian Joyce Appleby. Although she had come to L.A. from nearby San Diego, she told me that at the beginninng she had felt the same way, which meant that I was not the first to face that quandary. I decided that the task ahead was both a scholarly and a moral obligation: it helped me to adapt.

UCLA, a splendid institution, was (and remains) an enclave in an urban immensity that does not reject it, but celebrates very different gods, notwithstanding the links between the university and the city kept by former graduates, sporting events, the film school, the Medical Center, and well-known artistic programs.

The L.A. campus is a small town in and of itself whose students, faculty, and staff number about fifty thousand people; in terms of the architecture of buildings and the layout of gardens, the harmony of the whole is striking; it is possibly the most impressive of the University of California's ten campuses. As for the Department of History, it was and remains probably one of the largest such departments in the country. Depending on who heads it, keeping this vast medley of historical fields coherently and creatively together is not always successful; I have experienced the best and the worst.

In principle, my chair was part of Jewish history, but in fact I was almost entirely independent and could craft the curriculum as I wished, without having to watch left and right whether I trod on anybody's toes. At the outset, however, difficulties arose from an unexpected direction: my sponsors.

The "Holocaust chair," as it was called, had been endowed by members of the "1939 Club" of Los Angeles. Most of the original members of that group were Polish Jews who had spent the war in ghettos, camps, forced labor details, and the like; they had seen it all before reaching the States in the late forties or early fifties. They endowed the chair in the mid-seventies to counter the spread of Holocaust denial, particularly in California.

The core members of the club were activists and wanted the chair incumbent to "show results," like inviting President von Weizsäcker for a lecture or some such event. It took time to convince them that my role was to teach, to foster research, to spread knowledge, and not to cater to "events." In short, for a few years my sponsors wanted to have a say in the way the chair incumbent was fulfilling his task; they tried to convince the dean of humanities to establish a supervising committee that would guide me. After these rocky beginnings, they came to rely on the way I handled my duties. These were good people, devoted to a worthy goal; they annoyed me at times but I liked them.

As I am writing, I have been living longer in Los Angeles than in any other city in the world, and I have taught here longer than anywhere else. There is some logic in my having ultimately landed in the simulacrum of a real place, in a city that, despite countless areas of natural beauty, (almost) everlasting spring weather, and the magnificent ocean coast, does not touch you, take hold of you, doesn't make you sigh ecstatically, even for a brief moment. You know the song "I left my heart in San Francisco"; I hardly can imagine anybody singing, "I left my heart in Los Angeles." It may be the same in Kansas City, St. Louis, or, for that matter, Iowa City.

Can all of this be compensated by the sense of freedom you get in this vast anonymity, by living your life, teaching your classes, and writing your books while geographically away from a constant reminder of the past? During the early years, I wasn't convinced.

What I just wrote about the reminder of the past may appear contradictory. On the one hand, I left Geneva to devote more time to writing and teaching the history of the Holocaust, while on the other hand I found a saving grace in Los Angeles in the relative absence of that past in the environment and common discourse.

My reasoning may have been tortuous, but it followed some logic nonetheless. Staying in Geneva was no longer a viable option. I could have chosen to remain in Tel Aviv, but even there, a regular course on the Holocaust may have encountered difficulties, as it was already being taught in the Jewish history department. And I simply cringed at the idea of regularly teaching a subject that carried the possibility of political exploitation, particularly by the nationalist right that I abhorred. Finally, being only in Tel Aviv was difficult, as usual: I had to have an exit strategy. Thus for the following ten years, I divided my time between Tel Aviv and Los Angeles before moving exclusively to L.A. when mandatory retirement from Tel Aviv became imminent.

During the earliest phase of my stay, I was mostly alone, as Hagith had to take care of an ailing father. From the second or third year on, she would stay in L.A. for three months at a time. We rented a town house in Santa Monica and usually managed to sublet it when both of us were back in Israel.

*Santa Monica, April 1992.* We turned on the television for the evening news, while awaiting the arrival of some friends for dinner. We watched some scuffles next to a van that had stopped in the middle of a street in what appeared to be a predominantly African-American neighborhood. Our friends arrived, and within minutes we were all glued to the TV screen: the L.A. riots had started as a reaction to the acquittal of the four policemen responsible for viciously beating an African-American, Rodney King, following a high-speed freeway chase.

I don't remember whether it was on that first night or later on that houses were set on fire and wide-scale looting began. You saw it all live as it happened, and yet, for us, this dramatic outburst of violence appeared unreal, as if occurring on another planet. There was no contact, no proximity (geographically and socially) between Santa Monica and South Central L.A.: these two worlds simply never met, which, obviously, was at the heart of the problem. On my first stay in the States, in 1957, I skimmed through Gunnar Myrdal's *An American Dilemma*; it carried a pessimistic view of the evolution of race relations in the United States. As seen from the perspective of the 1992 riots, it was still to the point. Immense progress had been made since the fifties and yet, deep down, a chasm remained and remains between both worlds.

2

I hadn't personally met one of the most brilliant advocates of the Palestinian cause, the Palestinian-American professor of English literature at Columbia, excellent music critic, and fiery public intellectual, Edward Said, before our UCLA encounter in early 1994. We had participated in a written exchange in a French periodical a few years beforehand and even earlier Said had written a moderate review of *Arabs and Israelis* (although positive only regarding Mahmud Hussein and negative as far as I was concerned). The Center of Comparative History and Social Theory had organized a debate between the two of us. The organizers were well-known Marxist historians, Robert Brenner and Perry Anderson.

The debate took place in the euphoric atmosphere following the 1993 Oslo agreements and in the perspective of peace between Israel and the Palestinians on the basis of a two-state solution to the conflict. Said was a great debater, I still had some energy left, the personal contact between us was good, and a very attentive audience packed Royce Hall. It is then, however, that I noticed what had already been told to me previously about Said's position: he rejected the two-state solution and advocated a general "right of return" of Palestinian refugees to what was now Israel; it meant the extinction of Israel and the emergence of a binational state as the only possible outcome. To me this was completely unrealistic; thus, notwithstanding the friendly rapport, we fundamentally disagreed.

As time went by, post-Oslo euphoria gave way to increasing pessimism among the moderate Israeli left, which had pinned its hopes on the feasibility of the two-state solution. Pessimism was capped by tragedy when, on November 5, 1995, a right-wing religious fanatic assassinated Itzhak Rabin, the prime minister who could have convinced the majority of the population to accept some difficult decisions for the sake of peace. His successors, including Shimon Peres and Ehud Barak, did not inspire the same trust. Furthermore, when Barak took the huge risk of agreeing to almost all of the Palestinian demands in exchange for peace and was rebuffed by Yasser Arafat at Camp David in July 2000, the belief spread among Israelis that there was no partner on the other side.

I should have previously mentioned that when the Gulf War started in early 1991 and Saddam Hussein's Scud missiles were launched at Israeli cities, I decided to skip a week at UCLA and fly back to Israel. It was a gut reaction, an imperative expression of solidarity, although the danger was minimal and the missiles did not hit any of their intended targets. Some Scuds were shot down by batteries of Patriot antimissile missiles that the Americans had transferred to Israel, others fell into the sea or in uninhabited areas, and a few hit houses in Ramat Gan, a city bordering Tel Aviv, but, rather miraculously, without directly killing anybody. Nonetheless, people were frightened and when sirens announced an oncoming Scud, many took refuge in sealed rooms and put on gas masks (the assumption being that some of the Scuds may have been carrying gas-filled warheads, which they were not). A few persons died of heart attacks, others left Tel Aviv for safer areas, particularly in Europe.

Israel did not react, to avoid hampering the Arab anti-Saddam coalition set up by the United States. In the Palestinian territories, the population cheered the Scuds and celebrated the destruction of the Jewish state.

Within days, I was back in L.A. Yet, for my leftist colleagues, rushing to Israel meant that I was not on their side of the barricade. Nonetheless, I was asked to debate Said three years later. Over the following years, however, the hostility toward Israel that spread among some faculty members became painful to watch. Edward Said came again and his speech was much more aggressive than the first time. It was enthusiastically greeted. I did not attend.

## 3

*January 1993.* I had just returned to L.A. from my semester in Tel Aviv. It was the first Saturday of the month and within four days my lecture course would start. The weather was mild, I was in good spirits and decided to drive from Santa Monica to Westwood, the area surrounding UCLA, to park there and walk the rest of the way to the research library. I didn't get very far. As I was crossing Gayley Avenue, a car that had begun a left turn ahead of the green arrow hit me hard enough to propel me a few meters away. I didn't lose consciousness, but remained sitting in the midst of the street while the female driver stood next to me, howling, "Oh my God, what did I do, what did I do!" Within minutes I was at the UCLA hospital emergency room, diagnosed with a fractured kneecap but without a brain concussion. This was the good news.

The cardiologist who saw me before the knee operation (as my file indicated heart problems) gave me the bad news: it was high time for open-heart surgery to replace an aortic valve, defective from birth, which had substantially deteriorated. The surgery was scheduled for late April, once my knee would allow me to stand up and even walk around on crutches.

Strangely enough, I remained rather indifferent to this fourth major surgery of my life. As I was exchanging jokes with the anesthetist, I heard, "Wake up, Mr. Friedländer, wake up! All went very well." I woke up, and four days later I left the hospital. As I am writing, exactly twenty-two years later, the artificial valve is still nicely clicking and I still swallow a blood-thinning pill every day. As for the knee, the surgeon had warned me that I could get arthritis some twenty years after the operation; he was right, on the dot.

In the early eighties, our two boys were almost on their own, Eli at the Hebrew University and soon at Harvard, David, almost out of Lebanon, on his way to Paris, to Langues Orientales. Only Michal, a teenager by then, was still at home: in a sense she was keeping the family together, as our marriage was slowly flickering out. Soon though, Michal would also be gone, to the army first and then to the New England Conservatory of Music, for a degree in piano performance.

Although Hagith and I traveled together to faraway destinations — Japan, China, Mexico — the lengthy periods we spent separated did not help. And yet we remained married into the early years of the new century. Naturally, Hagith was with me after the car accident and the two surgeries that followed. Later, as I said, she would spend three or four months every year in Los Angeles. We spoke of separation, although then we may not have believed in it.

In the mid-nineties, however, I met Orna Kenan. Orna, still married, was the mother of two teenage boys, Gil and Amir. She was born in Israel — as Hagith had been — and, after years in London, followed by an interlude back in Israel, she had arrived in Los Angeles with her family in the mid-eighties, as her husband had been assigned to the L.A. branch of the commodities company for which he worked. At some stage, Orna resumed the studies she had interrupted for many years: after a stint in English history, she opted for Jewish studies and more specifically for the history of the Holocaust. In 1994 she became my doctoral student and chose to work on the early phase of the Israeli historiography of the Shoah, before the Eichmann trial.

Shortly after we met, I discovered that Orna's marriage was in no better shape than mine; we found each other. It took us years to decide, though, and while Orna's husband asked for a divorce quite some time before I did, I eventually followed. As I am writing this, more than twenty years have gone by since I met Orna.

During the emotional roller coaster of the nineties and the early years of the new millennium, work went on, more focused now on the major project I had planned after Berlin and Broszat. At the outset of that period, however, I took it upon myself to convene a conference that would have its intellectual significance as far as I was concerned — and possibly for some others as well.

My initiative came on the spur of the moment and was triggered by a debate involving two main protagonists: Carlo Ginzburg and Hayden White.

Carlo had joined the Department of History at UCLA more or less at the time I did, and like me, he spent a few months every year teaching at another university, in his case in Bologna. To historians, Carlo's name is familiar: he's the founder of "microhistory," and his early book *The Cheese and the Worms* remains a classic. His erudition was (and is) formidable and his mind a constant font of new ideas. Add to it an exuberant and highly engaging personality and lectures that were (and are) intellectual adventures, with unexpected twists and turns, leaving the audience pondering many riddles. He and I, and his wife Luisa, became friends.

Our friendship was strengthened by the fact that, albeit unbeknownst to me for quite some time, he had found a copy of *When Memory Comes*, liked it, and passed it on to his mother, the well-known Italian novelist Natalia Ginzburg. (I had read two of her autobiographical books, *Tutti i nostri ieri* [*All Our Yesterdays*] and *Lessico famigliare* [*Family Sayings*].) She translated my memoir into Italian. This touched me deeply. We twice agreed to meet and twice it became impossible. The first time, as I was in Rome for a short visit, a meeting of the Council of Europe close to where she lived set the area out of bounds for two days or so. Alas, the second time Carlo informed me that his mother had been hospitalized for what was to be a terminal illness.

I keep a handwritten letter from Natalia Ginzburg asking for some explanations about this or that tiny detail in my book; it is also an answer to a letter of thanks I had written to her. She uses a quaint French that gives her words a particular charm; her letter ends as follows: "I too would be very happy to make your acquaintance. Yet I have the impression of knowing you so well already, through the pages of your book! It is I who thanks you. I hope it is well translated, or at least not too badly. At times it was a little difficult. I think of you with much friendship."

As exuberant and engaging as Carlo could be, he did not hide his feelings when some irritation arose. This is precisely what happened in 1990, on the occasion of Hayden White's lecture on history and fiction (I don't remember the exact title of the lecture). The gist of White's argument was that, necessarily, every historian has to adopt a specific rhetorical mode — a literary category — for his or her narration (tragic, comic, ironic, etc.). The mode thus chosen determines the historian's specific selection of facts and the subsequent narrative ("emplotment") and interpretation. In other words, each historian opts for his or her rhetorical mode and thus for his or her own "objectivity." Ultimately, the generic distinction between history and literature (fiction) disappears. White had been developing his thesis for almost twenty years, since the publication of *Metahistory* in the early seventies; the title of one of his more recent books said it all: *The Content of the Form*. For Carlo, this was too much.

The exchange between Hayden and Carlo, following White's lecture, took epic proportions in front of a mesmerized audience. On the morrow of the confrontation, I asked Hayden whether he would be willing to participate in a conference that would put his ideas to the test in a discussion of the historical representation of Nazism and of the Holocaust (if one pushed his theories to their limit, it would make it difficult to reject the Holocaust deniers' narratives). He agreed, as did Carlo and a phalanx of scholars from various domains. The conference took place in 1991. I introduced it and later edited a volume of the texts entitled *Probing the Limits of Representation: Nazism and the "Final Solution."*

The conference was quite successful by the standards of such events and some of the presentations would be widely quoted over the following years. Yet, on the spot, one "performance" left me amazed, that of Jacques Derrida, the guru of deconstruction. I knew Derrida from his annual seminars at UC Irvine, some of which I attended. They were ritualized occasions: the master preached but mostly listened to the discussions and kept silent, surrounded by the veneration of his disciples. Otherwise, in our frequent conversations over lunch, Derrida behaved like an affable mortal. I invited him to give the keynote lecture at the conference and he accepted.

I assumed that although the lecture was scheduled for a mid-week evening, it would be well attended. I reserved a hall of four hundred seats and at about 8 p.m. went to fetch Derrida at the UCLA Guest House. We walked to the hall, and when we came near, we saw a huge throng of people blocking the entrance, trying to push their way into the packed auditorium. Students were sitting on every possible spot: in the seats, on the floor, in the aisles, on the stage. Unfazed, Derrida reached the podium while the crowd inside and outside fell silent. Without any introduction, he launched directly into a two-hour lecture on a notoriously opaque text on violence that Walter Benjamin had written in the early twenties. Nobody moved, nobody left. The crowd hung on to words that the immense majority certainly did not understand. I had never seen the like of it. Derrida strung interpretation upon interpretation like some venerated rabbi commenting on a particularly difficult Talmudic text to his awestricken followers.

A few years beforehand, Derrida had spent two weeks in Jerusalem. When an interviewer asked him about his background, he answered, *"Je suis juif, probablement"* (I am a Jew, probably). Deconstruction doesn't allow for any certainty.

I started writing *Nazi Germany and the Jews* in 1990 and completed the second volume in 2006. When I happened to mention the project to my colleagues, either one of two reactions was common: "What can be said that isn't already known?" or the slightly derisive "You're biting off more than you can chew." I well remember these remarks, not so much out of annoyance (after all, colleagues are colleagues) as rather because, in my heart of hearts, I shared the same doubts.

The motivation that sustained the project was, as I already mentioned, my recurrent sense of not having fulfilled what I felt as a deep obligation. The immediate triggers were Berlin and Broszat. The appointment to the chair at UCLA offered the "window of opportunity." In short, the very early nineties were indeed the right time (and, objectively, the last possibility) to start.

The conception of the history I was planning had occurred to me long before I seriously undertook to write it. Such a history had to be global and integrated; it had to include and render the intertwined evolution of Nazi policies, of reactions stemming from all European and a few other governments and societies (be they initiatives or abstentions), and, even more so, of Jewish attitudes and reactions, from wherever they came, throughout the entire period. I presented that conception of Holocaust history to the conference that took place in New York in March 1975 in a lecture entitled "Aspects of the Historical Significance of the Holocaust." Then I promptly forgot about the conference and about the idea. The time was not yet ripe.

And yet my teaching and reading over the years had given me detailed knowledge of the evolution of diplomacy and war throughout the Nazi years and, within that overall context, of the changing fate of the Jews of Germany and then of occupied and satellite Europe. *Nazi Anti-Semitism* and the later acceptance and defense of moderate "intentionalism" (as discussed in relation to the Stuttgart conference) familiarized me with minute details of Hitler's brand of anti-Jewish ideology (that I defined as "redemptive anti-Semitism"). The work on the Vatican and debates about Swiss refugee policy during the war following the publication of *When Memory Comes* added to my knowledge of the complex ramifications of diffuse but, more often than not, militant and widespread anti-Semitism in Western society. In short, contentwise, the problems could be overcome. These, however, were but minor difficulties. In any case, I had taken a guarantee against the eventuality that the entire project would never be completed by dividing it into two volumes, beginning with the "years of persecution," which would essentially deal with policies and reactions before the war and would therefore concentrate on Germany, Austria, and, ultimately, Bohemia and Moravia. This was the "easy" part. As for the war period and the Shoah as such, I had only very tentative insights when I started.

Yet even the easy part presented a challenge that would follow me throughout the entire enterprise, to the very last page. Sometime from 1938 on, my narrative met my individual experience and my personal memory: I remembered the monstrous sound of Hitler's threats against Czechoslovakia in his broadcast speeches of September 1938; I remembered the sense of an ending (if I may use the term) of my truncated first school year; the gas masks; the German troops marching along the Vltava, under our windows; and the swastika flag swaying in the breeze above our terrace. I remembered the preparations for departure, our false start toward the Hungarian border, the night train journey through Germany, the German border and customs police, the crossing of the Rhine, the first French uniforms, the arrival in Paris, and on. I remembered the fear, the all-pervasive fear around me, penetrating and cold. I remembered everything.

Memory goaded me on, but at the same time its impact had to be acknowledged. I wasn't writing on the moon; I was a Jew writing the history of his time, of his family, of the Jews of Europe on the eve of their extermination. I had to keep constantly aware of my subjectivity, remain on guard against it as much as possible, and show that even the victims "and their descendants" (to use Broszat's expression) were able to write that history.

I started to write almost at the very time I began teaching at UCLA. In the undergraduate courses, I taught the history I wrote about; it looked simple but was not. From my brief stint in 1982, I knew that Southern California undergraduates knew very little about European history, even if UCLA admitted only the very best that the state's high schools had produced. These students knew many other things but lived, in fact, in an environment that was not historically minded. As long as the majority of my charges were of European Jewish background, some basic facts were vaguely familiar to them, but even that changed by the mid-nineties. The new cohort of Jewish students, by then mainly of Iranian background, did not have grandparents able to share their memories and experiences of the war; at the same time, by the by, the demographic composition of the two-hundred-plus student body in my lecture courses evolved: soon a growing proportion was of Asian, Latin American, or non-Jewish American background. I had to be very careful in not assuming a basic knowledge that indeed wasn't there. But as I was a rather experienced teacher by then, all of that was not the major problem.

The real problem that my teaching entailed was by far more personal. When I discussed the conditions of my appointment, I had asked to teach the undergraduate lecture course every second year only. Even in their simplified form, these lectures did leave a trace. In the lecture hall I avoided any appeal to emotions; it didn't mean, however, that I managed to stay disconnected from what I was explaining, and that took its toll. Unfortunately, I soon discovered that no colleague was ready to alternate with me, and in any case, the only one who would have been capable of doing so (in terms of specific knowledge) was too busy with his own teaching. In short, the department chair had agreed to a request he had not the least intention of fulfilling. Thus, year in, year out, I taught a lecture course that compelled me to give a simplified rendition, and a thoroughly detached one, of events that were far from simple and, as I said, far from leaving me indifferent. Over time, it became quite a burden.

The graduate students, about fifteen to twenty in each seminar, were an entirely different breed, certainly as talented as the best graduates I had had in Geneva, Jerusalem (except for the 1967–68 seminar at the Hebrew University that I described previously), or Tel Aviv. Ironically, one of the most brilliant presentations I remember in a seminar on European intellectuals and fascism was on Carl Schmitt, one of the most contentious on Paul de Man. Almost all these graduates made it to doctorates and many among them advanced well beyond in the academic world.

5

When I think of the early years in Los Angeles, I remember them as somehow wrapped in a thin veil of sadness, as I alluded to at the beginning of this chapter. I felt in exile. But exiled from where and from what? The children came to visit, and I still regularly returned to Israel and had many occasions to stop over in Europe. The sadness probably did not stem from such potentially obvious and definable reasons. It wasn't a mild depression either, although during that period, among other medicines, I moved to daily Zoloft and Klonopin. Yet a sense of exile persisted. I often attempted to grasp its nature, then and later, always in vain. I probably missed a medley of tiny elements that belonged to several worlds and to diverse phases of the farthest past, those early years that Robert Brasillach called *le matin profond* (the deep morning). I had always missed it but the blandness of Los Angeles, its real and symbolic distance from familiar domains of sensibility, and, also, the emotional loneliness that I experienced at that time, created the kind of void that allowed for the rise of a low-grade *tristesse*.

# CHAPTER FOURTEEN

# Dilemmas

*Mid-January 1994.* I was peacefully asleep in the house we had bought just before my surgeries in the posh Bel Air area. It was a very small house, however, on top of the hill, invisible among the estates that define this part of the city.

On that morning I woke up a few minutes before 5 a.m., and while I was wondering about the time, the rumbling of a freight train engulfed the room, the house, everything. Then the world shook and shook hard. I won't go on describing the Northridge earthquake of January 17, 1994, except that the waves in the pool looked threatening and I needed the help of a neighbor to find where and how to shut off the gas. It was a peculiar awakening, a distinct addition to the charm of Los Angeles.

*1*

Notwithstanding the minor (and not so minor) vicissitudes I mentioned, work on volume one of *Nazi Germany and the Jews* was progressing apace. It may be remembered that this first part was relatively easy because of the unity of place (Germany, annexed Austria, and Bohemia-Moravia). It could be dealt with as a single entity in regard to anti-Jewish policies, the attitude of various sectors of the surrounding society, particularly of the German intellectual and spiritual elites, and the reaction of the Jews. Within this context, the creation of a unified narrative was not a major problem.

I took a few months of unpaid leave to plunge into the vast collection of microfilms kept at the Institute of Contemporary History in Munich. I searched for details in various domains and found far more than I could use. Yet, although nothing in this boundless sea of sadism and stupidity jolted me as much as would be the case later on, while working on *The Years of Extermination*, I couldn't help mulling over some marginal yet deeply puzzling issues, like the story of the Jewish *Kulturbund* (Cultural Association), for example.

Jews were not allowed to perform for Germans, nor were they allowed to attend cultural events of any kind, except within the four walls of their own cultural association, the *Kulturbund*. This, you would think, was in line with their segregation, their exclusion from German society. But it was just one facet of an overall policy. Soon the audiences of the *Kulturbund* were forbidden to watch German plays, to have readings of German literature, to listen to German music, and so on. These growing restrictions implied magical thinking: by listening to Mozart or watching a play by Schiller, the Jews were thought to pollute these fonts of German culture. How? Nobody ever explained it, as this was in the realm of sheer voodoo. In my mind, it offers the key to an aspect of the Nazi worldview and practice: the use of bureaucratic measures to enforce magical beliefs.

The first volume of *Nazi Germany and the Jews*, subtitled *The Years of Persecution (1933–1939)*, was published by HarperCollins in early 1997. The reviews were positive and translations followed. The city of Munich awarded me their Geschwister Scholl Prize (the "Siblings Scholl" prize), established to honor the memory of Hans and Sophie Scholl, who, together with other members of the small White Rose group, spread anti-Nazi propaganda in the Bavarian capital in 1942, particularly at the university. They were caught and beheaded in 1943.

2

Although I was intent on avoiding any chore — apart from my teaching and sundry administrative obligations, of course — that would deflect me from concentrating upon the second (and crucial) volume of my project, I had to answer an unexpected invitation. In 1996, I was officially asked in the name of the Swiss *Conseil fédéral* (the Swiss government) to become a member of the Independent International Experts Commission established upon the recommendation of the Swiss parliament to investigate the relations between Switzerland and Nazi Germany, particularly during the war. I would be the Israeli historian, along with eight colleagues from Switzerland, the United States, and Poland. The president of the commission was the Swiss economic historian Jean-François Bergier, who was the editor of the *Revue Suisse d'Histoire* in 1963, when they accepted my first strictly scholarly article.

The commission was established in a contentious atmosphere. For several years, Jewish institutions — particularly the World Jewish Congress — were demanding an inquiry into the handling by most Swiss banks of dormant accounts that had belonged to Jews exterminated during the Holocaust; the banks used all available means to avoid restitution of that money to the murdered Jews' legal heirs. The pressure on the banks escalated in the mid-1990s when U.S. officials — mainly in New York — threatened to limit the American activities of Swiss financial institutions that opposed the inquiry. The banks had no choice but to accept the investigation by a commission presided over by Paul Volcker, a highly respected former chairman of the Federal Reserve Board. As I remember him, Volcker had a no-nonsense approach, yet eased by a very friendly personality.

As a necessary sequel, the Swiss parliament, followed by the government, decided to establish the independent historians' commission to shed light on the overall network of relations between the confederation and the Third Reich. All relevant archives would be opened and no interference with the work of the commission permitted.

A substantial budget allowed for the hiring of excellent researchers in a wide variety of domains ranging from refugee policies to gold transactions, from the deals of Swiss insurance companies in Germany to the sale of weapons to the Reich. The atmosphere within the commission and among the researchers was convivial and essentially nonpolitical; its work, however, encountered suspicion and hostility from influential segments of Swiss society, be they politicians, historians, journalists, or the wider public. Thus, the most influential Swiss newspaper, the *Neue Zürcher Zeitung*, was mostly critical whenever the commission published any of its findings.

One of the most sensitive issues, partly within the commission but mainly in terms of outside reactions, was the Swiss wartime refugee policy. The subject touched me directly, and that did not escape the attention of the external censors. At some stage, after the commission had left me out from the initial comments to the press, at the presentation of the report on the refugees, my relations with my Swiss colleagues underwent a (brief) crisis; I considered the possibility of resigning. The internal issue was cleared up, but in the meantime, Gian Trepp, a journalist of the leftist *Wochenzeitung* (*WoZ*), accused me of exercising some kind of "sinister" influence on the work of the commission, particularly regarding the report on the refugees.

The anti-Semitic measures taken by the Swiss authorities from 1938 on were notorious (the Swiss demanded that Nazi Germany stamp all Jewish passports with a red *J*, which allowed the border police to refuse entry to Jews fleeing the Reich, mainly after the annexation of Austria). It is the number of Jews sent back at the border from mid-1942, when the major deportations to the extermination camps started (the Swiss government knew of the exterminations), that caused intense controversy. While the commission reached the conclusion that over twenty thousand Jews had been driven back, its critics brandished outlandish calculations to "prove" that the number was much lower.

Another issue threw a particularly lurid glare on the confederation's wartime behavior: its banks' — particularly its Central Bank's — gold transactions with the Reich's Central Bank. The Swiss bought considerable amounts of German gold, thus allowing the Reich to use vast sums in Swiss francs to acquire raw materials and other essential goods. Thereby, not only did the Swiss significantly help the German war effort, but in buying German gold they knew that they were acquiring gold looted from the central banks of occupied countries and probably ingots smelted from gold teeth, wedding rings, and other personal possessions of Germany's murdered victims.

Bergier became the main target of vicious attacks, mainly once our final report was published. He was an utterly honest scholar and, not being a specialist of twentieth-century European history and even less so of the Third Reich, he may have been taken aback by some of the information uncovered by the commission. Yet, although he was a Swiss patriot of the traditional mold, he never made the least attempt to influence the publication of the commission's findings. He stood behind the report and the accompanying monographs, although some of it may have wounded his feelings. In a way, he was too sensitive for the job, and I know that he suffered considerably from the hostility he encountered. For many a Swiss conservative nationalist, Bergier was a traitor. He wrote me a very touching letter a few years after the end of our task and I planned to visit him on a forthcoming trip to Europe. He died quite suddenly of cancer in October 2009, before I had a chance to meet him again.

I often think of Bergier's death. And, although our friendship was merely professional, I remember him with emotion, possibly because he was treated so unjustly. Other members of our commission are not alive anymore: Sybil Milton, a font of knowledge about the Shoah and the Nazi persecution and extermination of the Sinti and Roma; and Wladyslaw Bartoszewski, one of those heroic Poles who actively helped Jews during the war, at the risk of his life, and who later supported the change of regime, becoming a highly respected public personality (for a time the foreign minister of Poland).

3

I hate to admit that even before I was done with the Swiss commission, I accepted another invitation of the same kind, this time to chair a commission set up to investigate the history of the Bertelsmann publishing company during the Third Reich. Why did I accept? I trusted — correctly — that as in the case of the Swiss commission, I would be able to pursue my work on volume two and get a better insight into the business world of the Third Reich. Moreover, as the subject was a publishing company, I hoped to get further knowledge about the channeling of Nazi propaganda via the book industry.

Incidentally, the rumor spread that I was offered a substantial honorarium; it was offered indeed and I refused it, as it could have put in question the objectivity of the entire inquiry. I asked for myself and for the members of the commission to be paid exactly as I had been for the Swiss commission: a salary equivalent to that of a senior Swiss civil servant. And so it was.

Like the Swiss, Bertelsmann's owners, the Mohn family, took the initiative of setting up the inquiry following growing allegations about the collaboration of the company with the Nazi regime, particularly during the war. Clearing up the issue proved essential once Bertelsmann became massively present in the American book market, after the acquisition of Random House and a string of other U.S. publishers.

The CEO of the company, Thomas Middelhoff, asked me to accept their offer sometime in 1998. I chose the three other members of the group, who in turn chose the researchers. Our historian was my friend Norbert Frei, at the time professor at the Ruhr University in Bochum, an outstanding specialist of the Third Reich and postwar Germany; Norbert had been Broszat's main assistant but kept his total independence of mind. I had known him since 1983, when Broszat delegated him to a conference I had organized in Tel Aviv about the comparative history of twentieth-century "seizures of power" (remember that 1983 was fifty years after the Nazi accession to power).

This time the commission needed a theologian, as Bertelsmann had for a long time been essentially a publisher of religious books and remained rooted in and later still influenced by Pietism. Several colleagues recommended Trutz Rendtorff, one of the most respected theologians in Germany; he accepted. Reihard Wittmann became our media and book trade specialist; I knew him from a conference in Hamburg and as member of the Scholl Prize committee. We established our "headquarters" in Munich and, although we all were in constant contact on the Internet, I had to fly to Germany several times a year and, at the final stage, stay in Munich for a few months.

The research progressed apace as we had full access to the company's archives for the Nazi years and before. The difficulties we encountered were minor: at times, we had to remind Thomas Middelhoff not to use bits and pieces of our work to prove, mainly in his speeches in the States, how wonderfully transparent Bertelsmann had become regarding its past.

Ultimately, we showed in great detail how Heinrich Mohn, the owner of the company during the Hitler years and, soon after 1933, honorary member of the SS, aligned it with the demands of the regime. Bertelsmann became the largest publisher of books for the Wehrmacht, with some well-known Nazi propagandists among its authors. The company also used slave labor, including Jewish slave labor, in its production infrastructure. It was closed in 1944, not due to some political opposition on its part, but following the discovery of shady dealings with the paper stock allocated to it (the use of paper was severely limited in Germany during the last years of the war).

At the end of the war, British authorities did not allow Heinrich Mohn to stay as owner and head of the company; his son Reinhard took over, and Bertelsmann expanded as never before, in part by launching its "readers' circles" (*Leserkreise*). Referring to the company's Pietist beginnings in the 1830s, Norbert Frei described Bertelsmann's evolution in a perfect formula: "From the Bible reading groups to the Nazi *Volksgemeinschaft* [racial community] and from the racial community to the readers' circles." In short, Bertelsmann knew how to adopt and use the traditional need for "togetherness" of an important segment of German society, particularly in the postwar years. In 2003, two heavy volumes summed up our research; unlike what happened with the Swiss report, there was no significant controversy.

## 4

At the end of 1995 my friend Amos Funkenstein died. He had remarried in 1987. We didn't spend much time together at UCLA, as he moved to Stanford just when I arrived for good and then to Berkeley. I used to visit him and his wife Esti in one place after the other, as frequently as possible once he fell ill. And we met in L.A. and in Tel Aviv, where he went on teaching almost to the end.

I witnessed Amos's struggle with lung cancer during two years at least, which meant following the course of physical deterioration step by step. The only thing you can do is to assure the friend you are manifestly losing that his looks are improving and that, without any doubt, the chemotherapy will work and he will soon be healthy again. I don't know what Amos really believed, but he did make plans for the future, and shortly before his passing he told me of the courses he intended to teach in Tel Aviv during the coming academic year. He still managed to travel to Jerusalem to receive the Israel Prize, but then he had to return to Berkeley for further treatment. His heart suddenly gave way.

From the mid-nineties to the turn of the century, everyday life followed its course with its teaching chores, the added load of the two commissions, and constant work on *The Years of Extermination*. My frequent trips to Munich allowed me to see more of my German publisher Wolfgang Beck and his wife Mahrokh: we established a warm relationship. I had an excellent *Lektor* and chief editor for the German edition of the first volume, Peter Wieckenberg; after his retirement, I came under the "supervision" of his successor, Detlef Felken, a brilliant chief editor if there ever was one. Over the years, we not only worked together but Detlef also became a close friend of mine and of Orna's.

In 1997 or 1998, I retired from Tel Aviv University. From the outset, as I told, I had liked the Tel Aviv campus and, apart from my close friends Uriel Tal and Amos Funkenstein, I was lucky to have had some great colleagues: Zwi Yawetz, the historian of Rome, cofounder of the university, and permanent chair of the Department of History, whose exuberant personality and foul language barely hid an utterly generous core; and Shulamit Volkov, the highly respected historian of modern Germany and of German anti-Semitism, but, to me, a font of ever good advice and of decades-long friendship. I could mention other names, also those of some wonderfully talented students, who all add to my warm memory of the university. Let me just mention that some very special bonds still keep me close to it: my son Eli has, until recently, chaired its Department of Philosophy, and his wife Michal is professor of musicology in its Academy of Music.

Unfortunately, the conviviality that existed in Geneva and in Tel Aviv didn't characterize UCLA's Department of History in the early 2000s and later, as far as I experienced it, mainly after

Carlo chose to return to Italy, with the exception of our friendship with Sanjay Subrahmanyam and his wife, Caroline Ford. It could well be that I myself partly chose to keep my distance, as I noticed the growing anti-Israel drift among those to whom I had felt close at the outset, or because, increasingly, I was otherwise engaged. UCLA had now become my only academic home, but I felt less and less part of the department's life, if there was any left. I retired in 2011, without regret.


On September 11, 2001, I was still living in my small Bel Air house when "it" happened. It must have been about 6 a.m. L.A. time when I got up and, still half asleep, switched on the TV morning news, I was so taken aback by what I saw that, now as then, everything remains a blur. I am almost certain, though, that I saw the destruction of the second tower: the plane, the cloud of smoke, the collapse of the building. I was horrified. Orna was sitting beside me on the sofa facing the television. I remember that we practically didn't exchange a word; like hundreds of millions of people all over the world, we were in shock.

The collapsing buildings were the worst, but the street scenes were also terrifying: people running, fleeing in all directions, the blaring of sirens, firefighters, ambulances, police cars, pandemonium. I can't distinguish now between what was shown at the moment and images that were broadcast later, for days and days. In that jumble of camera shots, I see people falling from the towers; they escape from the smoke, the fire, and the crumbling floors by jumping to their death!

What did I think when President Bush finally emerged, slightly ridiculous in the midst of that tragedy? No, he wasn't FDR addressing the nation after Pearl Harbor. And there wasn't a Japan to fight, only terror groups, mostly in hiding. Yet Afghanistan under the Taliban was a sanctuary, so that invading Afghanistan made sense at the time. But did the invasion of Iraq, two years later, make sense? To me, it did, although some of my friends expressed outrage. I simply couldn't believe that U.S. intelligence agencies would be so wrong about Saddam Hussein's stockpile of weapons of mass destruction. The invasion was a terrible mistake, but that wasn't apparent in 2003.

I never felt "truly" American. How could I? I came here too late in life. The rules of baseball are a mystery to me, and I do not set up a barbecue on the Fourth of July or on any other day, for that matter. The main question, however, is different; it has little to do with national customs and relates, directly and simply, to the political and social texture of the country one has opted for.

I like what the United States strives to be; I say "strives," as it still is far from the goals that a majority of Americans hope to reach. It is easy to list America's glaring failures: racism, everyday violence, the role of money in politics (a problem from hell), and so on. I could go on about what is so frequently bandied about, such as the country's materialism and its so-called lack of culture; the failures are real, but much of the "cultural" criticism comes down to cartoonlike tags pretending to sum up major features of a huge and diverse country.

That Denmark has established a model society is admirable but hardly astonishing: it is small and ethnically homogeneous. The United States is a fumbling colossus that, with all its deficiencies, is a working democracy where people are free, have, nowadays, access to the justice system and usually get a fair hearing, where nothing stops the media from the most iconoclastic inquiries, where gay marriage is being recognized now throughout the country, and where, notwithstanding the still widespread racism, a decisive majority of the electorate — and that should never be forgotten — twice voted for an African-American president.

And one should not forget either that the United States has shown its readiness to defend countries that otherwise could not defend themselves. Of course such policies serve the American interest, as is true for the foreign policies of every other nation, but try to imagine the world today, with China's might and Putin's ambitions, without the United States' active presence as a deterrent.

I remember that some ten to twelve years ago, on the eve of Thanksgiving, I phoned a former student of mine from the time I started teaching in Tel Aviv, who had become a well-known historian and professor at Brown, Omer Bartov. At the end of the conversation, as one "exile" to the other, I wished him a happy Thanksgiving, to which he answered, "Yes, thank God for America!" I never forgot that unexpected answer, and, indeed, I often feel the same.


## 5


My major aim during the early years of the new century was to complete *The Years of Extermination*. Instead of dealing essentially with one country, as in the first volume, I undertook the challenge of writing an integrated history that would encompass *simultaneously* Nazi policies and those of their collaborators in each and every occupied country, the attitudes of surrounding societies, and, above all, the reactions of the Jews. The measures taken by the Allies and the neutrals also had to be included.

Showing the simultaneity of these diverse elements was the only way of conveying some of the dimensions of the events. It was obvious that no single conceptual framework could apply to such entirely diverse historical developments.

Yet how could a narrative aiming at the integration of policies and reactions, at their simultaneity all over occupied Europe and beyond, be structured without turning into a chaotic presentation that would become incomprehensible to all but the most specialized readers? It took me some time to grasp that without a unified conceptual framework, without a unity of place (there was one in the first volume), and without a unity of agency (again, only one uncontested agency dominated the first volume), there remained a single possible solution: to create very tight units of time spreading over six months each, at most. It would allow the reader to tie together the events narrated in each sequence and thus from sequence to sequence. This, however, was but one of my main challenges.

The other major challenge was to write as precise a historical rendition as possible, and at the same time re-create for the reader a momentary sense of disbelief that history has a tendency to eliminate in the case of extreme events. In fact, I had considered this problem for several years, well before conceiving of my project. How could such contradictory aims be reconciled? It was only after mulling over a number of solutions, each one as unconvincing as the next, that the most obvious, and the simplest, answer occurred to me: to introduce into the historical narrative not only the Jewish dimension as such but the "raw voices" of the victims. In other words, not only would I narrate collective Jewish reactions to the events in order to illustrate the vast array of Jewish attitudes, the multiple facets of the Jewish dimension, but, at various moments, I would introduce extracts from diaries or letters that, mostly without the intermediary of postwar memory, carried the incomprehension or the fear, the despair or the hopes of the trapped victims. These cries and whispers would puncture, so to say, the normalizing pace of the historical narrative, and jolt, albeit briefly, the distanced intellectual understanding conveyed by historical narration as such.

Once I assimilated these various answers, work progressed rapidly, and in the spring of 2006 I completed volume two. Detlef managed to organize a swift (and excellent) translation, so that the German edition was ready for the Frankfurt Book Fair in October and for the Leipzig Book Fair later on. The American edition, the original, came out later, in 2007. This second volume was very well received by reviewers and was translated into many languages. It brought some major recognition: the award for nonfiction at the Leipzig Book Fair, the Peace Prize of the German Book Trade Association (Frankfurt, 2007), and the Pulitzer Prize for general nonfiction (Columbia University, 2008).

The German Peace Prize (*Friedenspreis*), established in the early 1950s, was a very official accolade, awarded in the St. Paul Church in Frankfurt (the seat of the short-lived liberal parliament of 1848/49) in the presence of some thousand guests and of the German president or, alternatively, the chancellor. The laureate had to make a speech (broadcast live on television) of about half an hour, which on occasion could be an explicit political statement.

Ten years or so before I was awarded the prize, the German novelist Martin Walser received the award and used the occasion to launch an assault against the constant (according to him) reference to the Holocaust in the German public sphere, as "a moral cudgel" in his words. The remarkable aspect of that ceremony was not what Walser declared so openly, but rather the standing ovation that greeted his words. Only the chairman of the Central Council of Jews in Germany, Ignatz Bubis, remained seated and did not applaud.

It occurred to me that, among other reasons, I had been awarded the Peace Prize as a kind of indirect counterweight to the Walser accolade. Whatever the reason may have been, my address had to be a statement about the Shoah that would carry some significance and some resonance. I decided to read — in the original German — with as few comments as possible, family letters not published previously (with two exceptions), including a letter from my aunt Martha, who had remained in Prague, working at the local Jewish Community office. In early 1943, Martha wrote to my grandmother in Sweden, telling her that all community employees had been slated for deportation. She was happy, she wrote, to depart for the East as she would be closer to Elli and Hans (my parents) and could eventually meet them . . .

My work on the Holocaust had come to an end.

# CHAPTER FIFTEEN

# The Time That Remains

In 2005 I sold the house in Bel Air. Orna and I moved to a cozy and very quiet house in the hills of West Hollywood, off Laurel Canyon (even those who do not know L.A. may have heard of Laurel Canyon, the home of the Doors, the Mamas and the Papas, and sundry other rock bands). When you went to buy a thing or two at the local store, you met veterans of the 1960s; they did not seem to have outgrown those magic years, and Laurel Canyon was a good place for dreams to linger in their original habitat.

To reach the entrance of our house, however, you had to climb quite a number of double-height steps. Over the years, I was becoming increasingly breathless during such climbings, and I could easily foresee the moment I would have to give up. So, in 2014, we regretfully moved again.

In the meantime, though, in December 2008, we decided to give up living in sin and to get married. Where could we marry quickly and discreetly, if not in Las Vegas? From L.A. to Vegas, the drive took some five hours along Death Valley and through desert, most of the way. But Vegas was no desert. We left our suitcase at the Bellagio and went in search of a marriage office. We found one, stood in line (as at the post office), signed something, paid something, and were married. Not so fast, though: for the procedure to be complete, we had to undergo a "spiritual" introduction to married life. You had "chapels" all over town. We settled for the first we saw and, again, waited in line, signed something, and were ushered into a private room where a very young lady, dressed in a light blue "graduation" gown, explained to us that in married life there were summits and valleys . . . The insight cost us twenty dollars and, this time, we were married for good. The following day we were back in the Hollywood Hills.

2

Many questions have remained unanswered and it's closing time.

My own work on the history of the Shoah was done, although the decision had not been easy. Historians of my generation have contributed their share, each according to his/her specific approach, and, sometimes, under the impact of individual experience. Some of them are still wonderfully active, as agewise they are in between the old and the new groups, like Christopher Browning, for example, Hilberg's outstanding disciple.

The "young cohort" (historians between their forties and sixties) has already been on stage for some time. I admit that it is not always easy to keep hands off; occasionally, the new productions annoy me. I go on reading though (how could I otherwise?), and slowly get used to the fact that no history remains static and that, in any case, the memory of the Shoah is undergoing a major change: "the era of the witness" (Annette Wieviorka) is over. I also know that in due time, the pendulum of historiography will swing back, at least part of the way.

Putting an end to my work on the Shoah didn't mean to stop writing; that would have been impossible. I looked for a new but minor project, a brief essay on Kafka for example, as time was getting short. Actually, time could have been much shorter than I even thought. In 2012, my physician informed me that blood tests and the biopsy that followed showed high-risk prostate cancer. Weeks of radiation and hormone therapy became the unavoidable sequel: it worked, for now. Then, a few months ago (spring 2015), a ministroke added its contribution to the pleasures of old age . . . Am I hearing a knock at the door? (No bells do toll in Los Angeles.)

Why Kafka? I remember clearly my wish to write something on my revered compatriot during the stay in Paris in the spring of 1960, as I was organizing the conference on Soviet Jewry, that is, before I had written a single line about anything. Luckily, I didn't reveal my idea to anybody. But it remained over the decades without my doing much about it, except reading all I could. This is how, in the 1990s, after I went through most of the German critical edition of Kafka's novels, diaries, letters, fragments, and so forth, I became convinced that Max Brod, his lifelong friend and literary executor, had grievously censored his writings.

Brod's intention was clear and explicit: turn Kafka into a saint and, therefore, delete anything that smacked of sexuality from his autobiographical writings (the more so that Kafka was more attracted to men than to women and, at times, fantasized about children). In fact, much of Kafka's sexual life — apart from his frequent visits to brothels — was more fantasy than reality.

For Brod, there was no difference: K.'s expressions of desire or descriptions that were too explicit had to disappear. In short, Brod was robbing his friend of his humanity; he was also robbing all of us of an access — one of many — to Kafka's texts. As my project became part of the Yale series of "Jewish Lives," meant to present short biographies of important Jewish figures, I deemed it essential to reinstate the words, lines, or entire paragraphs that Brod had excised, and pursue a few themes that, to my mind, dominated Kafka's life and, indirectly, his work.

Although the slim volume got some strongly expressed support in its English, German, and French versions, the old guard of Kafka specialists was not amused. I had foreseen it and was hardly surprised.

I was still very much entangled in Kafka matters when, sometime in 2013, I started fiddling with the first elements of this memoir. There was no compelling reason for starting it (except for the need to work on something) and there were actually a few good reasons for not undertaking it. I hesitated about the Berlin imbroglio, for example, but then got on my way. I was aware, as I wrote in the prologue, that my perspective on issues very close to many people's passionate attention was both that of an insider of sorts but also of one sufficiently detached to be credible, or so I hope. The practical option was to write as much of a draft as possible and then take the advice of people I relied on, as my own judgment could have become a problem. And now, of course, as I plod ahead, the prospect of being unable to complete this text is never far from my mind. Starting projects should not mean taking for granted *le temps qui reste* (the time that remains).

In 2014 Orna and I moved from the Hollywood Hills to the "Valley," a suburb of the suburb that is Los Angeles. Two generous awards, the Dan David Prize of Tel Aviv University and the Edgar de Picciotto Prize of the Geneva institute allowed us to buy a house somewhat more expensive than the previous one but also more spacious, with easy access by car to the entrance (just in case) and with enticing grounds. As nothing required us to drive regularly to UCLA anymore, living in the Valley had advantages that the city could not offer for the same price. Moreover, both of us prefer to be on our own, without many social obligations, in moderate isolation. Like Voltaire's Candide, I take care of my garden. Voltaire may have meant gardening as a metaphor for writing, although he apparently was also a constant gardener. Orna loves gardening and I love watching her and writing about it.

We are not shut off from "civilization," though. Everything on Ventura Boulevard, the endless main artery of the Valley, is on hand in the Tarzana segment of it or in nearby Woodland Hills to the left of Vanalden Avenue, our street, or in Encino to the right. Everything, from medical centers to Mexican, Thai, Chinese, Japanese, Korean, Vietnamese, Italian, Persian, Armenian, Indian, and Israeli restaurants, to gas stations, banks, movie theaters, parking lots, car dealers, liquor stores, real estate offices, army recruiting centers, food supermarkets, shopping malls, cobblers, dentists, bakeries, optometrists, beauty salons, kung fu centers, hair salons, massage salons, nail salons, mattress stores, futon stores, insurance companies, New York bagel stores, delicatessens, and again gas stations, banks, parking lots, and car dealers.

You've got the idea, and I am sure that you would easily recognize the difference between Ventura Boulevard and avenue de l'Opéra, for example. I forgot to mention that on Ventura you also have churches, synagogues, yeshivas of various Orthodox groups, at least four Israeli restaurants in Tarzana alone, an Israeli *shuper-sal* (supermarket), and, of course, a lot of Israelis. How many? It's hard to tell: probably fewer than Mexicans, Nicaraguans, Salvadorans . . . , but if I have to venture a number on the basis of the all-day-long crowd at Humus Bar and Grill, Tel Aviv, Big Itsik, or Aroma, all places where we eat at times, Israel must have exported at least half of its population (including us) to the Valley.

### 3

Israelis, those who came here as adults, mostly keep a divided identity: "They live in the West but their heart is in the East," to quote the much overwrought sentence of Yehuda Halevi, the greatest Jewish medieval poet (who himself lived in Spain). Indeed, although most Israelis do well economically, send their children to American schools, strive to acquire U.S. citizenship, and willingly adopt and celebrate the quintessential American holidays, the Fourth of July and Thanksgiving, they continue to speak Hebrew at home, congregate with other Israelis, shop at Israeli supermarkets, and patronize Israeli restaurants; they read Israeli newspapers or follow the daily news from Israel on the Internet and celebrate Israel's Independence Day. Sometimes their children keep the same divided identity, but mostly they become simply Americans. You will say that this is the way of the American melting pot; it is.

The question that remains hard to answer is that of the "residue": How many of those Americans belonging to the second generation of ex-Israelis will continue to regularly visit the "old country"? How many would rush back in time of crisis? Logic and common sense say: fewer and fewer with each passing generation.

In the sixties, a French Jewish sociologist, Georges Friedmann, published a widely discussed essay: *La fin du peuple juif?* (*The End of the Jewish People?*). The gist of Friedmann's argument was that in Israel, a new kind of Jewish existence was emerging, growing increasingly different from that of the Diaspora. As years go by, these two Jewish worlds will have ever less in common, and thus, of necessity, the Jews will disappear as one overall entity. At the time, Friedmann's thesis was contradicted by the outburst of solidarity that the Six-Day War engendered among Diaspora Jews. I am much less certain, with the passage of time, whether Friedmann's prognostication is not proving true, also as far as successive generations of ex-Israelis are concerned.

The picture I am drawing is too schematic: any number of American Jews, without Israeli heritage, feel very close to Israel for political or religious reasons, and a small minority spends time there in various frameworks, also as volunteers in the army. Some American Jews, a few hundred per year, even end up living in Israel. They are usually on the right side in politics and on the Orthodox side (not ultra-Orthodox) in religion. In fact, U.S. Jewry has provided Israel with some of the most dangerous fanatics among the settlers in the occupied territories. Some were notorious racists and anti-Arab agitators (Meir Kahana), even mass murderers, such as the infamous Baruch Goldstein; now a new Jewish terrorist group, with Kahana's grandson as a leading member, has surfaced.

Make no mistake, however: the immense majority of American Jews, a near totality in fact, be they liberals or conservatives, are Americans first and foremost. They may criticize Israel or support it, they may contribute money and try to mobilize U.S. politicians to their camp, but from afar.

What I just mentioned should help define where we, Orna and I, stand. We are no different from the majority of Israelis who have lived in the States for decades (in Orna's case over thirty years). And we too are divided between our integration in America and our constant attention to what is happening in Israel, even far beyond the daily news.

Most paradoxically, for example, it is here, thanks to Orna, that I discovered the vast expanses of recent Hebrew literature. I had read the modern classics: A. B. Yehoshua, Amos Oz, David Grossman, but only in translation. Once I even lectured on one of Yehoshua's books (*The Lover*, if memory serves me right) in Zurich and in German (I had read it in German). Among the "classics," I particularly admired Grossman's *To the End of the Land* and Oz's *A Tale of Love and Darkness*, but, again, in their English translations.

Regarding the more recent writers that Orna reads in the original, I had never heard of them before; now that I have heard so much about the quality of some, I wait impatiently for the English and, in the meantime, keep their names in mind: thus I remember Yochi Brandes, thanks to another Brandes, Nietzsche's early interpreter.

I have no compunction in reading Hebrew prose in translation: it goes so much faster and, after all, prose is prose and a good translation catches many of the nuances. My problem is poetry: I would feel ashamed of reading Yehuda Amichai, for example, in English when with minor effort I could read him in Hebrew. I won't have a chance to tell you how it went, but now is the time to try.

On several occasions we toyed with the idea of returning to Israel. We are well aware of Israel's immensely attaching aspects: the energy and the astounding creativity, among much else. And we miss families and friends. Wouldn't living there make more sense for the two of us than playing Candide in faraway California? In practical terms, returning to Israel would be but slightly more difficult than staying put, but the drift toward an increasingly nationalist-religious society and the political initiatives it shamelessly displays are repelling. Under such conditions, one must express oneself or, to me at least, the political environment would quickly become unbearable, even within the bubble of sanity that Tel Aviv appears to be. Unfortunately, I feel too old and too much of an outsider (even if I devoutly follow most of what goes on) to contribute anything of significance to the public debate. Notwithstanding my literary discoveries, I have lost touch, also with the slang (for "very good," when do you say *haval al hazman*, or *Sababa*, or *Achla?*).

As for family, soon only Eli and his wife Michal will be staying in Tel Aviv. Omer and Elam, their twin boys, will be studying in Europe and in the States for several years to come. Otherwise, as I already wrote, David, Isabelle, and Thom live in Paris; Michal, Karl, Yoni, and Ben, in Berlin. Orna's two boys, Gil and Amir, and her granddaughter Una, live in L.A. Hence, moving to Tel Aviv would solve only part of that problem. Going for longer stays in Europe and in Israel may be the only viable solution at this stage.

There are also the friends. It is sad to say, but, among my friends, the closest I had in Israel have died: Uri Tal, Amos Funkenstein, Shabtai Teveth, and Meir Rosenne. Meir passed away a few months ago, suddenly, possibly from a hospital-generated infection. We had reconnected only during the last few years; I had kept my distance, as from the seventies on, Meir explicitly leaned to the Likud kind of right. But, of course, all this became irrelevant once we met again, also with his wife Vera.

I was told only very recently of Shabtai Teveth's death. In 2002 Sabi suffered a stroke, and since then he could not communicate anymore. I visited him once. He seemed happy to see me but there was no way of knowing whether he recognized me or not, whether he recognized anybody. Here was somebody who had been an outstanding journalist, a prolific writer, a most thorough biographer of Ben-Gurion, suddenly incapable of saying anything except a single, incomprehensible word. I hope that he didn't understand what was going on with him or around him, otherwise every minute of his life, for thirteen years, would have been a horrible torture. Sabi was possibly the closest friend I have had for so long. It is painful to write about his last years: for him, death was truly deliverance.

## 4

Here, the local ideological scene is not without its problems either, mainly regarding Israel and particularly in academe. Thus, the University of California campuses have got the reputation, justified or not, of being a fount of anti-Israel activity. Some faculty members of my Department of History certainly do their best to enhance that notoriety. Criticizing Israel's policies is not only justified, it is necessary. However, questioning Israel's right to exist is a very different matter. Sometimes one gets the feeling that, in the American academic environment, the first attitude easily leads to the second one. As for the second attitude, it often smells of more than a whiff of anti-Semitism. The dilemma is obvious and has to be dealt with case by case.

A few years ago, Orna became a target of this kind of politics. She had been teaching the history of Israel at UCLA for six years when the issue of tenure came up. Her students wrote glowing reports, but tenure was refused on the grounds, among other highly problematic arguments, that her courses showed too much of a pro-Israel bias, which meant, in the context, not doubting the state's very legitimacy.

The Israeli-Palestinian conflict in and of itself exacerbates the anti-Israel activism. This activism will spread without a solution. Is there, nowadays, any chance of reaching such a solution? Let me try, at the end of this memoir, to venture a few brief remarks on the present situation, as I see it from afar.

On both sides, radicalization has made deeper and possibly irreversible inroads. The conflict openly remains one between two nationalisms, but on both sides, the nationalist frenzy is increasingly laced with religious fanaticism. In other words, extremist rabbis and imams become more than ever the inciting voices in a highly volatile situation, in which young hotheads play a decidedly aggressive role on both sides. While half a million or more Jewish settlers, backed by extreme right-wing parties, turn violent, several endogeneous Islamic movements, possibly inspired by the so-called Islamic State, are deeply influencing a new generation of Palestinians, born after the end of the second Intifada, including some Arab-Israeli citizens.

Egypt, Jordan, and the Gulf States (including Saudi Arabia) keep open or covert relations with Israel, but rejection of any compromise with the "Zionist entity" is the official stance in Iran and among its allies: Assad's Syria, Hamas in Gaza, Hezbollah in Lebanon, as well as among the more diffuse Islamist movements, both Shiite and Sunni, all over the region.

This situation provides the main argument against revival of the peace process for many Israelis on the right and even among some on the left. If, the reasoning goes, under current conditions the West Bank becomes a Palestinian state, it will fall into the hands of Hamas or some other extremist group, as happened in Gaza, given the notorious weakness of the president of the Palestinian Authority; Israel will then be surrounded on all sides by militants determined to destroy it. That Israel is in part responsible for the radicalization of the Palestinians is irrelevant to those who so argue; the present situation is what has to be faced.

Preaching from afar or reading tea leaves from half a world away is anything but admirable. Yet, as I have been quite outspoken about my political opinions over the years, it would be less than candid not to say here whether these opinions have remained the same or whether they have evolved and, in both cases, for what reasons.

On the central issue of our relations with the Palestinians, I remain resolutely in favor of the two-state solution, which means putting an immediate end to the expansion of settlements and, beyond that, of being ready, on principle, to accept difficult concessions regarding the withdrawal of some settlements, an exchange of territory, and even a political (not social) division of Jerusalem.

A very recent resurgence of a Jewish terrorist movement that has existed for decades but lain low for most of the time adds a dangerous twist to a situation already complicated enough. After the burning down of a church in Galilee and the setting on fire of a Palestinian house in which an eighteen-month-old toddler was burned alive (the father succumbed a few days later and the mother shortly thereafter), the existence of this terror group was confirmed and denounced by the Israeli government. Seemingly adequate orders were given to the security service. Whether this sudden decisiveness will be sustained and lead to results, given the country's political and religious landscape, remains to be seen. Jewish terrorism is not only a threat to the Palestinians; as these ultra-fanatics are ready to use violence to scuttle any agreement, they may become one more disastrous obstacle to any move toward peace. This "hilltop youth" (so they call themselves at times) is, in the words of Israeli president Reuven Rivlin, a cancer that threatens to devour Israeli society itself.

Another recent growth that feeds Jewish violence in the occupied territories is developing within Israel: right-wing groups have started denouncing left-oriented initiatives as treasonous, as externally financed, at times accusing individuals, among them the best-known writers and artists in the country, of being "planted" agents of anti-Israeli elements. Simultaneously, ministers belonging to the far right have begun excluding from the school curriculum books they consider subversive (such as a novel telling of a love story between an Israeli woman and a Palestinian man); this is nothing else but outright Israeli McCarthyism, if not worse. And while this is going on, the left-wing parliamentary opposition watches passively the onset of its own doom.

If the present trend is not reversed, if the settlements policy is not stopped, if a government guided by a vision of peace is not elected, then, metaphorically speaking, regarding the values Israel once held dear, regarding the survival of an Israeli democracy, there is nothing more to say than "God help us."

# 5

The impact of the Shoah has determined the course of my life, but, for a long time now, it does not impinge on the everyday. My everyday is as gray or as sunny as that of many of my contemporaries. Well, almost. There is, for example, a recurrent dream theme that probably has nothing to do with the past. But who knows?

Usually, I don't remember my dreams, perhaps as a result of medication, but one theme has become so pervasive, under slightly different guises, that it has engraved itself deeply enough to resurface at any recall. I am in a city that I do not know, a mix of Prague, Geneva, and some touches of Tel Aviv. I must go somewhere and meet somebody, but each time I either get lost as I try one street after another, or miss the bus that would have taken me to the right place, or am misled by people I ask for directions (I am not sure that they want to mislead me, but I never find the way they indicate). In some variations, I know that at the end of a road once taken (no Robert Frost involved), there is a sudden opening onto a magnificent mountain landscape. I promised some people that I would show them the landscape, but, of course, I never find the road again . . .

A dream of childhood bliss never recovered? Of something essential missing in my life? I will never know, as, each time, I suddenly wake up without finding my goal. So let's leave the land of unpenetrable dreams and return to the everyday. In that everyday, I try to live in the present, in the minute happenings of the present. It's a process that, as I discover, is far from easy and certainly does not come naturally, at least not to me.

An embargo on the past is impossible: the past can never be banished, for "The past is never dead. It's not even past"

(William Faulkner). Moreover, who would want to miss all the wonderful time that the past carries entwined with all the sadness? Time spent with the woman you love, with your children, with your grandchildren, with all those who are close to you or whose memory you cherish. The past has to be let in, as it is. It should be accepted as a whole.

The future? You create it, willingly or not, as you go on living. About one of its aspects you may feel safe at my stage: the distant future is closed; there is no doubt about that. It is the near future that cannot be shaken off. There's the rub. You have matters to take care of, but as you tend to forget, you have to write it all down, and part of the present is spent listing the chores of the near future and, mainly, being consumed by the gnawing feeling that you forgot a few things, as, some time ago, you forgot the Hebrew name for "aubergines" and as you go on forgetting so many other words, occurrences, faces, and names.

Of course, there is one thing that I do not forget: death. I think of it all the time, so to say. Am I afraid? Less than I was during my anxiety crises in the faraway past, but yes, I am certainly not indifferent to the sounds of its steady and approaching steps. I know there may be worse to come and that's what often keeps me awake around three in the morning: trying to remember names or just those terribly simple, ordinary words that seem to have gone . . .

Back to the past: you cannot help examining your life, wondering whether on given moments you made the right decision or expressed your true thoughts firmly enough; you ask yourself if, by your own standards, you really fulfilled at least part of what you intended to accomplish. I could go on; it's unnecessary.

As for the present, its flashes are in fact intractable: not only do past and future constantly prey on it but, whether you want it or not, a constant stream of information reaches you with its ever repeated sources of worry and its too frequent news of some tragedy. How could I, for example, get out of my mind that Jews in Israel burned a Palestinian toddler alive?

Saving some moments from that constant flow is the most you can hope for. There must be endless individual methods for isolating and protecting that precious gift: a sliver of peacefulness. In the past, I tried to empty my mind of all thought; it doesn't work anymore. My method has become more down-to-earth: a double dose of humor when possible, otherwise a double dose of Zoloft ...

You can also fall back on more traditional ways, those you have used throughout your adult life (on top of the above): a great book, some music, and a glass of whiskey. As far as whiskey goes, my taste is very simple, I prefer mild Irish whiskey, let's say Jameson, to all the Scottish single malts — and to add insult to injury, with a lot of ice. The books? I just read the excellent Patrick Modiano's *Pedigree*. I would love to say more about it (particularly as I have recently started and abandoned several highly praised and very mediocre productions), but it wouldn't fit here.

At this penultimate stage, I realize that I have said very little about the music I love (apart from mentioning some religious music, *Parsifal*, and Richard Strauss's *Four Last Songs*). It's a shame, as music was always very present in my life; alas, I cannot simply take the plane from L.A. to hear our daughter Michal, for example in the Shostakovich piano concerto she just performed or in the concerts of her chamber music ensemble. Shall I admit my love for Mozart, Chopin, and for chamber music from Beethoven to Brahms? As in many other things, I am hopelessly old-fashioned and conventional, but it's what I love.

Strangely enough, I remember that my uncle Willy, who also lived in Nirah and who apart from being a good chemist was a very good violinist, once told me that King Boris of Bulgaria (poisoned by the Nazis) had asked that Anton Bruckner's Eighth Symphony be performed at his funeral. Over the years, I discovered the reason for this odd request: the performance could easily have lasted until the resurrection of the dead.

Add to these strategies for grasping the present something Orna and I chose without being fully aware of the importance it would take: Bonnie, our chocolate Labrador puppy. We cherish that innocent, trusting, loving little being (not so little anymore). You can get her to obey any demand if you promise her a "treat," but if your explanations are too elaborate her green eyes will stare at you and she will incline her head first to the left, then to the right, to try and understand what is expected now of the "very good girl."

Mainly, as a young dog, she loves to play. While I was writing this, she dashed across the living room with one of Orna's slippers in her jaws; she immensely enjoys being chased around and, needless to say, is much faster than both of us. Yet after a while, she will be tired, fall asleep, faintly snore, and suddenly twitch as she dreams.

SAUL FRIEDLÄNDER is an award-winning Israeli historian and currently a professor of history at UCLA. He was born in Prague to a family of German-speaking Jews, grew up in France, and experienced the German Occupation of 1940–1944. His historical works have garnered much praise and recognition, including the 2008 Pulitzer Prize for General Non-Fiction for his book *The Years of Extermination: Nazi Germany and the Jews, 1939–1945*.

Four months before Hitler came to power, Saul Friedländer was born in Prague to a middle-class Jewish family. In 1939, seven-year-old Saul and his family were forced to flee to France, where they lived through the German Occupation, until his parents' ill-fated attempt to flee to Switzerland. They were able to hide their son in a Roman Catholic seminary before being sent to Auschwitz, where they were killed. After an imposed religious conversion, young Saul began training for the priesthood. The birth of Israel prompted his discovery of his Jewish past and his true identity.

Friedländer brings his story movingly to life, shifting between his Israeli present and his European past with grace and restraint. His keen eye spares nothing, not even himself, as he explores the ways in which the loss of his parents, his conversion to Catholicism, and his deep-seated Jewish roots combined to shape him into the man he is today. Friedländer's retrospective view of his journey of grief and self-discovery provides readers with a rare experience: a memoir of feeling with intellectual backbone, in equal measure tender and insightful.